The Dilemma:

Modern Conundrums

Talmudic Debates

Your Solutions

JLI

JEWISH LEARNING INSTITUTE

STUDENT TEXTBOOK

COURSE EDITOR
Rabbi Mordechai Dinerman

COURSE DEVELOPMENT TEAM
Rabbi Lazer Gurkow
Rabbi Sholom Ber Hertzel
Rabbi Eli Raksin
Rabbi Shmuel Super
Rabbi Boruch Werdiger

EDITORIAL BOARD
Rabbi Yisrael Rice
Mrs. Rivkah Slonim
Rabbi Ari Sollish
Rabbi Avrohom Sternberg

CURRICULUM COORDINATOR
Mrs. Rivki Mockin

The Dilemma:

Modern Conundrums

Talmudic Debates

Your Solutions

JLI

JEWISH LEARNING INSTITUTE

STUDENT TEXTBOOK

PRINCIPAL BENEFACTOR

GEORGE ROHR
New York, NY

ADVISORY BOARD OF GOVERNORS

YAAKOV AND KAREN COHEN
Potomac, MD

YITZCHOK AND JULIE GNIWISCH
Montreal, QC

BARBARA HINES
Aspen, CO

DANIEL B. MARKSON
S. Antonio, TX

DANIEL AND ROSIE MATTIO
Seattle, WA

DAVID MINTZ
Tenafly, NJ

DR. STEPHEN F. SERBIN
Columbia, SC

LEONARD A. WIEN, JR.
Miami Beach, FL

PILLARS OF JEWISH LITERACY

KEVIN BERMEISTER
Sydney, Australia

The Rohr Jewish Learning Institute acknowledges the generous support of the following individuals and foundations:

PABLO AND SARA BRIMAN
Mexico City, Mexico

YOSEF GOROWITZ
Redondo Beach, CA

DR. VERA KOCH GROSZMANN
S. Paulo, Brazil

HERSCHEL LAZAROFF
Baltimore, MD

JENNY LJUNGBERG
New York, NY

DAVID MAGERMAN
Gladwyne, PA

DR. MICHAEL MALING
Deerfield, IL

YITZCHAK MIRILASHVILI
Herzliya, Israel

LARRY SIFEN
Virginia Beach, VA

YAIR SHAMIR
Savyon, Israel

PARTNERING FOUNDATIONS

WILLIAM DAVIDSON FOUNDATION

MEROMIM FOUNDATION

KOHELET FOUNDATION

CRAIN-MALING FOUNDATION

WORLD ZIONIST ORGANIZATION

AVI CHAI FOUNDATION

OLAMI WORLDWIDE—WOLFSON FOUNDATION

RUDERMAN FAMILY FOUNDATION

THE ESTATE OF ELLIOT JAMES BELKIN

SPONSORS

MARK AND REBECCA BOLINSKY
Long Beach, NY

DANIEL AND ETA COTLAR
Houston, TX

SHMUEL AND SHARONE GOODMAN
Chicago, IL

FRANK AND FRUMETH POLASKY
Saginaw, MI

DR. ZE'EV RAV-NOY
Los Angeles, CA

ALAN ZEKELMAN
Bloomfield Hills, MI

THE ROHR JEWISH LEARNING INSTITUTE

gratefully acknowledges
the pioneering support of

George and Pamela Rohr

Since its inception,
the Rohr JLI has been
a beneficiary of the vision, generosity,
care, and concern
of the Rohr family.

In the merit of
the tens of thousands of hours of Torah study
by JLI students worldwide,
may they be blessed with health,
Yiddishe nachas from all their loved ones,
and extraordinary success
in all their endeavors.

The course
THE DILEMMA
has been approved
in these states and provinces
for fulfillment of
the continuing education
requirements
for legal and ethics credits:

United States
Alabama
Alaska
California
Colorado
Connecticut
Delaware
Georgia
Idaho
Illinois
Kentucky
Minnesota
Nevada
New Jersey
New York

North Carolina
Ohio
Oregon
Pennsylvania
Rhode Island
South Carolina
Tennessee
Utah
Virginia
Washington
Wisconsin

Canada
British Columbia
Saskatchewan

Endorsements

Many thanks for sharing with me the exciting curriculum and for the excellent idea of bringing the treasure of Jewish law, a major point of Jewish life and Jewish ethos, to the attention of interested people. The idea is relevant and timely, and I am confident that this venture will enjoy great success.

HON. ELYAKIM RUBINSTEIN
Vice President, Supreme Court of Israel

The JLI Program admirably merges Torah learning with American jurisprudence. It encourages Talmudic scholars and beginners to appreciate American law and stimulates lawyers and laymen to treasure the wisdom of the Torah.

NATHAN LEWIN, ESQ.
Past President, American Association of Jewish Lawyers and Jurists

As an international law professor and lawyer, I often reflect on general principles that transcend particular cultures and societies. Too often, people look at law and ethics as separate and distinct spheres. However, law and ethics are institutions that evolve together. The beauty of the JLI course is that it shows us the potential of law to inspire a more ethical world.

LUIS OLAVO BAPTISTA
Professor of International Trade Law
University of S. Paulo Law School
Member, Permanent Court of Arbitration at the Hague

This course deals with timeless problems that have excited the minds of great thinkers. The debates they engender help reveal the values that we want a legal system to promote and the limitations inherent in any legal system to deal effectively with conflict. The rich discussions in the Talmud and in later Jewish writings offer fascinating insights to these problems, sometimes foreshadowing ideas that have surfaced in secular legal writings only in the past decades. At other times, the Jewish sources offer unique insights reflecting the duties owed not only to others but to G-d. The JLI courses that I am familiar with are of high quality, integrating traditional learning and modern secular thought. This course offers each participant the opportunity to sample the traditional method of Talmudic study, a close reading of texts with a study partner. It can be highly rewarding where the total can be more than the sum of its parts.

STEVEN F. FRIEDELL
Professor of Law
Rutgers Law School

The Rohr Jewish Learning Institute's new course, *The Dilemma: Modern Conundrums, Talmudic Debates, Your Solutions,* is an excellent project designed to relate the timeless ethical code of the Talmud to the timely concerns of society. It offers what professional education sometimes lacks, the opportunity to reflect and focus on the ethical underpinnings of the law. In my work with Jewish and legal organizations, I have found the JLI CLE curricula to be fascinating and relevant and a valuable element in our programming.

HAROLD L KAPLAN, ESQ.
Foley & Lardner, LLP
National Chair, JNF's Lawyers for Israel Society

Any program that seeks to enhance ethical awareness and helps to resolve legal conflicts among well-intentioned people in an intelligent, thought provoking manner is worth attending and endorsing.

BENJAMIN BRAFMAN, ESQ.
Brafman & Associates, PC

The Rohr Institute's new six-week CLE program *The Dilemma* engages participants by combining practical legal questions with Jewish ethical principles. Capitalizing on its characteristically thoughtful approach to educational programming, the format is sure to engage lawyers by demonstrating the contemporary applications of Jewish law's ancient ethical commitments.

MICHAEL A. HELFAND
Associate Professor, Pepperdine University School of Law
Associate Director, Pepperdine University Glazer Institute for Jewish Studies

Determining what is "just" is often more than simply determining the facts and applying the law. Each case has variables that may cause us to question whether we are arriving at a conclusion that is both legally and ethically right. What should be most significant to our analysis: the act itself, the intent with which the act is done or the consequences of the act? What about a failure to act when the circumstances would seem to require it? Through this course, the Jewish Learning Institute helps us to find some of the answers; or, at least, a better way to analyze the questions.

HON. ANDREW C. KAUFFMAN
Los Angeles County Superior Court, Retired

The Rohr Jewish Learning Institute has a well-earned reputation for producing outstanding materials and courses on the application of Jewish law and ethics to contemporary social issues ranging from end of life decision making to business ethics and marriage. Their most recent endeavor matches and perhaps surpasses their record of success. The authors have put together six cases that pose complex ethical dilemmas that escape easy or superficial resolution…. The materials and the course will once again show compellingly that our Torah and rabbinic tradition provide guidance and direction even in the thorniest issues of life because G-d's Torah is indeed a Torah of Life. Congratulations on this wonderful work!

RABBI YITZCHAK A. BREITOWITZ
Kehillat Ohr Somayach, Jerusalem
Professor Emeritus, University of Maryland School of Law

This is a law class for everyone. Life is full of moral dilemmas. How we confront these ethical challenges defines each person's humanity. The Rohr Jewish Learning Institute brings Jewish ethics from theory to application into our everyday lives. With clear, concise teaching each lesson will help you live a fuller and enriched life.

CARY B. CHEIFETZ, ESQ.
Diplomate, American College of Family Trial Lawyers
Director, AAML Foundation

The Dilemma is exactly what is needed today. This series presents an opportunity to focus on ethics at a time when moral norms are increasingly disputed; to draw vital connections between the ancient and the modern; and to illuminate to a broad audience the esoteric wisdom of the Jewish tradition. It epitomizes what lifelong learning should be: engaging, informative and relevant.

MARTIN PRITIKIN
Dean, Concord Law School

Contents:

LESSON 1 1

No Good Deed Unpunished
What If a Crime Has an Upside?

LESSON 2 39

Above the Law
*The Ethics of Taking Matters
into Your Own Hands*

LESSON 3 79

Windfall Wrangles
*Determining Ownership
for Exotic Finds*

LESSON 4 105

Between Proximate and Remote
*Is One Responsible for Causing
an Indirect Loss?*

LESSON 5 149

Making the Right Turn
*Engineering Ethics into
Driverless Vehicles*

LESSON 6 187

Hastening the Inevitable
*Is One Responsible for Expediting
Inescapable Harm?*

Lesson

1

NO GOOD DEED UNPUNISHED

WHAT IF A CRIME HAS AN UPSIDE?

Legal theorists have long struggled to come up with a coherent account of culpability. Are criminals punished for their intentions, for their actions, or for causing harm? This lesson bursts into the discussion with three real-life cases that share a curious common feature: a criminal whose malicious actions result in an unplanned positive outcome for the intended victim. Drawing on biblical and Talmudic literature, we consider the interplay between these elements—intention, action, and outcome—in law, ethics, and life.

CASE STUDY A

SOURCES: IDAN DOYEV, "VICTIM OF TERROR ATTACK IN RISHON L'TZIYON: 'THE STABBING SAVED MY LIFE,'" WWW.NRG.CO.IL/ONLINE/1/ART2/736/941.HTML, NOVEMBER 11, 2015; YARON DORON, "THREE WOUNDED IN TERROR-STABBING ATTACK IN RISHON L'TZIYON," WWW.NRG.CO.IL/ONLINE/1/ART2/735/002.HTML, NOVEMBER 2, 2015

Daniel Cohen, aged thirty-one, was waiting for his bus near the Central Bus Station of Rishon L'Tziyon, Israel. It was a Monday in early November 2015, and the country was dealing with a frenzy of hate-filled acts of terror against Jews, the majority of them knife attacks on unsuspecting civilians.

Suddenly, Cohen felt an arm wrap around his neck, cutting off his ability to breathe. Gasping for air, he struggled with his attacker, a young twenty-something Arab man who had now produced a knife and was aiming for his neck. The blow glanced off his jaw, and his attacker persisted to stab him repeatedly along the left side of his upper body. Still Cohen fought back, until a passerby came to help and chased the terrorist away.

After receiving first aid from a bus driver in the area, who helped to stop the flow of blood, Cohen was rushed off by a Magen David Adom ambulance. When he woke up in a hospital room some time later, Daniel Cohen's life had been saved—twice. It turned out that in the course of a four-hour procedure, while Cohen's doctors were working on his spleen and liver, they discovered a cancerous growth above his large intestine, which they subsequently removed. As Cohen later put in an interview with the NRG news site, "That terrorist attack saved my life."

The terrorist, a native of the town of Hebron, was subsequently taken into police custody.

POLL 1

Should the attacker be granted a more lenient sentence?

1 Yes

2 No

3 Not sure

CASE STUDY **B**

SOURCES: JOE WARD AND LINZE RICE, "IF THIEVES HADN'T ACCIDENTALLY SAVED DOG FROM HOT CAR, BAR OWNER WOULD HAVE," JULY 28, 2016, WWW.DNAINFO. COM/CHICAGO/20160728/WEST-TOWN/IF-THIEVES-HADNT-ACCIDENTALLY-SAVED-DOG-FROM-HOT-CAR-BAR-OWNER-WOULD-HAVE; CHRISTOPHER BRENNAN, "THIEVES ACCIDENTALLY SAVE DOG FROM HOT TRUCK BY BREAKING WINDOW TO STEAL LAPTOP," *NEW YORK DAILY NEWS*, JULY 28, 2016, WWW.NYDAILYNEWS.COM/1.2729895

On Monday, July 25, 2016, a group of young men were walking outside of Irish Nobleman Pub on Chicago's West Side when they spotted a laptop in a pickup truck. Surveillance footage posted by pub owner Declan Morgan showed the thieves breaking into the vehicle to steal the computer, but they don't appear to notice the animal they've accidentally rescued.

The German shepherd was left in the car at around 9 a.m. on a morning when temperatures reached into the high 80s (Fahrenheit). The truck's window was smashed about twenty minutes later, but it was not until an hour after first leaving the canine in the car that its owner came back and noticed the damage. The American Veterinary Medical Association notes that when temperatures outside a vehicle are in the 80-degree range, after an hour, the vehicle's inside can reach temperatures as high as 125 degrees, leading to a high risk of heatstroke for pets.

"I truly believe that if they didn't break the window, the dog would have died," Morgan said. "I asked the guy why he left his dog in the car, and he said he thought he parked in the shade."

Chicago Police Officer Bari Lemmon said that they saw the video but had not received any report from the victim. Some have speculated that the unidentified truck owner is not coming forward about losing his laptop for fear of possible animal abuse charges.

"If I would have seen the car [with the dog], I probably would have smashed [the window]," Morgan said.

POLL 2

Should these men be exempt from compensating the car owner for his window?

1 Yes

2 No

3 Not sure

CASE STUDY C

SOURCES: RABBI CHAIM SEGALOWITZ, *RESPONSA MEKOR CHAYIM* 33; "ALCOHOL MONOPOLY," *ENCYCLOPEDIA OF RUSSIAN HISTORY*, WWW.ENCYCLOPEDIA.COM/ DOC/1G2-3404100043.HTML; "RUSSIA," *THE JEWISH ENCYCLOPEDIA*, WWW. JEWISHENCYCLOPEDIA.COM/ARTICLES/12943-RUSSIA

In 1894, Czar Alexander initiated the establishment of a strict government liquor monopoly throughout the Russian Empire. Before that time, the sale of alcohol had been taxed heavily, but the monopoly meant that the state would become the sole seller of all spirits for the internal market. Taverns were shut down and state-managed liquor stores took over an industry in which Jewish people had long been an integral part, and upon which they relied so heavily for their livelihood. Thousands of families were suddenly left destitute.

Some Jews felt that they had no choice but to take their taverns underground and to sell spirits illegally. One day, one such Jew living in Lithuania was visited by a fellow Jew, who, to the vendor's utter dismay, destroyed his barrel of alcohol.

The liquor seller was livid, but only at first. Unbeknownst to both vandal and vendor, a government official had been doing rounds at that time, checking compliance with the liquor laws. He entered the vendor's store seconds after the vandal broke the barrel. Thus the vendor was saved from being found in violation of the law and escaped paying the harsh penalties that would have far exceeded the value of the alcohol that had just been in his possession. All of this, thanks to a destructive vandal.

POLL 3

Should the vandal be exempt from paying for the alcohol?

1 Yes

2 No

3 Not sure

BABYLONIAN TALMUD

A literary work of monumental proportions that draws upon the legal, spiritual, intellectual, ethical, and historical traditions of Judaism. The 37 tractates of the Babylonian Talmud contain the teachings of the Jewish sages from the period after the destruction of the 2nd Temple through the 5th century CE. It has served as the primary vehicle for the transmission of the Oral Law and the education of Jews over the centuries; it is the entry point for all subsequent legal, ethical, and theological Jewish scholarship.

TEXT 1

TALMUD, NAZIR 23A

מִי שֶׁנִּתְכַּוֵּון לַעֲלוֹת בְּיָדוֹ בְּשַׂר חֲזִיר, וְעָלָה בְּיָדוֹ בְּשַׂר טָלֶה, טָעוּן כַּפָּרָה וּסְלִיחָה.

One who reaches out to take pork with the intention of eating it, but accidentally takes lamb instead, stands in need of atonement and forgiveness.

QUESTION FOR DISCUSSION

How might this Talmudic passage apply to our case studies?

TEXT 2a

GENESIS 37:17–28, 39:1 🚶🚶

וַיֵּלֶךְ יוֹסֵף אַחַר אֶחָיו, וַיִּמְצָאֵם בְּדֹתָן.

וַיִּרְאוּ אֹתוֹ מֵרָחֹק, וּבְטֶרֶם יִקְרַב אֲלֵיהֶם, וַיִּתְנַכְּלוּ אֹתוֹ לַהֲמִיתוֹ. וַיֹּאמְרוּ אִישׁ אֶל אָחִיו, הִנֵּה בַּעַל הַחֲלֹמוֹת הַלָּזֶה בָּא. וְעַתָּה לְכוּ וְנַהַרְגֵהוּ, וְנַשְׁלִכֵהוּ בְּאַחַד הַבֹּרוֹת, וְאָמַרְנוּ חַיָּה רָעָה אֲכָלָתְהוּ . . .

וַיְהִי כַּאֲשֶׁר בָּא יוֹסֵף אֶל אֶחָיו, וַיַּפְשִׁיטוּ אֶת יוֹסֵף אֶת כֻּתָּנְתּוֹ, אֶת כְּתֹנֶת הַפַּסִּים אֲשֶׁר עָלָיו. וַיִּקָּחֻהוּ וַיַּשְׁלִכוּ אֹתוֹ הַבֹּרָה, וְהַבּוֹר רֵק אֵין בּוֹ מָיִם.

וַיֵּשְׁבוּ לֶאֱכָל לֶחֶם, וַיִּשְׂאוּ עֵינֵיהֶם וַיִּרְאוּ, וְהִנֵּה אֹרְחַת יִשְׁמְעֵאלִים בָּאָה מִגִּלְעָד . . .

וַיֹּאמֶר יְהוּדָה אֶל אֶחָיו, מַה בֶּצַע כִּי נַהֲרֹג אֶת אָחִינוּ וְכִסִּינוּ אֶת דָּמוֹ. לְכוּ וְנִמְכְּרֶנּוּ לַיִּשְׁמְעֵאלִים, וְיָדֵנוּ אַל תְּהִי בוֹ, כִּי אָחִינוּ בְשָׂרֵנוּ הוּא, וַיִּשְׁמְעוּ אֶחָיו.

. . . וַיִּמְשְׁכוּ וַיַּעֲלוּ אֶת יוֹסֵף מִן הַבּוֹר, וַיִּמְכְּרוּ אֶת יוֹסֵף לַיִּשְׁמְעֵאלִים בְּעֶשְׂרִים כָּסֶף, וַיָּבִיאוּ אֶת יוֹסֵף מִצְרָיְמָה . . .

וְיוֹסֵף הוּרַד מִצְרָיְמָה, וַיִּקְנֵהוּ פּוֹטִיפַר סְרִיס פַּרְעֹה שַׂר הַטַּבָּחִים אִישׁ מִצְרִי מִיַּד הַיִּשְׁמְעֵאלִים אֲשֶׁר הוֹרִדֻהוּ שָׁמָּה . . .

Joseph went after his brothers and found them in Dothan.

They saw him in the distance, and before he reached them, they were plotting to kill him. "Here comes the dreamer!" they said to one another. "Now we have the chance. Let's kill him and throw him into one of the wells. We can say that a wild beast ate him." . . .

When Joseph came to his brothers, they stripped him of the long colorful coat that he was wearing. They took him and threw him into a pit. The pit was empty; there was no water in it.

The brothers sat down and ate a meal. When they looked up, they saw an Arab caravan coming from Gilead. . . .

Judah said to his brothers, "What will we gain if we kill our brother and cover his blood? Let's sell him to the Arabs and not harm him with our own hands. After all, he's our brother, our own flesh and blood."

His brothers agreed. . . . [The brothers] pulled Joseph out of the pit. They sold him to the Arabs for twenty pieces of silver. . . .

Joseph was brought down to Egypt, and Potiphar, one of Pharaoh's officers, the captain of the guard, purchased him from the Arabs who had brought him there. . . .

TEXT 2b

GENESIS 41:15–40

וַיֹּאמֶר פַּרְעֹה אֶל יוֹסֵף, חֲלוֹם חָלַמְתִּי וּפֹתֵר אֵין אֹתוֹ, וַאֲנִי שָׁמַעְתִּי עָלֶיךָ לֵאמֹר, תִּשְׁמַע חֲלוֹם לִפְתֹּר אֹתוֹ . . .

וַיֹּאמֶר יוֹסֵף אֶל פַּרְעֹה חֲלוֹם פַּרְעֹה אֶחָד הוּא, אֵת אֲשֶׁר הָאֱלֹקִים עֹשֶׂה הִגִּיד לְפַרְעֹה . . . הִנֵּה שֶׁבַע שָׁנִים בָּאוֹת, שָׂבָע גָּדוֹל בְּכָל אֶרֶץ מִצְרָיִם. וְקָמוּ שֶׁבַע שְׁנֵי רָעָב אַחֲרֵיהֶן, וְנִשְׁכַּח כָּל הַשָּׂבָע בְּאֶרֶץ מִצְרָיִם, וְכִלָּה הָרָעָב אֶת הָאָרֶץ. וְלֹא יִוָּדַע הַשָּׂבָע בָּאָרֶץ, מִפְּנֵי הָרָעָב הַהוּא אַחֲרֵי כֵן, כִּי כָבֵד הוּא מְאֹד . . .

וְעַתָּה יֵרֶא פַרְעֹה אִישׁ נָבוֹן וְחָכָם, וִישִׁיתֵהוּ עַל אֶרֶץ מִצְרָיִם. יַעֲשֶׂה פַרְעֹה וְיַפְקֵד פְּקִדִים עַל הָאָרֶץ, וְחִמֵּשׁ אֶת אֶרֶץ מִצְרַיִם בְּשֶׁבַע שְׁנֵי הַשָּׂבָע. וְיִקְבְּצוּ אֶת כָּל אֹכֶל הַשָּׁנִים הַטֹּבוֹת הַבָּאֹת הָאֵלֶּה, וְיִצְבְּרוּ בָר תַּחַת יַד פַּרְעֹה אֹכֶל בֶּעָרִים וְשָׁמָרוּ. וְהָיָה הָאֹכֶל לְפִקָּדוֹן לָאָרֶץ, לְשֶׁבַע שְׁנֵי הָרָעָב אֲשֶׁר תִּהְיֶיןָ בְּאֶרֶץ מִצְרָיִם, וְלֹא תִכָּרֵת הָאָרֶץ בָּרָעָב . . .

וַיֹּאמֶר פַּרְעֹה אֶל יוֹסֵף, אַחֲרֵי הוֹדִיעַ אֱלֹקִים אוֹתְךָ אֶת כָּל זֹאת, אֵין נָבוֹן וְחָכָם כָּמוֹךָ. אַתָּה תִּהְיֶה עַל בֵּיתִי וְעַל פִּיךָ יִשַּׁק כָּל עַמִּי, רַק הַכִּסֵּא אֶגְדַּל מִמֶּךָ . . .

Pharaoh said to Joseph, "I had a dream, and there is no one who can interpret it. I heard that when you hear a dream, you can explain it." . . .

Joseph said to Pharaoh, "Pharaoh's dream has a single meaning. God has told Pharaoh what He is about to do. . . . Seven years are coming, during which there will be a great surplus of food all over Egypt. These will be followed by seven years of famine, when all the surplus in Egypt will be forgotten. The famine will ravage the land. The ensuing famine will be so terrible that there will be no way of telling that there was once a surplus in the land. . . .

"Now Pharaoh must seek out a person with insight and wisdom, and place him in charge of Egypt. Pharaoh must then take further action, and appoint officials over the land. A rationing system will have to be set up over Egypt during the seven years of surplus. Let the officials collect all the food during these coming good years, and let them store the grain under Pharaoh's control. The food will be kept in the cities under guard. The food can then be held in reserve for the land when the seven famine years come to Egypt. The land will then not be depopulated by the famine." . . .

Pharaoh said to Joseph, "Since God has informed you about all this, there can be no one with as much insight and wisdom as you. You shall be in charge of my government, and food will be distributed to my people by your orders. Only by the throne will I outrank you." . . .

TEXT 2c

GENESIS 50:14–21

וַיָּשָׁב יוֹסֵף מִצְרַיְמָה, הוּא וְאֶחָיו וְכָל הָעֹלִים אִתּוֹ לִקְבֹּר אֶת אָבִיו, אַחֲרֵי קָבְרוֹ אֶת אָבִיו.

וַיִּרְאוּ אֲחֵי יוֹסֵף כִּי מֵת אֲבִיהֶם, וַיֹּאמְרוּ לוּ יִשְׂטְמֵנוּ יוֹסֵף, וְהָשֵׁב יָשִׁיב לָנוּ אֵת כָּל הָרָעָה אֲשֶׁר גָּמַלְנוּ אֹתוֹ . . .

וַיֵּלְכוּ גַּם אֶחָיו, וַיִּפְּלוּ לְפָנָיו, וַיֹּאמְרוּ הִנֶּנּוּ לְךָ לַעֲבָדִים.

וַיֹּאמֶר אֲלֵהֶם יוֹסֵף אַל תִּירָאוּ כִּי הֲתַחַת אֱלֹקִים אָנִי. וְאַתֶּם חֲשַׁבְתֶּם עָלַי רָעָה, אֱלֹקִים חֲשָׁבָהּ לְטֹבָה, לְמַעַן עֲשֹׂה כַּיּוֹם הַזֶּה לְהַחֲיֹת עַם רָב. וְעַתָּה אַל תִּירָאוּ, אָנֹכִי אֲכַלְכֵּל אֶתְכֶם וְאֶת טַפְּכֶם, וַיְנַחֵם אוֹתָם וַיְדַבֵּר עַל לִבָּם.

After he buried his father, Joseph returned to Egypt along with his brothers and all those who went with him to his father's burial.

Joseph's brothers began to realize [the implications] of their father's death. "What if Joseph is still holding a grudge against us?" they said. "He is likely to pay us back for all the evil we did to him." . . .

They came and threw themselves at his feet. "Here!" they said, "We are your slaves!"

"Don't be afraid," said Joseph to them. "Shall I take God's place? You might have meant to do me harm [but] God made it come out good. [He made] it come out as it actually did, where the life of a great nation has been preserved. Now, do not worry. I will fully provide for you and your children." He thus comforted them and spoke kindly to them.

QUESTION FOR DISCUSSION

How might this biblical story apply to our case studies?

POLL 4

Based on the story of Joseph, should the attacker in Case Study A be granted a more lenient sentence?

1 Yes

2 No

3 Not sure

POLL 5

Based on the story of Joseph, should the men in Case Study B be exempt from compensating the car owner for his window?

1 Yes

2 No

3 Not sure

POLL 6

Based on the story of Joseph, should the vandal in Case Study C be exempt from paying for the alcohol?

4 Yes

5 No

6 Not sure

CHAVRUTA B

TEXT 3

TALMUD, MENACHOT 64A

לֹא שָׁמַע שֶׁטָּבַע תִּינוֹק בַּיָּם, וּפָרַשׂ מְצוּדָה לְהַעֲלוֹת דָּגִים . . . וְהֶעֱלָה
תִּינוֹק וְדָגִים - רַבָּה אָמַר פָּטוּר, וְרָבָא אָמַר חַיָּב.

רַבָּה אָמַר פָּטוּר - זִיל בָּתַר מַעֲשָׂיו. וְרָבָא אָמַר חַיָּב - זִיל בָּתַר מַחְשַׁבְתּוֹ.

Say a child has fallen into the sea on Shabbat but a particular fisherman was unaware of this. He spreads his net to catch fish . . . but in addition to catching fish he also saves the child. Rabah says he is not liable, but Rava says he is liable.

Rabah says he is not liable because we decide the matter by his actual deed. Rava says he is liable because we decide the matter by his intention.

RABAH BAR NACHMANI (RABAH)
CA. 270–330

Third-generation Talmudic sage (*amora*). Rabah headed the Talmudic academy of Pumbedita, Babylonia. His prodigious ability to debate, resolve, and apply earned him the nickname "uprooter of mountains." He was known for beginning his Torah lectures with a witticism to put his students in a good mood.

ABBA BEN YOSEF (RAVA)
CA. 280–352

Fourth-generation Talmudic sage (*amora*), referred to in the Talmud as Rava (short for Rabbi Abba). Rava is one of the most oft-cited rabbis of the Talmud. He lived in Machoza, Babylonia. He was famous for his debates with his study-partner, Abaye; their debates are considered classic examples of Talmudic dialectical logic. Out of hundreds of their recorded disputes, the law was decided according to Rava's opinion in all but six cases.

? QUESTION FOR DISCUSSION

How might this text apply to our case studies?

Figure 1.1

Intention — Action — Outcome

	NEGATIVE INTENT	ACT	POSITIVE OUTCOME
Talmud's Case	Desecration of Shabbat	Fishing	Saving life of child
Case Study A	Murder	Stabbing	Discovering harmful tumor
Case Study B	Burglary	Breaking car window	Saving life of dog
Case Study C	Vandalism	Destroying barrel of alcohol	Averting penalty

TEXT 4

MAIMONIDES, *MISHNEH TORAH,* LAWS OF SHABBAT 2:16 📖

נִתְכַּוֵּן לְהַעֲלוֹת דָּגִים, וְהֶעֱלָה דָגִים וְתִינוֹק, פָּטוּר. אֲפִילוּ לֹא שָׁמַע
שֶׁטָּבַע, הוֹאִיל וְהֶעֱלָה תִּינוֹק עִם הַדָּגִים פָּטוּר.

If a fisherman lowers his net to catch fish, and he happens to also save a child, he is not liable—even if he did not know that the child had fallen into the water.

**RABBI MOSHE BEN MAIMON
(MAIMONIDES, RAMBAM) 1135–1204**

Halachist, philosopher, author, and physician. Maimonides was born in Cordoba, Spain. After the conquest of Cordoba by the Almohads, he fled Spain and eventually settled in Cairo, Egypt. There, he became the leader of the Jewish community and served as court physician to the vizier of Egypt. He is most noted for authoring the *Mishneh Torah,* an encyclopedic arrangement of Jewish law, and for his philosophical work, *Guide for the Perplexed.* His rulings on Jewish law are integral to the formation of halachic consensus.

TEXT 5

RABBI CHAIM SEGALOWITZ, *RESPONSA MEKOR CHAYIM* 33

נִרְאֶה לִי דְּפָטוּר מִטַּעַם כֵּיוָן עַל יְדֵי שֶׁשּׁוֹבֵר נִיצַל מִלְשַׁלֵּם עוֹנֶשׁ, וְטוֹבָה גְדוֹלָה עָשָׂה לוֹ בָּזֶה.

וְחֵילֵי דִילִי מֵהַהִיא דִמְנָחוֹת... אַלְמָא אַף דְּכַוָּנָתוֹ הָיָה לְאִיסּוּר... וְיוּכַל לִהְיוֹת שֶׁגַּם תְּחִלַּת מַעֲשָׂיו הָיָה בְּאִיסּוּר, כְּגוֹן שֶׁהַמְצוּדָה יָרַד לַמְצוּלָה וְצָד דָּגִים, וְאָז חַיָּיב אַף שֶׁלֹּא הוֹצִיאָהּ עֲדַיִין מֵהַיָּם, כֵּיוָן שֶׁכְּבָר הֵם נִיצוֹדִים וְעוֹמְדִים, בְּכָל זֶה, אִם אַף בַּחֲזִירָתוֹ הַמְצוּדָה מֵהַיָּם הֶעֱלָה תִּינוֹק אָז פָּטוּר, וְנִתַּקֵּן הָאִיסּוּר, כֵּן מַשְׁמַע מֵהַגְּמָרָא...

וְאִם כֵּן, גַּם כָּאן בְּנִידוֹן דִּידַן, אַף שֶׁמִּתְּחִלָּה עָבַד לוֹ הֶיזֵק שֶׁשָּׁבַר לוֹ הַכְּלִי יֵין שָׂרָף, בְּכָל זֶה אִם אַחַר כָּךְ נִמְצָא שֶׁעָשָׂה לוֹ טוֹבָה בָּזֶה, אֲזַי פָּטוּר.

RABBI CHAIM SEGALOWITZ
1844–1925

Rabbi Chaim Segalowitz served as rabbi in Salcininkai, near Vilna, from 1870–1884, and later moved to Vilna, where he served until his passing in 1925. In 1894 he published his work *Mekor Chayim*, which includes halachic responsa as well as Talmudic commentaries and his homilies.

It would seem to me that the vandal is not liable, because by breaking the barrel of alcohol, he saved the vendor from a penalty, and thus did him a great service.

My proof is from the Talmudic passage about the fisherman. . . . In that case, his intentions were to commit a prohibition. . . . In fact, it is possible that his net first caught fish—at which point he would be liable—and only afterward he caught the child. And nevertheless, if at some point during his lowering of the net he saved the child, his transgression is corrected and he is exempt. So it is implied in the Talmud. . . .

Therefore, in our case, although at first the vandal caused the vendor damage by breaking the barrel of alcohol, nevertheless, if it emerges thereafter that he thereby did him a favor, the vandal is exempt.

TEXT 6

RABBI SHLOMO HAKOHEN OF VILNA, *RESPONSA BINYAN SHLOMO,* VOL. II, *CHOSHEN MISHPAT* 5

מַה דְּהֵבִיא רְאָיָה מֵהָא דְּפוֹרֵשׁ מְצוּדָה לְהַעֲלוֹת דָּגִים וְהֶעֱלָה תִּינוֹק
וְדָגִים, דְּקַיְימָא לָן כְּרַבָּה דְּפָטוּר, דְּאָזְלִינַן בָּתַר מַעֲשָׂיו, שָׁאֲנִי הָתָם
דְּבְאוֹתָהּ מְלָאכָה דְּצֵידָה גוּפָא הָיָה בָּהּ פִּיקּוּחַ נְפָשׁוֹת.

וְאַף דְּהַדָּגִים נִיצוֹדִין מִתְּחִילָּה קוֹדֶם שֶׁהֶעֱלָה הַתִּינוֹק, מִכָּל מָקוֹם מִידֵּי
סְפֵיקָא לֹא נַפְקָא, דְּשֶׁמָּא הֶעֱלָה תִּינוֹק מִתְּחִילָּה בְּתוֹךְ הַמְּצוּדָה וְאִי
אֶפְשָׁר לְחַיְּיבוֹ . . .

אֲבָל אִם יָדוּעַ לְהֵיפֶךְ, שֶׁהֶעֱלָה הַדָּגִים מִתְּחִילָּה, גַּם לְרַבָּה חַיָּיב, דְּהָא
בְּכַהַאי גַּוְונָא מַחֲשַׁבְתּוֹ וְגַם הַמַּעֲשֶׂה הָיָה בְּאִיסּוּר, אַף דְּאַחַר כָּךְ הֶעֱלָה
גַּם תִּינוֹק, מִכָּל מָקוֹם אִי אֶפְשָׁר לְפוֹטְרוֹ מֵחֲמַת הַמַּעֲשֶׂה שֶׁעָשָׂה
בַּתְּחִילָּה . . . וְהִלְכָּךְ גַּם לְרַבָּה חַיָּיב.

וּמִמֵּילָא בְּנִידוֹן דִּידַן נַמִי, דְּהַמַּחֲשָׁבָה וְגַם הַמַּעֲשֶׂה הָיָה לְהַזִּיק לַחֲבֵירוֹ,
גַּם לְרַבָּה חַיָּיב לְשַׁלֵּם. וּבַמֶּה שֶׁאַחַר כָּךְ הָיָה הַהֶיזֵק לְטוֹבָתוֹ, אִי אֶפְשָׁר
לְפָטְרוֹ מֵחֲמַת זֶה.

RABBI SHLOMO HAKOHEN
1828–1905

Supreme judge of the Vilna rabbinical court. Rabbi Shlomo Hakohen was the editor of the Vilna Edition of the Talmud, by far the most common printed edition of the Talmud and still in use today. He sought to produce the most accurate version of the Talmud without the errors that were present in previous editions.

You cite a proof from the Talmudic passage about the fisherman who casts his net to catch fish and who inadvertently rescues a child in the process. In this case, we rule according to Rabah that the fisherman is not liable because he is judged by his deed, not his intention.

However, that case is different [from our case of the liquor vandal] because the act of fishing itself saved a life.

Although it is possible that the fish were caught before he brought up the child, one cannot be certain of this; it is possible that he first caught the child, and so he cannot be held liable. . . . However, if it is known for sure that he first caught fish, even Rabah would deem him liable, because both his intent and action were forbidden. Even though he subsequently caught and rescued the child in the same haul, he cannot be exonerated of his original prohibited action. . . . Therefore, even Rabah would agree that he is culpable.

Therefore, it follows that in our case [of the liquor vandal], where the intent was to cause damage and the deed caused damage, he is liable to pay. The fact that the damage later turned out to be for the vendor's benefit cannot exonerate the vandal of his already-established culpability.

QUESTION FOR DISCUSSION

How would Rabbi Shlomo Hakohen rule in the first two case studies of this lesson?

POLL 7

Would Rabbi Shlomo Hakohen treat the attacker in Case Study A leniently?

1 Yes

2 No

3 Not sure

POLL 8

Would Rabbi Shlomo Hakohen treat the burglars in Case Study B leniently?

1 Yes

2 No

3 Not sure

Figure 1.2

Summary of Rabbi Shlomo Hakohen, *Responsa Binyan Shlomo*

	LIABLE	EXONERATED
Talmud's Case		✓
Case Study A (stabbing)	✓	
Case Study B (dog)		✓
Case Study C (alcohol)	✓	

KEY POINTS

1 Those who intend to transgress, but inadvertently perform a neutral act instead of a transgressive act, are not penalized. They do, however, require atonement and forgiveness.

2 Joseph did not punish his brothers for selling him into slavery, pointing out that this act ultimately effected a positive result. While Joseph possibly intended to exonerate them in a legal sense, this was more likely his personal attitude regarding revenge, and does not teach us how such a case should play out in a court of law.

3 Although fishing on Shabbat is forbidden, one is obligated to throw a net into the water to save a life. But is it only the *intention* to save a life that overrides the Shabbat prohibition? Or does the mere *act* of saving the life, even without intention, override the prohibition? The final halachic ruling follows the latter interpretation.

4 A corollary of this ruling: If someone commits a crime, but the act immediately and directly leads to a greater positive benefit, this person will not be held liable in a court of law. According to the halachic consensus, this ruling does not apply if the positive benefit occurred after the criminal act.

5 Although, in some cases, a criminal will be exempt in a court of law, the court still has the right to administer extrajudicial penalties to ensure a more peaceful society, and the criminal still holds moral responsibility and ought to repent.

6 The primary goal of Judaism is to better the world. Therefore, Judaism recognizes the primacy of actions and results over intentions.

Continue your
learning experience
ONLINE
Visit www.myJLI.com/dilemma1
for insightful and inspiring videos,
articles, and readings on this topic.

Appendix

TEXT 7

IMMANUEL KANT, *GROUNDWORK OF THE METAPHYSICS OF MORALS* 4:394, MARY GREGOR, ED. (CAMBRIDGE: CAMBRIDGE UNIVERSITY PRESS, 1998), P. 8

A good will is not good because of what it effects or accomplishes, because of its fitness to attain some proposed end, but only because of its volition. . . . Even if, by a special disfavor of fortune . . . this will should wholly lack the capacity to carry out its purpose—if with its greatest efforts it should yet achieve nothing and only the good will were left (not, of course, as a mere wish but as the summoning of all means insofar as they are in our control)—then, like a jewel, it would still shine by itself, as something that has its full worth in itself.

IMMANUEL KANT
1724–1804

One of the most influential Western philosophers, Kant's contributions to metaphysics, epistemology, ethics, and aesthetics have had a profound impact on almost every philosophical movement that followed him. His most famous work, Critique of Pure Reason, deals with questions concerning the foundations and extent of human knowledge.

TEXT 8

ADAM SMITH, *THE THEORY OF MORAL SENTIMENTS,* PART II, SECTION III, CH. II,
(LONDON: A. STRAHAN, T. CADELL, 1812), PP. 172–173

The thief, whose hand has been caught in his neighbour's pocket before he had taken any thing out of it, is punished with ignominy only. If he had got time to take away a handkerchief, he would have been put to death. The house-breaker, who has been found setting a ladder to his neighbour's window, but had not got into it, is not exposed to the capital punishment. The attempt to ravish is not punished as a rape. The attempt to seduce a married woman is not punished at all, though seduction is punished severely. Our resentment against the person who only attempted to do a mischief, is seldom so strong as to bear us out in inflicting the same punishment upon him, which we should have thought due if he had actually done it. In the one case, the joy of our deliverance alleviates our sense of the atrocity of his conduct; in the other, the grief of our misfortune increases it. His real demerit, however, is undoubtedly the same in both cases, since his intentions were equally criminal; and there is in this respect, therefore, an irregularity in the sentiments of all men, and a consequent relaxation of discipline in the laws of, I believe, all nations, of the most civilized, as well as of the most barbarous.

ADAM SMITH
CA. 1723–1790

A Scottish philosopher, Smith is most famous for his book, *An Inquiry into the Nature and Causes of the Wealth of Nations.* Published in 1776, this work established economics as an autonomous subject and launched the economic doctrine of free enterprise. The book had a profound influence on modern economics and the concept of individual freedom.

TEXT 9

JUDGE RICHARD POSNER, *MILNER V. APFEL,* 148 F. 3D 812, 815 (7TH CIR. 1998)

Take two cases. In one a reckless driver narrowly misses hitting a child; in the other, a no more reckless driver hits a child. As far as mental state is concerned, both are equally blameworthy; but the second driver will be punished much more heavily. . . . The reason is that the community attaches moral significance to consequences as well as to states of mind.

RICHARD POSNER
1939–

American jurist. Posner serves as a judge on the United States Court of Appeals for the Seventh Circuit and is a senior lecturer at the University of Chicago Law School. A leading scholar in the fields of law and economics, he was identified by the Journal of Legal Studies as the most cited legal scholar of the 20th century.

TEXT 10a

TALMUD, BAVA METSI'A 101A

> הַיּוֹרֵד לְתוֹךְ שְׂדֵה חֲבֵירוֹ וּנְטָעָהּ שֶׁלֹּא בִּרְשׁוּת, אָמַר רַב: שָׁמִין לוֹ, וְיָדוֹ
> עַל הַתַּחְתּוֹנָה.
>
> וּשְׁמוּאֵל אָמַר: אוֹמְדִין כַּמָּה אָדָם רוֹצֶה לִיתֵּן בְּשָׂדֶה זוֹ לְנוֹטְעָהּ.
>
> אָמַר רַב פָּפָּא: וְלֹא פְּלִיגֵי. כָּאן בְּשָׂדֶה הָעֲשׂוּיָה לִיטַּע, כָּאן בְּשָׂדֶה שֶׁאֵינָהּ
> עֲשׂוּיָה לִיטַּע.

If one enters a neighbor's field and plants trees without permission, Rav said: An assessment is made, and the laborer is at a disadvantage. [Meaning, we assess both the laborer's costs and the value of the improvements, and the field owner pays for the cheaper of the two (RASHI).]

Shmuel said: We estimate how much a person is willing to pay for such a job [and the field owner pays this amount].

Said Rav Papa: The two sages do not disagree. Shmuel refers to a field that is meant to be planted while Rav refers to a field that is not meant to be planted.

TEXT 10b

RABBI YOSEF CARO, *SHULCHAN ARUCH, CHOSHEN MISHPAT* 175:2

אָמַר לֵיהּ בַּעַל הַשָּׂדֶה: עֲקוֹר אִילָנָךְ וָלֵךְ, שׁוֹמְעִין לוֹ.

If, however, the owner of the field says, "Remove your trees and leave me alone," we listen to this claim [and the field owner need not pay anything].

RABBI YOSEF CARO (MARAN, *BEIT YOSEF*)
1488–1575

Halachic authority and author. Rabbi Caro was born in Spain, but was forced to flee during the expulsion in 1492 and eventually settled in Safed, Israel. He authored many works including the *Beit Yosef*, *Kesef Mishneh*, and a mystical work, *Magid Meisharim*. Rabbi Caro's magnum opus, the Shulchan Aruch (Code of Jewish Law), has been universally accepted as the basis for modern Jewish law.

QUESTION FOR DISCUSSION

How might Texts 10a and 10b relate to Case Study B? Can the burglars demand payment for saving the dog?

TEXT 11a

TALMUD, SANHEDRIN 91A

אִי קָאֵימְנָא - בָּעֵיטְנָא בָּךְ וּפָשִׁיטְנָא לְעַקְמוּתָךְ מִינָךְ.

אָמַר לֵיהּ: אִם אַתָּה עוֹשֶׂה כֵּן - רוֹפֵא אוּמָן תִּקָּרֵא, וְשָׂכָר הַרְבֵּה תִּטוֹל.

"If I stand up, I will kick you so hard that I will straighten out your hunchback."

Said Geviha, "If you do this, you will be called a skilled physician and command a large payment."

TEXT 11b

RABBI CHAIM YOSEF DAVID AZULAI, *PESACH EINAYIM,* AD LOC.

נִרְאֶה דְּאִם זֶה שֶׁעָשָׂה הַטּוֹבָה כִּיוֵן לְצַעֲרוֹ, אֶלָּא דְּהַטּוֹבָה בָּאָה מִמֵּילָא, אֵינוֹ חַיָּיב לְשַׁלֵּם, כֵּיוָן דְּיָדַע דְּאִיהוּ לְצַעוּרֵיהּ קָמְכַוֵּין.

וְהָכָא קָאָמַר "אִי קָאֵימְנָא בָּעִיטְנָא וְכוּ'", וְכַוָּנָתוֹ לְצַעֲרוֹ. וְהַגַּם דְּמִמֵּילָא בָּאָה טוֹבָה מְרוּבָּה, דְּפָשִׁיט לֵיהּ, לֹא יִתְחַיֵּיב שָׂכָר כִּמְדוּבָּר. וְהַיְינוּ דְּקָאָמַר לֵיהּ, אַף שֶׁכַּוָּנָתְךָ לְהָרַע, לֹא יִקָּרֵא שִׁמְךָ מְצַעֵר לַחֲבֵירוֹ אֶלָּא רוֹפֵא אוּמָן תִּקָּרֵא, וְשָׂכָר הַרְבֵּה תִּטּוֹל, אַף שֶׁאֵינוֹ מִין הַדִּין.

It seems to me that if the one who does you a favor intended to harm you, and you know this, you need not compensate the benefactor for the favor.

Here, the heretic said, "If I stand up, I will kick you, etc.," and his intention was to harm Geviha. Although he would have derived a great benefit, Geviha would not have been responsible to pay the heretic. Geviha thus said, "Although you would have intended harm, you would not be deemed an assaulter, but rather an expert physician. And you will ask for a large fee, though I would be under no obligation to give it to you."

RABBI CHAYIM YOSEF DAVID AZULAI (CHIDA) 1724–1806

Talmudist and noted bibliophile. Born in Jerusalem, scion to a prominent rabbinic family, he studied under Rabbi Chaim ibn Atar. A prolific writer on various Jewish topics, his *Shem Hagedolim* is particularly famous, chronicling short biographies of Jewish authors with overviews of their works. He traveled extensively in Europe to raise funds on behalf of the Jewish community in the land of Israel, and died in Italy.

Additional Readings

CRIMES, CONSEQUENCES, AND CULPABILITY
DETERMINING LIABILITY WHEN A CRIME LEADS TO A BENEFIT

MENACHEM SANDMAN

I. Moral Luck

On a hot day in July 2016, a group of young men on Chicago's West Side broke into a pickup truck and stole a laptop. Unbeknownst to the thieves, there was a dog in the car that might have died in the heat had they not broken the window. The car was parked for about an hour before the owner's return, long enough to cause heatstroke in pets according to the American Veterinary Medical Association.[1]

These alleged thieves did a good thing (saving the dog's life) without meaning to do so, which brings us to the concept of "moral luck." "Moral luck" is a term of recent vintage, but it describes an ancient philosophical concept. The *Stanford Philosophy Encyclopaedia*[2] defines moral luck in the following terms: "Moral luck occurs when an agent can be correctly treated as an object of moral judgment despite the fact that a significant aspect of what she is assessed for depends on factors beyond her control."

To better understand the concept of moral luck, let us consider and contrast two scenarios.

Scenario A: A driver is speeding recklessly down the road and narrowly misses hitting a pedestrian, who managed to dart out of harm's way at the last second.

Scenario B: A driver is speeding recklessly down the road, no more recklessly than the driver in Scenario A, and hits a pedestrian.

We have here two drivers. They are equally blameworthy for driving as recklessly as they did. The only

MENACHEM SANDMAN

Attorney at law, Sandman Law Group in New Haven, Connecticut. While at University of Connecticut School of Law, Sandman clerked for Judge James Bentivegna of the Connecticut Superior Court.

difference is that the pedestrian in Scenario A was nimble enough to avoid being hit, whereas the pedestrian in Scenario B was not so lucky. But despite their identical moral culpability, the driver in Scenario B will be punished far more heavily than the driver in Scenario A.

People intuitively sense that this should be the case—after all, driver B hit someone!—but why? Why does it matter that one scenario had a victim while the other did not? The "moral luck" experienced by the victimless driver was just that—luck. Why should he be treated less harshly by the law simply because of circumstances beyond his control?

In cases of this sort, society has chosen to consider the consequences of actions. We look at what you did (hit a pedestrian) as much as what you meant to do. As Judge Richard Posner, one of the most prolific living judges, explained, "The community attaches moral significance to consequences as well as to states of mind . . . [this] reflects a moral intuition that is deeply rooted in the traditions of the American people (and probably every other people as well)."[3]

This can then raise a question regarding our case in Chicago: Should the thieves in the news story get credit for freeing the dog even though they had no intention to do so? In law, will their unintended benevolence minimize their criminal or civil liability? Would it be a mitigating factor in sentencing?

It is possible to analyze both criminal law and civil law through an intention-or-consequences lens. Another way of describing those lenses would be action-or-results. Do we look at the person's action (driven by intentions), or at the *results* of the person's action?

II. Talmudic Law
What might the Talmud say about the Chicago thieves?

The Talmud brings a tidy example of this issue concerning the laws of Shabbat. It is forbidden for a Jew to fish on Shabbat. Obviously, as in any case of life-and-death, it is permitted to lower a net into the water in order to save a child even if this means that the actor will raise fish as well. And we thus arrive at a Talmudic dispute between Rabah and Rava.

> Say a child has fallen into the sea on Shabbat but a particular fisherman was unaware of this. He spreads his net to catch fish . . . but in addition to catching fish he also saves the child. Rabah says he is not liable, but Rava says he is liable.
>
> Rabah says he is not liable because we decide the matter by his actual deed. Rava says he is liable because we decide the matter by his intention.[4]

This is a case of pure luck. The fellow simply wanted to catch a fish for dinner, and the next thing he knows, he's saved a child's life.

Rava says that the prohibition of fishing on Shabbat is suspended only if you intend to save a life, because to Rava, intentions are paramount. It is true that the fisherman saved a child, but he also fished, and fishing was what he intended to do; so the fishing prevails. According to Rava, the actor is guilty of desecrating Shabbat and is liable to bring a sacrifice of atonement,[5] because that's what he intended to do. He gets no credit for rescuing the child. We can assume that this line of reasoning would lead to the conclusion that the thieves should get no credit for saving the dog's life when they broke into the car.

But Rabah says that the prohibition of fishing on Shabbat is suspended if you intend to save a life *or* if you do in fact save a life. To Rabah, outcome is paramount. It is true that the fisherman caught fish, but the prohibition is overlooked when a life is saved. We can assume that this line of reasoning would say that the thieves should indeed get credit for rescuing the dog when they broke into the car.

Rambam, in his codification of Jewish law, agrees with Rabah: "If a fisherman lowers his net to catch fish, and he happens to also save a child, he is not liable—even if he did not know that the child had fallen into the water."[6]

III. Criminal Law
A. Prosecution and Sentencing

How may the criminal justice system deal with our Chicago case? Would it look at the overall results of the situation or just the crime? The short answer is (probably) the crime (and not the positive outcome), and what follows is a brief explanation.

It is a tenet of our legal system that crimes are a wrong not against the individual, but against society as a whole. This is what distinguishes a person who steals from a person who breaches a contract. Thus, criminals are prosecuted not by the person who was wronged, but by the state on behalf of the people. That's why in the U.S., criminal cases are formulated as "The People" or "The State" v. Smith and the like, and in Commonwealth countries it will be "The Queen" (representing society) v. Smith.

The Crown Prosecution Service, which prosecutes crimes in the United Kingdom, sums up this idea: "The Crown Prosecution Service does not act for victims or the families of victims in the same way as solicitors act for their clients. We act on behalf of the public and not just in the interests of any particular individual."[7] Or, as the American Bar Association puts it: "The idea that the criminal law, unlike other branches of the law such as contracts and property, is designed to vindicate public rather than private interests is now firmly established."[8]

A salient example of this concept is a scenario in which one would think there is no victim because the "victim" consented to the perpetrator's actions. English case law shows that judges have long struggled with the question of whether a person can consent to assault.

> When one person is indicted for inflicting personal injury upon another, the consent of the person who sustains the injury is no defence to the person who inflicts the injury, if the injury is of such a nature, or is inflicted under such circumstances, that its infliction is injurious to the public as well as to the person injured. But the injuries given and received in prize-fights are injurious to the public, both because it is against the public interest that the lives and the health of the combatants should be endangered by blows, and because prize-fights

are disorderly exhibitions, mischievous on many obvious grounds.[9]

Given that a criminal case is prosecuted on behalf of the community as a whole, it should lead us to give less weight to the positive consequences of a criminally intended act. The unintended positive consequences of a crime impact the *individual* victim, whether it is the person who was assaulted or robbed and the like. However, the state's prosecution of a crime is not (primarily) to secure retribution for the victim, but for the betterment of society at large. In other words, criminal law seeks to sanction people for reasons beyond the isolated crime—and an unintended positive outcome to the individual has little relevance for the broader society.

At the same time, a prosecutor would have the authority to refrain from bringing charges or he may choose to bring lesser charges, considering the positive outcome:

> *Prosecutorial discretion is a central component of the federal criminal justice system. Prosecutors decide which cases to pursue and plea bargains to accept, determining the fates of the vast majority of criminal defendants who choose not to stand trial. Prosecutors' decisions are generally not, however, subject to judicial review.*[10]
>
> *Whether to prosecute and what charge to file or bring before a grand jury are decisions that generally rest in the prosecutor's discretion.*"[11]

Assuming the prosecutor does bring charges against these young men and they were found guilty, would the positive outcome have any impact on sentencing? To answer this we need to address the purposes of punishing an offender:

> *In general, there are four justifications for criminal sanctions: deterrence, incapacitation, rehabilitation, and just deserts. Since the American Founding, the influence of the four justifications of criminal punishment has varied. While closely aligned with utilitarianism, the deterrence and incapacitation models seek to reduce future crime. Deterrence seeks to make crime more costly, so less crime will occur. Incapacitation does not try to change behavior through raising costs; it simply*

removes the offender from society. The criminal behind prison bars cannot harm those of us on the outside. At its modern extreme, the rehabilitative model assumes crime is determined by social forces and not the decisions of criminals. The just deserts model asserts that punishments should be commensurate with the moral gravity of offenses.[12]

Given the four aims of sentencing, should criminal law focus more on intention, consequences or neither? Should dumb luck (rescuing a dog by breaking into a car) help reduce a person's sentence?

From the perspective of retribution alone, one could make a good argument that sentencing should be lenient considering the offender's dumb luck. However, the other three aims would lead to an opposite result: In these aims, the criminal sentencing goals are to deter people who are considering breaking into cars, to incapacitate those who have shown a tendency to break into cars, and to rehabilitate those who are of a mind to break into cars. Dumb luck should not help the criminal under these theories.

B. Victim Impact Statements

Our analysis might lead one to conclude that criminal law focuses primarily on intentions and minimally on the consequences of a criminal act. However, this not really the case as consequences are taken into account in many ways. Earlier, we saw how the law treats two acts of similar recklessness differently because of the differing results. And another good example of this is the use of victim impact statements.

> *Victim impact statements are written or oral information from crime victims, in their own words, about how a crime has affected them. All 50 states allow victim impact statements at some phase of the sentencing process. Most states permit them at parole hearings, and victim impact information is generally included in the pre-sentencing report presented to the judge.*
>
> *Purpose: The purpose of victim impact statements is to allow crime victims, during the decision-making process on sentencing or parole, to describe to the court or parole board the impact of the crime. A judge may use information from these statements to help determine an offender's sentence;*

a parole board may use such information to help decide whether to grant a parole and what conditions to impose in releasing an offender.[13]

Victim impact statements were once barred by the U.S. Supreme Court because they were found to be emotionally charged testimony that would divert the jury's attention from the defendant's actions. The court held that "the victim impact statements information in question may be wholly unrelated to the blameworthiness of a particular defendant, and may cause the sentencing decision to turn on irrelevant factors such as the degree to which the victim's family is willing and able to articulate its grief, or the relative worth of the victim's character. Thus, the evidence in question could improperly divert the jury's attention away from the defendant. Moreover, it would be difficult, if not impossible, to provide a fair opportunity to rebut such evidence without shifting the focus of the sentencing hearing away from the defendant."[14]

However, just a few years after it handed down its decision in *Booth v. Maryland*, the Supreme Court changed its mind. In a 5-to-4 decision, the U.S. Supreme Court ruled in *Payne v. Tennessee,* 501 U.S. 808 (1991) that crime victims' family members can deliver victim impact statements at capital sentencing hearings, reversing its own decision of just two years earlier in *Booth v. Maryland*. The *Booth* decision had barred the statements, viewing them as emotionally charged testimony that would divert the jury's attention from the defendant's responsibility for the crime and focus it on the character and identity of the victim. The *Payne* decision not only dismissed this concern, but found that the statements were valuable precisely because they remind sentencing juries and judges "that the victim is an individual whose death represents a unique loss to society and in particular to his family." Ultimately, the Supreme Court rejected the argument that the statements would influence sentencing based on irrelevant factors, such as the victim's attractiveness, respectability, social class, or race.

How does this bear on our intention-vs.-consequences discussion? It would seem that victim impact statements allow a shift from the intention of the crime to the ultimate consequences of the crime.

Although the judicial debate in the *Booth* and *Payne* decisions did not frame the issue that way, it is easy to conceive of a victim impact statement scenario where it becomes apparent that we are looking more to the consequences than the criminal intent that ultimately triggered those consequences.

Let us compare-and-contrast two scenarios. In both scenarios, the defendant shoots his victim dead. In Scenario A, the victim was an 18-year old straight-A student, in a large family, well-liked by his peers, admired by his teachers, and about to enter college. He had a bustling social life, busy extracurricular schedule, and was going to be part of the basketball team. In that case a victim impact statement would detail the devastation that the shooting wrought on the young man's family and friends, and how it cut off his promising future. In Scenario B, the victim was a chronically unemployed 60-year-old man with a drug problem, an unsociable hermit who had little family and few friends. Any victim impact statement would be far less heartbreaking and would probably elicit much less sympathy than in Scenario A.

Put differently, the downstream consequences of the defendant's criminal behavior in Scenario A were far more grievous than in Scenario B—and because victim impact statements are allowed, the defendant may receive a harsher sentence for the very same crime.

C. Considering Intent in Crimes

While Victim Impact Statements seem to push criminal law toward consequences, another area of law seems to focus on intent. At present, most states have enacted hate crime penalty-enhancement laws. Under these laws, "a perpetrator can face more severe penalties if the prosecutor can demonstrate, beyond a reasonable doubt, for the trier of fact that the victim was intentionally targeted on basis of his personal characteristics because of the perpetrator's bias against the victim. Almost every state penalty-enhancement hate crime law explicitly includes crimes directed against an individual on the basis of race, religion, and national origin/ethnicity."[15]

This means that there can be a situation where two individuals commit the same exact crime, but in one an offender will be punished in a harsher manner even though the outcomes of both crimes were the same. What the law is doing here is looking not only at the consequences of the criminal's act, but at the criminal's intention and punishing the criminal more severely due to his intention.

We see that, at least in America, there are crimes where we focus heavily on the person's intention. That summation may sound a little too much like a "thought crime," which has been the criticism leveled at hate crime legislation generally. As syndicated columnist Richard Cohen put it:

Almost as bad as hate crimes themselves is the designation. It is a little piece of totalitarian nonsense, a way for prosecutors to punish miscreants for their thoughts or speech, both of which used to be protected by the Constitution (I am an originalist in this regard). It is not the criminal act alone that matters anymore but the belief that might have triggered the act. For this, you can get an extra five years or so in the clink.[16]

IV. Civil Law

We've taken a closer look at the ways intention and consequence are treated in criminal law. If there's one thing we can take away from that discussion, it is that there is no black letter law approach to favoring either intention or consequences. There are strong policy considerations in favor of focusing on one or the other.

Let us now look at civil law.

A significant branch of civil law is tort law. *Torts* means wrongs done by the defendant to the plaintiff. There are many types of torts (trespass to land, for example), but the one we'll focus our discussion on here is the tort of negligence.

The golden rule of negligence is that "damage is the gist of negligence." *Damages* describes what harm the defendant suffered. What this rule is saying is that you can't sue someone (for negligence) unless that person caused you harm in some way.[17] [18]

To put it in academic jargon, tort law:

. . . is a law that empowers victims to respond to wrongdoers whose wrongs have injured them. Absent an 'injuring,' there is no victim to complain of

the conduct, and hence no basis for a tort suit or tort liability. To say the same thing affirmatively, tort law requires that fortuities as to realization be considered in assessing liability precisely because tort law is a victim-based law of wrongs rather than a community-based or society-based law of wrongs.[19]

The money which a defendant will be ordered to pay a plaintiff is called *damages*. In a tort case, the kind of harm for which the victim will be compensated can be broadly categorized in two ways: special damages (economic or out-of-pocket losses) and general damages (noneconomic losses).[20] [21] Special damages are those which can be calculated precisely, such as the medical expenses incurred from the injury that the defendant caused. General damages are harder to assess, such as compensation for pain and suffering.[22]

This brings us to the following question regarding our case: The vandals broke a person's car window. But, when they did so, the dog that had been forgotten in the back seat and was near death was saved. If the car owner were to sue the vandals who broke the window and won, what should the damages be? The cost of repairing the window? Or perhaps the costs of repairing the window, minus the value of the dog, which would have died had the defendant not broken the window?

Let us attempt to answer this question by analyzing the concept of "reasonable foreseeability." When A sues B for something B did that caused harm to A, the suit will be successful only if it is proven that it was reasonably foreseeable to B that B's actions would cause that harm to A. Just because B's actions caused harm to A does not mean that B will always be liable. The injury or damage must be foreseeable.

An example: A ship has pulled into the harbor. It begins leaking oil into the harbor. In normal circumstances, that oil should not have caused any damage, as it was nonflammable. But elsewhere at the wharf, metal workers were welding. Sparks from their acetylene torches fell onto bits of cotton waste that had made its way into the water. This fluke allowed the cotton to ignite, which then in turn set the oil on fire. This resulted in damage to several ships docked at the wharf. Although the leaking oil caused the damage (if not for the oil, nothing would have happened), the leaking ship was not liable, because the damage was not reasonably foreseeable.[23]

How does the concept of reasonable foreseeability impact our intention-vs.-consequences discussion? The simple response is that the positive outcome was not foreseeable to the vandals and therefore it should not be a factor for minimizing civil liability in our case.

But the analysis might change when we look at another well-known rule—the eggshell skull rule. If a person punches another person who is a lot more harmed than an average person because he has an eggshell-thin skull, the assailant is liable for all the damages even though any other victim's injuries would have been much less. The rule is that "we take the victim as we find him [or her]." A common example is a hemophiliac who bleeds to death after the defendant stabbed him, although nearly any other person would have survived easily.

In the context of torts, the eggshell skull rule is a counterbalance to the requirement of reasonable foreseeability. The leading case in this area is *Smith v. Leech Brain*. An employee suffered a burn from a splash of molten lead while he was at work, which triggered cancer from which he eventually died. The employee had a predisposition to cancer. The employer admitted that it had negligently caused the initial injury from the splash of molten lead, but argued that it should not be liable (in negligence) for the employee's ultimate death because it was not reasonably foreseeable.

The court rejected this argument. We must take the victim as we find the victim, no matter whether he or she has an eggshell-thin skull or a predisposition to cancer or hemophilia.[24]

Turning to our case: If we can say (to the defendant's detriment) that the defendant is civilly liable for the consequences of his or her actions, even beyond those that are reasonably foreseeable, why can we not also say (to the defendant's advantage) that a court trying a defendant for theft will take into account the fact that a dog was saved when that defendant broke

into the car? Why shouldn't good outcomes to bad behavior be rewarded in a civil context?

V. Conclusion

The jurisprudence behind many of the laws cited in this article may seem inconsistent when judging the matter through the lenses of intention and outcome. However, law is not only driven by abstract principles but also by public policy factors that, among other things, seek to reduce crime, compensate victims, and ensure societal benefits and overall gains. Ultimately, judging by these factors we see that unintended positive consequences would most probably not be taken into account to mitigate criminal or civil liability, while unintended negative consequences would be considered in rendering the punishment of someone who disturbs the peace.

Written for *The Dilemma: Modern Conundrums, Talmudic Debates, Your Solutions*

Endnotes

[1] http://tinyurl.com/zdjz7l7

[2] Nelkin, Dana K., "Moral Luck," *The Stanford Encyclopedia of Philosophy* (Winter 2013 Edition), Edward N. Zalta (ed.) (http://tinyurl.com/3mecsah).

[3] *Milner v. Apfel*, 148 F. 3d 812, 815 (7th Cir. 1998).

[4] Menachot 64 a

[5] See *Sefat Emet*, ad loc.

[6] Rambam, *Hilchot Shabbat* 2:15. This law was applied in actual civil cases. See Rabbi Chaim Segalowitz, *Responsa Mekor Chaim* 33; and Rabbi Shlomo Cohen, *Responsa Binyan Shlomo*, vol. II, *Choshen Mishpat* 5.

[7] "The Decision to Charge," http://tinyurl.com/hmetnxu.

[8] *ABA Standards for Criminal Justice*, Standard 3–2.1 cmt. (1979).

[9] *R v. Coney* (1882) 8 QB 534.

[10] Wayne R. LaFave, et al., *Criminal Procedure* §§1.9(c) and 13.2(g) (3d ed. 2007).

[11] *United States v. Batchelder*, 442 U.S. 114, 123-24 (1979) (citations omitted).

[12] The Heritage Foundation, *Theories of Punishment and Mandatory Minimum Sentences*, http://tinyurl.com/zd4s4pb. See also *United States v. Booker*, 543 U.S. 220, 268-270 (2005); Title 18 U. S. C. A. § 3553(a) (main ed. and Supp. 2004).

[13] Victim Impact Statements http://tinyurl.com/zd6kghd.

[14] *Booth v. Maryland* 482 U.S. 496, 505-508 (1987).

[15] See, "Hate Crime Laws — The ADL Approach," page 4. http://tinyurl.com/hl4xo4y.

[16] Richard Cohen, "Op-Ed: Hate-Crime Laws Turn Thoughts into Crimes," *The Washington Post*, October 19, 2010. http://tinyurl.com/3xsbp5h.

[17] See, e.g., *Comstock v. Wilson*, 257 NY 231, 235 (N.Y. App. 1931).

[18] There are some torts (such as trespass) that are actionable *per se*: this means that you can sue a person for the very fact that they committed the tort, even if they haven't caused you any harm. For example, imagine that someone constantly walks through your land as a shortcut. It is very likely that his action causes you no harm (meaning, legally there is no damage) but you want him to stop. Because trespass is actionable *per se*, you can sue him. The remedy might be an injunction restraining the person from walking through your land, or a nominal payment the trespasser must make which serves to acknowledge that it is your land and he had no right to walk through it.

This is not the case for the tort of negligence. An action in negligence can succeed only if there was damage.

[19] John C. P. Goldberg & Benjamin C. Zipursky, "Tort Law and Moral Luck," 92 *Cornell L. Rev.* 1123, 1135 (2007).

[20] We will not discuss punitive damages here.

[21] In Halachah: *tzar, ripui, and boishes* would all be called "damages."

[22] See, e.g., *Kenton v. Hyatt Hotels*, 693 S.W.2d 83 (Mo. 1985).

[23] See: *Overseas Tankship (UK) Ltd. v. Morts Dock and Engineering Co. Ltd.* or "Wagon Mound (No. 1)" [1961] UKPC 2.

[24] *Smith v. Leech Brain & Co.* [1962] 2 QB 405.

Lesson

2

ABOVE THE LAW
THE ETHICS OF TAKING MATTERS INTO YOUR OWN HANDS

We are blessed today to live under a system of laws that enables our orderly and peaceful society to function. But what are we to do when the proverbial long arm of the law suddenly seems to shrink—when a situation seems to call for us to take the law into our own hands to correct an injustice? Is there ever justification to do so? If God helps those who help themselves, should the law also help those who help themselves? In this lesson, we discuss the advantages and disadvantages of allowing citizens to self-help and how the Talmud addresses this matter.

CASE STUDY A

SOURCES: "HILLVIEW MAN ARRESTED FOR SHOOTING DOWN DRONE; CITES RIGHT TO PRIVACY," JULY 28, 2015, WWW.WDRB.COM/STORY/29650818/HILLVIEW-MAN-ARRESTED-FOR-SHOOTING-DOWN-DRONE-CITES-RIGHT-TO-PRIVACY; ANDREW BLAKE, "WILLIAM MERIDETH, 'DRONE SLAYER,' SEEKS TO DISMISS FEDERAL LAWSUIT," *THE WASHINGTON TIMES,* MARCH 8, 2016

It happened Sunday night, July 26, 2015 in Hillview, Kentucky. When police arrived at the scene, William Merideth told them that he had shot down a drone that was flying over his house. The drone was hit in mid-air and crashed in a field near Merideth's home.

Merideth reported that his girls, who were out on the back deck, came in complaining about a drone flying over their yard.

"I came out and it was down by the neighbor's house, about ten feet off the ground. I went and got my shotgun. I wasn't going to do anything unless it would come directly over my property. Within a minute or so, it came. It was hovering over my property, and I shot it out of the sky. I didn't shoot across the road; I didn't shoot across my neighbor's fences; I shot directly into the air."

It wasn't long before the drone's owner appeared. Merideth yelled, "If you cross my sidewalk, there is going to be another shooting."

The owner of the drone, David Boggs, claimed he was flying it to get pictures of a friend's house, and that the cost of the drone was over $1,800.

Merideth was arrested and charged with first degree criminal mischief and first degree wanton endangerment. But Merideth said he's offering no apologies for what he did.

"He didn't just fly over," he said. "If he had just kept moving, that would have been one thing. But when he came directly over our heads, and just hovered there, I felt like I had the right. When you're in your own property, within a six-foot privacy fence, you have the expectation of privacy. We don't know if he was looking at the girls. We don't know if he was looking for something to steal. To me, it was the same as trespassing."

As the incident made waves across the country, Mr. Merideth began marketing merchandise in which he referred to himself as the "drone slayer."

POLL 1

Was the homeowner justified in shooting down the drone?

1 Yes

2 No

3 Not sure

CASE STUDY B

SOURCE: AVI BAR, "HE CAUGHT A THIEF, ATTACKED, AND IS SERVING TIME," DECEMBER 30, 2014, WWW.BE106.NET/NEWS_INNER.PHP?CITY=233&ID=7699

A resident of Rechovot, Israel was enjoying a quiet evening in his home, located directly above his metal workshop. That is, until a chance glance at a security camera showed a burglar breaking into his workshop. The owner had recently suffered two burglaries, and expensive equipment was stolen. These burglaries caused him great distress, disrupting his business and harming his reputation by forcing him to miss deadlines on a number of jobs.

The owner grabbed a plank of wood and went downstairs to confront the burglar. Entering the workshop and making eye contact with the burglar, his blood boiled even further. He believed that this was the same man who had committed the two previous burglaries.

An altercation quickly developed. The owner struck the burglar with the plank of wood, and stabbed him five times in the back of his legs with a sharp object.

The owner was arrested and charged for attacking the burglar.

Attorney Yaron Forer asked the court to recognize that the defendant's actions did not transpire in a vacuum, but were a result of the accumulated frustration and distress of being a victim of multiple burglaries. He pointed out that the defendant was concerned that the police would not arrive in time to stop the burglar, and so he decided to take the law into his own hands to defend his belongings.

POLL 2

Was the workshop owner justified in using force to prevent the burglary?

1 Yes

2 No

3 Not sure

CASE STUDY C

SOURCE: SAM SHEFFER, "I CAUGHT THE THIEF WHO STOLE MY IPHONE," *THE VERGE,* NOVEMBER 11, 2014, HTTP://WWW.THEVERGE. COM/2014/11/11/7188365/I-CAUGHT-THE-THIEF-WHO-STOLE-MY-IPHONE

It was like any other Saturday night out in New York City. I was at a local bar around 3:00 AM, and was having some beers with my brother. Shortly after arriving, I noticed that I didn't have my iPhone on me. I hastily patted myself down, feeling each of my pants and jacket pockets, but there was no iPhone. I didn't remember putting it down anywhere, and my mind began to race.

My brother immediately pulled out his iPhone and called my phone. The call went through, but no one answered. Thankfully, I had Find My iPhone set up on my phone, so I grabbed his phone and downloaded the Find My iPhone app.

My heart was racing, and I was feeling terrible, angry, and overall confused. I signed into my iCloud account as soon as the download finished. And there it was, a flash of hope—my phone was somewhere in the bar.

When you track your iPhone using Find My iPhone, you are shown a map with the device's last known location, which seems to update every thirty seconds or so. The thing about the map is that it is not one hundred percent accurate to the point where you can track it to the inch, or even foot. Among other features, Find My iPhone also allows you to play a sound on your lost device.

I began hammering the Play Sound button, hoping I'd hear the ringing somewhere in the bar, but the bar was packed, the music was loud, and people were drunk.

It was nearing closing time, 4:00 AM, and as people were exiting the bar, I began asking if they had seen an iPhone. I was about to give up.

And then it happened: the phone icon jumped across the street. The person had left the bar. This was my chance.

We exited the bar and I noticed a group of people on the street with one man waving a handkerchief at a cab. Something came over me. I cannot explain exactly what, but I knew this was the guy.

I said to my brother in Hebrew, "I think that's him," and we began to follow him. I kept pressing the Play Sound button, and that's when my brother heard the ring. "It's him," my brother exclaimed.

I've never been in a fist fight and I've never confronted someone in a situation like this before. How do you approach a thief you know for a fact stole your $900 cell phone? What do you say? What do you do?

POLL 3

Does Sam have the right to forcibly grab his phone back?

1 Yes

2 No

3 Not sure

QUESTIONS FOR DISCUSSION

1 Have you ever (in your adult life) taken the law into your own hands? What were the results?

2 Were you ever tempted to take the law into your own hands but refrained from doing so? Why did you refrain? What were the results?

CHAVRUTA A

TEXT 1

TALMUD, BAVA KAMA 27B

שָׁלַח לֵיהּ רַב חִסְדָּא לְרַב נַחְמָן: הֲרֵי אָמְרוּ לִרְכוּבָה - שָׁלֹשׁ, וְלִבְעִיטָה - חָמֵשׁ, וּלְסַנוֹקֶרֶת - שָׁלֹשׁ עֶשְׂרֵה. לְפַנְדָּא דְמָרָא וּלְקוּפִינָא דְמָרָא מַאי? שָׁלַח לֵיהּ: ... אֵימָא לִי גּוּפָא דְעוּבְדָּא הֵיכִי הֲוָה?

שָׁלַח לֵיהּ: דְּהַהוּא גַּרְגּוּתָא דְּבֵי תְרֵי דְּכָל יוֹמָא הֲוָה דָּלֵי חַד מִנַּיְיהוּ, אֲתָא חַד קָא דָּלֵי בְּיוֹמָא דְּלָא דִּילֵיהּ. אָמַר לֵיהּ: יוֹמָא דִידִי הוּא. לֹא אַשְׁגַּח בֵּיהּ. שָׁקֵל פַּנְדָּא דְמָרָא מַחְיֵיהּ.

אָמַר לֵיהּ: מֵאָה פַּנְדֵי בְּפַנְדָּא לִמְחַיֵּיהּ. אֲפִילוּ לְמַאן דְּאָמַר לֹא עָבֵיד אִינִישׁ דִּינָא לְנַפְשֵׁיהּ, בִּמְקוֹם פְּסֵידָא עָבֵיד אִינִישׁ דִּינָא לְנַפְשֵׁיהּ.

דְּאִתְּמַר: רַב יְהוּדָה אָמַר: לֹא עָבֵיד אִינִישׁ דִּינָא לְנַפְשֵׁיהּ. רַב נַחְמָן אָמַר: עָבֵיד אִינִישׁ דִּינָא לְנַפְשֵׁיהּ. הֵיכָא דְּאִיכָּא פְּסֵידָא כּוּלֵּי עָלְמָא לֹא פְּלִיגֵי דְּעָבֵיד אִינִישׁ דִּינָא לְנַפְשֵׁיהּ, כִּי פְּלִיגֵי הֵיכָא דְּלֵיכָּא פְּסֵידָא. רַב יְהוּדָה אָמַר: לָא עָבֵיד אִינִישׁ דִּינָא לְנַפְשֵׁיהּ, דְּכֵיוָן דְּלֵיכָּא פְּסֵידָא לֵיזִיל קַמֵּיהּ דַּיָּינָא. רַב נַחְמָן אָמַר: עָבֵיד אִינִישׁ דִּינָא לְנַפְשֵׁיהּ, דְּכֵיוָן דְּבְדִין עָבֵיד לֹא טָרַח.

BABYLONIAN TALMUD

A literary work of monumental proportions that draws upon the legal, spiritual, intellectual, ethical, and historical traditions of Judaism. The 37 tractates of the Babylonian Talmud contain the teachings of the Jewish sages from the period after the destruction of the 2nd Temple through the 5th century CE. It has served as the primary vehicle for the transmission of the Oral Law and the education of Jews over the centuries; it is the entry point for all subsequent legal, ethical, and theological Jewish scholarship.

RAV CHISDA
CA. 216–308

Third-generation Talmudic sage (*amora*). Rav Chisda lived in Kafri, Babylonia, near what is now the city of Najaf, Iraq. He grew up poor but earned great wealth as a brewer. The Talmudic sage Rava was his student and son-in-law.

Rav Chisda sent a question to Rav Nachman:

"The sages said that when one strikes another [the judges determine liability for humiliation according to the following formula]: For kneeing, the attacker must pay three *sela*; for kicking, five; and for striking with a saddle, thirteen. But for striking with the handle or top of a hoe, how much is the attacker liable to pay?"

Rav Nachman sent a reply to Rav Chisda. . . . "Tell me how the incident transpired."

Rav Chisda replied: "There was a water cistern that belonged to two people. They had an arrangement that they would each draw water from the well on alternate days. It once happened that one of the partners was drawing water on a day that was not his. The other partner protested: 'It is my day!' Yet the offending partner ignored him. The aggrieved partner then struck the offender with the handle of a hoe. [And I am not sure how much the payment for humiliation ought to be.]"

Rav Nachman responded to Rav Chisda: "Let him strike the offender even a hundred times! For even those who assert that you may not enforce the law for yourself agree that you may do so if inaction might result in an irretrievable loss. [And here, if the victim of the theft were to seek legal recourse, he would not be able to prove the damage in court, and so he will not be properly compensated.]"

As it was taught: Rav Yehudah says that you may not enforce the law for yourself, whereas Rav Nachman says that you may enforce the law for yourself. In a case where inaction might result in an irreparable loss, all agree that you may enforce the law for yourself. They only disagree in a case where inaction would not result in an irreparable loss. Rav Yehudah says that in such cases you may not enforce the law for yourself because there would be no loss by seeking recourse within the

RAV NACHMAN BAR YA'AKOV
CA. 250–318

Third-generation Talmudic sage (*amora*). Rav Nachman was a student of the Talmudist Aba Aricha, known as Rav, and of the Talmudist Shmuel, and he served as head of the academy in Nehardeah, Babylonia. The Talmud regards him as an expert in civil law, and *halachah* usually follows him in this area. Among his students were the Talmudic sages Rabah, Rav Yosef, and Rav Abah.

RAV YEHUDAH BAR YECHEZKEL
CA. 220–299

Third-generation Talmudic sage (*amora*). Rav Yehudah was born on the day that Rabbi Yehudah Hanasi, redactor of the Mishnah, passed away. He was one of the foremost disciples of the Talmudist Abba Aricha, known as Rav, and when he studied under the Talmudist Shmuel, the latter called him "the sharp one." He subsequently founded and headed the academy in Pumbedita.

justice system. But Rav Nachman says that you may enforce the law for yourself even in a case where inaction will not cause any irreparable loss, because if you are acting in accordance with the law, you do not have to trouble yourself to go before a judge.

QUESTIONS FOR DISCUSSION

1 Are we allowed to take the law into our own hands?

	RAV CHISDA	RAV YEHUDAH	RAV NACHMAN
Irreparable loss			
No irreparable loss			

2 Which of the three positions is most agreeable to you? Why?

POLL 4

Which of the three positions is most agreeable to you?

1 Rav Chisda

2 Rav Yehudah

3 Rav Nachman

TEXT **2**

DAVID WERNER AMRAM, "THE SUMMONS: A STUDY IN JEWISH AND COMPARATIVE PROCEDURE," *UNIVERSITY OF PENNSYLVANIA LAW REVIEW*, 68:1 (NOVEMBER 1919), P. 50

At first every man did what was right in his own eyes and used such force as was necessary to redress his wrongs. Thereafter the exercise of this force was controlled and legalized through a long period of legal evolution in which various forms were adopted under the influence of tribal, royal, ecclesiastical administrators. But the older practice of self-help never quite disappeared and even in our own times we find ample illustration in all contemporary legal systems of such primitive survivals of the days in which there were no courts of law.

DAVID WERNER AMRAM
1866–1939

Legal scholar. Amram published several books, including *The Jewish Law of Divorce According to Bible and Talmud* (1896). He served as director of the Federation of American Zionists and editor of *The Maccabean*, the official publication of the Zionist Organization of America.

TEXT **3**

EPHRAIM KISHON, "GET A BETTER LAWYER," IN *THE REDHEAD WITH THE KEY* (HEB.)
(YEDIOT ACHARONOT, 2002), P. 123

Ten years ago, Konstater borrowed twenty liras and promised to pay me back within twenty-four hours. When he didn't turn up, I gave him a call and he requested a one-week extension.

At the end of the week, I visited Konstater and demanded my money. He promised to have it all sorted out by Monday afternoon.

On Thursday evening I went to a lawyer, and he sent Konstater a letter saying that if the debt is not repaid within seventy-two hours, all necessary measures will be exercised.

Two months passed with no response from Konstater, and the lawyer said that nothing can be done. I transferred the case to a better lawyer, who summoned Konstater to court.

Five months later the hearing was held, but Konstater didn't turn up due to an illness. The case was adjourned to a date the following year. When the date came, the case couldn't be heard because Konstater had traveled overseas.

After waiting a year and a half, and seeing that he still hadn't returned, I turned to another lawyer, a very famous one. He attempted to move ahead with the

EPHRAIM KISHON
1924–2005

Israeli satirist, screenwriter, and film director. A concentration camp survivor, Kishon immigrated to Israel in 1949 from Hungary. For thirty years he wrote a regular satirical column called "*Chad Gadya*" in the daily Hebrew tabloid *Ma'ariv*. His satirical and humorous writings have been translated into 37 languages.

proceedings, but the judge was unwilling to hear the case in the absence of the defendant.

We appealed the decision to a higher court, but they refused to hear the case because they do not accept cases that concern less than fifty liras.

We waited another two or three years until Konstater returned from overseas. I then sent him a loan of thirty liras through a notary, which brought his debt to fifty liras. Now the higher court finally heard our appeal and ordered the lower court to conduct a case in the absence of the defendant. However, because Konstater had returned from overseas and was no longer absent, the case was delayed pending further investigation.

I hired an even more illustrious lawyer and we got the Supreme Court to summon the justice minister to explain why I couldn't get my fifty liras back. The justice minister appeared and explained that we need to go to court, so we renewed the case, but it was delayed because Konstater requested a delay.

I went to the best lawyer in the country and described the case to him. He listened to me closely and advised me to go over to Konstater and to hit him. I went over to Konstater and hit him. He immediately paid me fifty liras in cash.

You really need to hire a great lawyer. . . .

TEXT 4

MAIMONIDES, *MISHNEH TORAH*, LAWS OF THE SANHEDRIN 2:12

> יֵשׁ לָאָדָם לַעֲשׂוֹת דִּין לְעַצְמוֹ אִם יֵשׁ בְּיָדוֹ כֹּחַ. הוֹאִיל וְכַדָּת וְכַהֲלָכָה הוּא עוֹשֶׂה, אֵינוֹ חַיָּב לִטְרוֹחַ וּלְהָבִיא לְבֵית דִּין, אַף עַל פִּי שֶׁלֹּא הָיָה שָׁם הֶפְסֵד בִּנְכָסָיו אִלּוּ נִתְאַחֵר וּבָא לְבֵית דִּין.

RABBI MOSHE BEN MAIMON (MAIMONIDES, RAMBAM) 1135–1204

We may execute judgments for ourselves if we have the ability to do so. When our actions are proper according to the law, we are not obligated to assume the trouble of going to court, even if we would not suffer any financial loss by doing so.

Halachist, philosopher, author, and physician. Maimonides was born in Cordoba, Spain. After the conquest of Cordoba by the Almohads, he fled Spain and eventually settled in Cairo, Egypt. There, he became the leader of the Jewish community and served as court physician to the vizier of Egypt. He is most noted for authoring the *Mishneh Torah*, an encyclopedic arrangement of Jewish law, and for his philosophical work, *Guide for the Perplexed*. His rulings on Jewish law are integral to the formation of halachic consensus.

TEXT 5a

TALMUD, BAVA KAMA 28A

> שׁוֹר שֶׁעָלָה עַל גַּבֵּי חֲבֵירוֹ לְהוֹרְגוֹ, וּבָא בַּעַל הַתַּחְתּוֹן וְשָׁמַט אֶת שֶׁלּוֹ, וְנָפַל עֶלְיוֹן וּמֵת, פָּטוּר . . .
> דְּחָפוֹ לָעֶלְיוֹן וּמֵת, חַיָּיב.

If an ox climbed on top of another ox to kill it, and the owner of the lower ox pulled his ox out from underneath, causing the upper ox to fall and die—the owner of the lower ox is not liable. . . .

However, if the owner of the lower ox pushed the upper ox off and it died, he is liable.

QUESTIONS FOR DISCUSSION

1 What is the difference between these two cases?

2 Is this teaching compatible with the law that permits self-help?

TEXT **5 b**

TALMUD, BAVA KAMA 28A

שֶׁהָיָה לוֹ לִשָׁמְטוֹ וְלֹא שָׁמְטוֹ.

The owner should have pulled out his ox from underneath and failed to do so.

TEXT 6

TALMUD, BERACHOT 5B 📖

רַב הוּנָא תְּקִיפוּ לֵיה אַרְבַּע מְאָה דָּנֵי דְחַמְרָא. עַל לְגַבֵּיה רַב יְהוּדָה אֲחוּהּ דְרַב סַלָּא חֲסִידָא וְרַבָּנַן, וְאָמְרִי לֵיהּ רַב אָדָא בַּר אַהֲבָה וְרַבָּנַן, וְאָמְרוּ לֵיה: לְעַיֵּין מַר בְּמִילֵיה.

אָמַר לְהוּ: וּמִי חֲשִׁידְנָא בְּעֵינַיְיכוּ?

אָמְרוּ לֵיה: מִי חָשִׁיד קוּדְשָׁא בְּרִיךְ הוּא דְעָבֵיד דִּינָא בְּלָא דִּינָא?

אָמַר לְהוּ: אִי אִיכָּא מַאן דִשְׁמִיעַ עָלַי מִלְּתָא לֵימָא.

אָמְרוּ לֵיה: הָכִי שְׁמִיעַ לָן, דְּלָא יָהֵיב מַר שַׁבִישָׁא לַאֲרִיסֵיה.

אָמַר לְהוּ: מִי קָא שָׁבֵיק לִי מִידֵי מִינֵיה? הָא קָא גָּנֵיב לֵיה כּוּלֵיה!

אָמְרוּ לֵיה: הַיְינוּ דְאָמְרֵי אִינְשֵׁי: בָּתַר גַּנָּבָא גְנוֹב וְטַעְמָא טְעֵים.

אָמַר לְהוּ: קַבֵּילְנָא עָלַי דְיָהֵיבְנָא לֵיה.

RAV HUNA
CA. 206–296

Second-generation Talmudic sage (*amora*). Rav Huna served for 40 years as head of the Talmudic academy in Sura, Babylonia. Among his numerous students were the Talmudic sages Rav Yosef, Rabah, and Rav Sheshes.

Rav Huna had four hundred barrels of wine that soured and turned into vinegar. Rav Yehudah the brother of Rav Sala Chasida (others say it was Rav Adah bar Ahavah), as well as other sages, went to visit Rav Huna. They said to him, "Let our master examine his affairs [to determine whether a transgression might be the spiritual cause of this loss]."

Rav Huna said to them, "Am I suspect in your eyes?"

They responded to him, "Is God suspected of punishing unjustly?"

Rav Huna said to them, "If there is anyone that heard something about me that I must rectify, speak up!"

They responded, "We heard that you did not give the agreed-upon amount of branches to your tenant farmer."

Rav Huna said, "Did he leave me anything? He stole from me more than his rightful share!"

They said to him, "This is an example of the popular folk adage 'One who steals from a thief has a taste of theft.'"

Rav Huna said to them, "I accept upon myself to give him his share of the branches."

QUESTION FOR DISCUSSION

Is this teaching compatible with the law that permits self-help?

TEXT 7

RABBI MORDECHAI BEN HILLEL, BAVA KAMA 30

הֲלֹא מִן הַדִּין לָקַח, דְּקַיְימָא לָן עָבֵיד אִינִישׁ דִּינָא לְנַפְשֵׁיהּ?
וְיֵשׁ לוֹמַר: דְּהַיְינוּ דַּוְוקָא אוֹתוֹ דָּבָר עַצְמוֹ שֶׁנִּלְקַח לוֹ לְאָדָם, מוּתָּר לוֹ
לִיקָחֶנּוּ בְּכָל מָקוֹם שֶׁיָּכוֹל לְהַשִּׂיגוֹ . . . אֲבָל הָכָא לָקַח זְמוֹרוֹת אֲחֵרִים
שֶׁלֹּא גָּנַב לוֹ הָאָרִיס.

**RABBI MORDECHAI BEN HILLEL
CA. 1240–1298**

Rabbi Mordechai was a disciple of Rabbi Meir (Maharam) of Rothenburg, as was his brother-in-law, Rabbi Meir Hakohen, author of *Hagahot Maimoniyot*. His work on the Talmud—published in most editions of the Talmud—includes a collection of *tosafot*, responsa, halachic decisions, and commentary. During the Rintfleisch massacres of 1298, Rabbi Mordechai was killed in Nuremberg, Germany, together with his wife (daughter of Rabbi Yechiel of Paris) and their five children.

But Rav Huna acted in accordance with the law that we are allowed to enforce the law for ourselves!

We can answer this by qualifying the allowance of self-help: that we may only enforce the law for ourselves in order to recover the very object that was taken from us, no matter where it may be. . . . But in the case of Rav Huna, he didn't retrieve what was stolen from him but withheld branches that he was supposed to give to his tenant farmer.

TEXT 8

RABBI YOSEF CHAIM OF BAGHDAD, *RESPONSA RAV PE'ALIM* 3:5

אֵינוֹ יָכוֹל לִיטוֹל כִּי אִם רַק אוֹתוֹ דָּבָר שֶׁגְּזָלוֹ מִמֶּנּוּ מַמָּשׁ. אֲבָל דָּבָר אַחֵר, אֲפִילוּ שֶׁהוּא דָּבָר מְבוֹרָר, כְּגוֹן שֶׁגְּזַל מִמֶּנּוּ מָנֶה וְשׁוּב בָּא לְיָדוֹ מָעוֹת מִשֶּׁל אוֹתוֹ אָדָם שֶׁגְּזָלוֹ, לֹא יִקַּח מֵאוֹתָם הַמָּעוֹת מָנֶה כְּנֶגֶד מַה שֶּׁגְּזָלוֹ, אַף עַל פִּי שֶׁהוּא דָּבָר מְבוֹרָר, כֵּיוָן שֶׁאֵין זֶה הַדָּבָר שֶׁגְּזָלוֹ מִמֶּנּוּ מַמָּשׁ, דְּהֶחְמִירוּ בְּכָהַאי גַוְונָא... מִפְּנֵי דְחָשׁוּ אִם יַתִּירוּ לוֹ בְּכָךְ, יָבוֹא לִיקַּח גַּם בְּהֵיכָא שֶׁאֵין הַדָּבָר מְבוֹרָר. דְּהַיְינוּ אִם גָּזַל מִמֶּנּוּ חֵפֶץ, יָבֹא לִיקַּח חֵפֶץ אַחֵר שֶׁשָּׁם אוֹתוֹ לְפִי דַעְתּוֹ שֶׁשָּׁוֶה כְּמוֹ אוֹתוֹ חֵפֶץ הַנִּגְזַל מִמֶּנּוּ, אוֹ אִם גָּזְלוֹ מִמֶּנּוּ חֵפֶץ אַחֵר וְלוֹקֵחַ כְּנֶגְדּוֹ מָעוֹת כְּפִי שׁוּמָה שֶׁשָּׁם אֶת הַחֵפֶץ, עַל כֵּן אָמְרוּ... לֹא יוּכַל לִיקַּח דָּבָר אַחֵר אֲפִילוּ זוּזֵי בְּזוּזֵי, אֶלָּא דַּוְקָא אִם מָצָא הַחֵפֶץ שֶׁגְּזָלוֹ מִמֶּנּוּ בְּעֵין, יוּכַל לִיקַּח אוֹתוֹ שֶׁלֹּא בִּרְשׁוּת.

RABBI YOSEF CHAIM OF BAGHDAD
(*BEN ISH CHAI*) 1834–1909

Sefardic halachist and kabbalist. Rabbi Yosef Chaim succeeded his father as chief rabbi of Baghdad in 1859, and is best known as author of his halachic work, *Ben Ish Chai*, by which title he is also known. Also popular is his commentary on the homiletical sections of the Talmud, called *Ben Yehoyadah*.

It is forbidden to take anything back other than the item itself that was stolen from you. This is true even if someone stole from you one hundred coins and you have access to different coins belonging to this thief—you should not take these coins, because they are not the exact items stolen from you. The sages were very strict in this regard . . . because they were afraid that if they allowed you to take currency for currency, you might learn to act similarly in other cases. That is, if someone stole an item from you, you might take a different item from the thief that you estimate to be equal to the worth of your item, [and you might be mistaken]. Therefore, the sages said . . . that you may only take back the exact item that was stolen from you.

Figure 2.1

Self-Help for Theft

	TAKING TO OWN	TAKING AS COLLATERAL
The item itself	✓	n/a
Something else	✗	✓

TEXT 9

RABBI SHNE'UR ZALMAN OF LIADI, *SHULCHAN ARUCH HARAV, CHOSHEN MISHPAT,*
LAWS OF ROBBERY AND THEFT 29

וְכָל זֶה כְּשֶׁיָכוֹל לְבָרֵר שֶׁזֶה הַחֵפֶץ שֶׁלוֹ אִם יִתְבָּעֶנוּ הַלָה לְבֵית דִין. אֲבָל
אִם לֹא יוּכַל לְבָרֵר, אֵין צָרִיךְ לוֹמַר שֶׁאֵינוֹ רַשַׁאי לְהַכּוֹתוֹ, שֶׁאִם יְכֵהוּ
יַעֲנִישׁוּהוּ הַבֵּית דִין, אֶלָא אֲפִילוּ בְּלֹא הַכָּאָה אֵין הַצָלָתוֹ כְּלוּם.

The permission to enforce the law for yourself only applies when you can prove that the item is yours should you be challenged in court. If, however, you will not be able to establish your claim in court, there is no validity to your self-help action, and certainly you may not use violence in such an instance.

**RABBI SHNE'UR ZALMAN OF LIADI
(ALTER REBBE) 1745–1812**

Chasidic rebbe, halachic authority, and founder of the Chabad movement. The Alter Rebbe was born in Liozna, Belarus, and was among the principal students of the Magid of Mezeritch. His numerous works include the *Tanya*, an early classic containing the fundamentals of Chabad Chasidism, and *Shulchan Aruch HaRav*, an expanded and reworked code of Jewish law.

JUSTICE
JUSTICE
shall tou
pursue,
DEUT. 16:20

TEXT 10

RABBI SHNE'UR ZALMAN OF LIADI, *SHULCHAN ARUCH HARAV, CHOSHEN MISHPAT,* LAWS OF LENDING 7 ⓘ

הַמַּלְוֶה אֶת חֲבֵירוֹ, אֶחָד עָנִי וְאֶחָד עָשִׁיר, שֶׁלֹּא עַל הַמַּשְׁכּוֹן, וּכְשֶׁהִגִּיעַ זְמַן הַפֵּרָעוֹן, בָּא לְמַשְׁכְּנוֹ לִהְיוֹת בָּטוּחַ בִּמְעוֹתָיו אוֹ לִגְבּוֹת חוֹבוֹ מֵהַמַּשְׁכּוֹן, לֹא יְמַשְׁכְּנֶנּוּ בְּעַצְמוֹ בִּזְרוֹעַ, אֶלָּא עַל פִּי בֵּית דִּין שֶׁיִּשְׁלְחוּ שְׁלוּחָם.

וְאִם מִשְׁכְּנוֹ בְּעַצְמוֹ, בֵּין שֶׁחָטַף מִן הַלֹּוֶה בַּשּׁוּק, בֵּין שֶׁנִּכְנַס לְבֵיתוֹ (שֶׁלֹּא מִדַּעְתּוֹ) וְנָטַל מַשְׁכּוֹן, הֲרֵי זֶה עוֹבֵר בְּלֹא תַעֲשֶׂה. שֶׁנֶּאֱמַר (דְּבָרִים כד, י), "לֹא תָבֹא אֶל בֵּיתוֹ" וְגוֹ', וְאֵין צָרִיךְ לוֹמַר, לַנּוֹטֵל בִּזְרוֹעַ אֲפִילוּ בַּשּׁוּק.

Say you lend to a colleague, rich or poor, without collateral. When it is time for repayment, you wish to take collateral either as a security or from which to draw repayment. In such a case, be sure not to employ any force in taking the collateral yourself. Instead, charge the court with this responsibility.

If you do take the collateral yourself—whether you entered the borrower's home without permission or seized it on the street—you have violated the Torah's prohibition, "You shall not enter the borrower's home" (DEU-TERONOMY 24:10). This verse forbids entering the borrower's home without permission to find collateral, and it definitely forbids confronting the borrower directly, even on the street, to seize collateral by force.

POLL 5

According to Jewish law, was the homeowner justified in shooting down the drone?

1 Yes

2 No

3 Not sure

POLL 6

According to Jewish law, was the workshop owner justified in using force to prevent the burglary?

1 Yes

2 No

3 Not sure

POLL 7

According to Jewish law, does Sam have the right to forcibly grab his phone back?

1 Yes

2 No

3 Not sure

KEY POINTS

1 Enforcing the law for oneself might undermine peace and civility, and if applied improperly, will cause unwarranted pain and injustice.

2 The reality is that the justice system is often unable to address every claim expediently and efficiently. This has led some to advocate for the self-help legal doctrine in certain instances.

3 In terms of actual practice, when local governments enact civil laws for the benefit of society, *halachah* requires that Jews follow these laws.

4 While the Talmud expresses different views on the subject, the halachic consensus is that, with certain caveats, people are allowed to self-help in order to avoid the hassle of pursuing the matter through the justice system, even if going to the courts will cause no irreparable financial loss.

5 One is not allowed to employ self-help in the form of retribution or revenge. It is only permitted in order to protect oneself or one's assets from harm, or to retrieve something that was stolen.

6 A self-helper most choose the least harmful means to achieve justice. A clearly excessive reaction is unjustified.

7 Self-help justice is limited to the recovery of the actual item that was stolen. Taking a different item in lieu of a stolen item is forbidden, unless taken as collateral.

8 It is insufficient for self-helpers to know that they are definitely right; they must also have court-worthy evidence to back up their claims. Otherwise, if challenged in court, their actions would be reversed, and hence, unjustifiable.

9 If a debtor fails to repay a loan, the creditor may not act independently to seize the debtor's property, even as collateral. Jewish law is extra particular about shielding vulnerable debtors.

10 In terms of our overall mission in life, we ought to "take the law into our own hands" by taking personal responsibility, relying on no one but ourselves to make a real difference and ensure a better future.

Continue your
learning experience
ONLINE
Visit www.myJLI.com/dilemma2
for insightful and inspiring videos,
articles, and readings on this topic.

Appendix

TEXT **11**

RABBI MENACHEM MEIRI, *BEIT HABECHIRAH,* BAVA KAMA 27B

כָּל שֶׁאוֹנֵס דָּבָר לַחֲבֵרוֹ, וַחֲבֵרוֹ הָאָנוּס לְשָׁם וְרוֹאֶה בְּאָנְסוֹ, וְאֶפְשָׁר לוֹ
לְבָרֵר אַף לְאַחַר מַעֲשֶׂה שֶׁאוֹתוֹ עִנְיָן אוֹנֶס אֶצְלוֹ, יֵשׁ לוֹ רְשׁוּת לַעֲשׂוֹת
דִּין לְעַצְמוֹ וְלִדְחוֹתוֹ שֶׁלֹּא לַעֲשׂוֹת לוֹ אוֹנֶס זֶה, אֲפִילוּ הִכָּהוּ עַל זֶה כַּמָּה
הַכָּאוֹת אֵין לוֹ חִיּוּב . . . הוֹאִיל וְהוּא לְשָׁם בְּעוֹד שֶׁזֶּה אוֹנְסוֹ, עוֹשֶׂה דִּין
לְעַצְמוֹ, וּמַכֵּהוּ עַד שֶׁיְּדָחֶה מֵעָלָיו. הָא כָּל שֶׁעָבַר הָאוֹנֶס, כְּגוֹן שֶׁכְּבָר גְּזָלוֹ
אוֹ גָּנַב לוֹ אוֹ שֶׁכְּבָר הִלְוָהוּ וְאֵינוֹ רוֹצֶה לְפָרְעוֹ, אֵינוֹ בְּדִין זֶה. לֹא אָמַר זֶה
אֶלָּא בְּעוֹד שֶׁהוּא אוֹנְסוֹ.

RABBI MENACHEM ME'IRI
1249–1310

Talmudist and author. Me'iri was born in Provence, France. His monumental work, *Beit Habechirah,* summarizes in a lucid style the discussions of the Talmud along with the commentaries of the major subsequent rabbis. Despite its stature, the work was largely unknown for many generations, and thus has had less influence on subsequent halachic development.

If an individual attempts to dispossess you in your presence, and if you will later have the ability to prove in court that this would have been an unlawful dispossession, you are allowed to take the law into your own hands. Even if you struck the aggressor repeatedly, you are not liable for any damages. . . . So long as you are present at the time of the attempted dispossession, you can take the matter into your own hands, and strike the aggressor until you chase him away. But self-help is not allowed if the dispossession has already occurred, that is, if someone already stole from you or received a loan from you but now refuses to repay.

QUESTION FOR DISCUSSION

What might be the rationale of Meiri's ruling distinguishing between the time of the crime and afterward?

TEXT 12a

EPHRAIM GLATT, "GIVE ME BACK MY BICYCLE: THE USE OF FORCE TO RECAPTURE CHATTEL ACCORDING TO AMERICAN LAW AND JEWISH LAW," *THE GONZAGA JOURNAL OF INTERNATIONAL LAW*, MAY 15, 2013, WWW.LAW.GONZAGA.EDU/GJIL/2013/05/USE-OF-FORCE/

Numerous conditions must be present for a self-helper to use force to recapture chattel. . . . Courts . . . require that the attempted recapture occur immediately after dispossession or upon fresh pursuit of the wrongdoer. While the meaning of fresh pursuit has never been defined by the courts, it is clear that it is limited to prompt discovery of the dispossession, and prompt and persistent efforts to recover the chattel thereafter. An undue lapse of time during which it may be said that the pursuit has come to a halt would seemingly be outside the scope of the privilege. Notably, some leeway has been given. . . . If by reasonable diligence he could have known of it at an earlier time, force is not privileged, even when he acts promptly after he knows of his dispossession. . . .

JEFFREY EPHRAIM GLATT

Associate at Kasowitz, Benson, Torres & Friedman LLP. Glatt's practice focuses on complex commercial litigation in both federal and state courts, with experience in litigation involving contract disputes, unfair competition, and fraud claims. He has published and lectured on the interplay between American and Jewish law.

TEXT **12 b**

EPHRAIM GLATT, IBID.,

Many people find it natural to try and regain property wrongfully taken from them, and judicial imposition of liability on the wronged person for the results of such natural behavior arguably is inequitable.

Resorting to the frailties of human nature to justify the use of force when recapturing an item is logical in light of the many limitations placed on this privilege. Specifically, recognizing the natural impulse to pursue the taker of one's property helps explain the fresh pursuit limitation, since a delay obviously would allow the ire of the wronged party to subside, thereby negating the natural impulse justification. . . . Since the justification for this privilege is based on the frailties of human nature, this privilege logically only applies when the self-helper is still very upset over his loss.

TEXT 13

RABBI ADIN EVEN-ISRAEL (STEINSALTZ), *THE TALMUD: A REFERENCE GUIDE* (NEW YORK: RANDOM HOUSE, 1989), P. 215

The word *migu* literally means *from the midst of,* or *since,* and it refers to an important legal argument used to support the claim of one of the parties in a dispute. If one of the litigants could have made a claim more advantageous to his cause than he actually did, we assume he was telling the truth.

The *migu* argument may be summarized in the following way: "Since he could have made a better claim (for had he wanted to lie, he would presumably have put forward a claim more advantageous to himself), we assume that he must be telling the truth." For he could say: "What reason do I have to lie?"

There are, however, certain limitations governing the application of this principle; for example, "There is no *migu* where there are witnesses." In other words, *migu* is not effective where witnesses contradict the litigant's claim.

RABBI ADIN EVEN-ISRAEL (STEINSALTZ) 1937–

Talmudist, author, and philosopher. Rabbi Even-Israel Steinsaltz is considered one of the foremost Jewish thinkers of the 20th century. Praised by *Time* magazine as a "once-in-a-millennium scholar," he has been awarded the Israel Prize for his contributions to Jewish study. He lives in Jerusalem and is the founder of the Israel Institute for Talmudic Publications, a society dedicated to the translation and elucidation of the Talmud.

TEXT **14**

RABBI SHNE'UR ZALMAN OF LIADI, *SHULCHAN ARUCH HARAV, CHOSHEN MISHPAT,*
LAWS OF ROBBERY AND THEFT 29

אֶלָּא אִם כֵּן אֵין עֵדִים כְּשֶׁמַצִּיל מִיָּדוֹ, שֶׁאָז מוֹעֶלֶת לוֹ הַצָּלָה זוֹ שֶׁיִּהְיֶה
נֶאֱמָן בִּשְׁבוּעָה לוֹמַר שֶׁלִּי תָּפַסְתִּי בְּמִיגוֹ שֶׁהָיָה יָכוֹל לִכְפּוֹר וְלוֹמַר לֹא
תָּפַסְתִּי כְּלוּם, מֵאַחַר שֶׁאֵין עֵדִים.

If you do not have proof that the item is yours, your
taking of your item can still be effective if there are no
witnesses who observe your self-help seizure. The court
will believe your claim that you grabbed your own
item—if you will swear to this effect—because you have
a *migu* that you could have said, "I didn't take anything,"
a claim that would have been believed because there are
no witnesses to attest otherwise.

Additional Readings

GIVE ME BACK MY BICYCLE
THE USE OF FORCE TO RECAPTURE CHATTEL ACCORDING TO AMERICAN LAW AND JEWISH LAW

EPHRAIM GLATT

I. Introduction

Reuben buys an expensive new bicycle and rides it all over town. Simon eyes the bicycle enviously and makes plans to steal it. When Reuben locks the bicycle to a tree outside the ice cream store, Simon jumps at the opportunity. Using his bolt cutters, Simon cuts the lock and mounts the bicycle, leaving the bolt cutters on the ground. At that moment, Reuben comes out of the store and sees Simon sitting on his bicycle. Hoping to prevent Simon, whom he recognizes from the neighborhood, from riding off with his new bicycle, Reuben picks up the bolt cutters and hurls it at Simon. The bolt cutters hit Simon directly on the head, leaving him unconscious on the ground. Reuben retrieves his bicycle and rides off, noting the need to get a better lock for his bicycle. Simon is taken to the hospital and suffers numerous injuries from the hit.

Self-help in the law is often defined as "legally permissible conduct that individuals undertake absent the compulsion of law and without the assistance of a government official in efforts to prevent or remedy a legal wrong."[1] The above anecdote discusses one potential self-help scenario: Reuben retaking his stolen item on public property by use of force, absent any physical danger to Reuben. Yet, this "legally recognized alternative or substitute for a judicial remedy . . . may become unlawful when a self-helper oversteps the limits of the privilege."[2] It is thus incumbent on all legal systems to "identify potential self-help situations and the legal boundaries of appropriate self-help responses."[3]

Further contemplation of the Reuben and Simon anecdote helps underscore the need for these legal boundaries. Is Reuben criminally liable for throwing the bolt cutters at Simon? What if he had killed Simon? Must Reuben pay Simon's medical bills? Can Reuben wait until the next day to attack Simon and retrieve his bicycle? Assuming that Simon escaped with the bicycle, could Reuben legally keep the bolt cutters in lieu of the bicycle? These are only some of the many self-help questions with which every developed legal system must grapple.

Thankfully, "self-help is by no means a nascent legal phenomenon."[4] Rather, "in various forms, self-help has been a familiar remedy in society since the initial stages of civilization."[5] In fact, almost "every legal system addresses itself to the issue of self-help."[6] The American legal system and the Jewish legal system, or "Halacha," are no exceptions. Both of these systems have extensive laws regarding the self-help privilege, albeit with important differences. Studying these discrepancies, especially ones related to the limitations and justifications of the privilege, helps better our understanding of the complex legal theory behind this doctrine.

This Article discusses the American and Jewish legal systems' diverse views on the specific issue of retaking an item on public property by use of force, in the absence of physical danger to the self-helper. Part II of this Article details the history of American law in relation to the self-help privilege and gives the current state of the law in many jurisdictions. It focuses primarily on the American legal system's limitations

EPHRAIM GLATT

Associate at Kasowitz, Benson, Torres & Friedman, LLP. J.D., Benjamin N. Cardozo School of Law, 2012; Rabbinical Ordination, RIETS, Yeshiva University, 2009; B.A. Yeshiva University, 2006. A special thank you to my wife and daughters for all their support and encouragement.

and justifications of this privilege. Alternatively, part III of this Article examines the Jewish law's perspective on the self-help privilege. Examining the Talmud and its classical commentators, the section focuses on the Jewish system's limitations and justifications of this privilege. Part IV of this Article analyzes the discrepancies and identifies two observations.

II. American Law
A. Self-Help Privilege

"Self-reliance, perseverance, ingenuity, and the noble notion of rugged individualism have been pervasive themes in the American lifestyle since the precolonial era."[7] As such, an organized judiciary exists "despite its apparent contravention of American wherewithal and human nature, partly because the courts and laws provide an adequate and efficient alternative for redressing wrongs."[8] Yet, "the American legal system also owes its durability to its effective incorporation of a significant number of the common individual methods of dealing with others that predate the system's refinement to its current dignity."[9] "American courts were sophisticated enough to recognize that self-help was an efficient alternative to traditional judicial remedies, and it was later codified into various diverse areas of the law."[10] By adopting these lawful self-help privileges, the founders of America effectively alleviated "the long-standing tension between the imperatives of an established system of laws and the individual needs and desires to avoid and remedy injury as effectively and efficiently as possible."[11]

One of these privileges "recognized" in American law is "the privilege of an owner dispossessed of his chattel to recapture it by force against the person."[12] While reception of chattels is merely a small part of self-defense and defense of property law, many cases over the last two hundred years have developed this privilege quite extensively.[13] Since peaceful legal recourse is usually available through the judicial system, numerous conditions must be present for a self-helper to use force to recapture chattel, thereby severely limiting the use of self-help force.[14] "A self-helping . . . owner who cannot meet these prerequisites runs a risk of liability because the privilege to recover . . . will not have attached."[15]

B. Limitations on Recapture of Chattel
1. Wrongful Taking

"Courts view tortious dispossession . . . as a threshold requirement for recovering property."[16] Tortious dispossession occurs "without a claim of right" or taking "with a claim of right, but by force or . . . fraud."[17] Thus, an owner may use force to recover a stolen item, as the thief took it "without a claim of right."[18] Accordingly, force could be used against a third party who acquires the stolen goods, so long as the third party knows of the illegal origin of the goods.[19]

The parameters of recapture of an item taken from the self-helper "with a claim of right, but by force or . . . fraud" are less defined.[20] Although "actual violence" is unnecessary, there must be a "fraudulent misrepresentation made by the other" that "induces" the self-helper to give up the item.[21] Thus, courts were initially hesitant to allow a seller to forcefully retake goods from a buyer after a default, as this did not constitute "fraudulent misrepresentation."[22] Recent cases, on the other hand, have indicated that such force would be privileged.[23] It is certainly clear though, that a creditor may never use force to collect collateral from a debtor.[24]

2. Entitlement

Force is only privileged when the self-helper "is entitled as against the other to the immediate possession of the chattel."[25] "Since the actor must be entitled to immediate possession as against the other, an erroneous belief that he is so entitled, due to a mistake of law or fact, however reasonable, does not create the privilege."[26]

3. Timeliness

"Courts also require that the attempted recapture occur immediately after dispossession or upon 'fresh pursuit' of the wrongdoer."[27] While the meaning of "fresh pursuit" has never been defined by the courts, it is clear "that it is limited to prompt discovery of the dispossession, and prompt and persistent efforts to recover the chattel thereafter."[28] An "undue lapse of time during which it may be said that the pursuit has come to a halt" would seemingly be outside the scope of the privilege.[29] Notably, some leeway has been given.[30]

Additionally, "not only must the retaking be promptly made after discovery by the actor of his dispossession, but his discovery must be timely."[31] Therefore, "if by reasonable diligence he could have known of it at an earlier time," force is not privileged, even when "he acts promptly after he knows of his dispossession."[32]

4. Demand/Warning

"A resort to any force at all will not be justified until a demand has been made for the return" of the item.[33] The self-helper must "first request the other to give up possession" of the item.[34] An exception to this condition exists where the self-helper "correctly or reasonably believes a request to be useless, dangerous to himself or a third person, or likely to defeat the effective exercise of the privilege."[35]

5. Proper Purpose

Force is only privileged if "used for the purpose of regaining possession of the chattel."[36] Using force to simply prevent an escape after the goods are already retrieved is not protected.[37] In other words, this self-help privilege only exists where "the emergency justifies the risk of a breach of the peace."[38]

6. Amount of Force

The force used must be "reasonable under the circumstances."[39] If the item can be retrieved "without the use of force against the other," such force "is unnecessary and therefore unprivileged."[40] Consequently, "if the chattel is upon the other's table, and the actor, even though the other is present, can retake it without touching the other, he must do so unless the other interposes to prevent the taking."[41] However, "if the dispossessor forcibly resists, the person attempting recapture can exercise the privilege to meet and repel such force."[42]

"Force which causes a breach of the peace is unreasonable."[43] Deadly force is never allowed, because it is never reasonable to protect a property interest.[44] A noteworthy exception is if a life-saving "bottle of medicine" is stolen, "deadly force to regain possession of the medicine" may be used.[45] Also, if the dispossessor forcibly resists, the self-helper may apply "any force required to defend his own person."[46]

C. Justifications

"The chief historical justification for the privilege of recapture was the significance that the common law placed on physical possession as a determinate of ownership."[47] Since "the rightful owner needed a swift and effective cure for wrongful possession lest he lose his claim to the property because of a lack of adequate proof of ownership," using the court system was not an option.[48] "Courts rarely would compel the return of specific property, instead opting to award damages."[49] Further, "the judicial process was slow and the rightful owner suffered deprivation of his property for the length of the proceedings."[50]

Yet, in modern times "courts no longer consider physical possession the principal determinant of ownership, and they increasingly are more willing to use the remedy of specific performance."[51] Unfortunately, "the judicial remedy still may be slow . . . but delay alone is not a sufficient rationale for self-help because it would justify self-help in practically all cases."[52] Currently, "the present judicial remedy . . . does not evince the same degree of inadequacy" as previous remedies, leaving scholars searching for new justifications which may necessitate the self-help privilege. [53]

Perhaps privileged recapture continues to be recognized because "such a privilege comports with fundamental notions of fairness and 'the frailties of human nature.'"[54] Many people find it natural to try and regain property wrongfully taken from them, and "judicial imposition of liability on the wronged person for the results of such natural behavior arguably is inequitable."[55]

Resorting to "the frailties of human nature" to justify the use of force when recapturing an item is logical in light of the many limitations placed on this privilege. Specifically, recognizing "the natural impulse to pursue the taker of one's property" helps explain the "fresh pursuit" limitation, "since a delay obviously would allow the ire of the wronged party to subside, thereby negating the natural impulse justification."[56] Further, it is quite understandable that deadly force cannot be used to retake an item, as "the frailties of human nature" would surely never justify murder. Finally, it makes sense that only a "wrongful taking" invokes this privilege, as only such tortious dispossession stirs the ire of a self-helper.

III. Jewish Law

A. Talmudic Passage

To understand Jewish law's view on retaking an item through the use of force,[57] a lengthy passage of the Talmud must be dissected.[58] In Tractate Bava Kama,[59] the Talmud tells a story:

Rabbi Chisda dispatched [the following query] to Rabbi Nachman: . . . what is the [penalty] . . . for wounding with the blade of the hoe or with the handle of the hoe? . . . [Rabbi Chisda explains the background of the query]: There was a well belonging to two persons. It was used by them on alternate days. One of them, however, came and used it on a day not his. The other party said to him: 'This day is mine!' But as the latter paid no heed to that, he took a blade of a hoe and struck him with it. Rabbi Nachman thereupon replied: No harm if he would have struck him a hundred times with the blade of the hoe. For even according to the view that a man may not take the law in his own hands for the protection of his interests, in a case where an irreparable loss is pending he is certainly entitled to do so.

It has indeed been stated: Rabbi Yehudah said: No man may take the law into his own hands for the protection of his interests, whereas Rabbi Nachman said: A man may take the law into his own hands for the protection of his interests. In a case where an irreparable loss is pending . . . [all agree] that he may take the law into his own hands for the protection of his interests; the difference of opinion is only where no irreparable loss is pending. Rabbi Yehudah maintains that no man may take the law into his own hands for the [alleged] protection of his interests, for since no irreparable loss is pending let him resort to the [court system]; whereas R. Nachman says that a man may take the law into his own hands for the protection of his interests, for since he acts in accordance with [the prescriptions of the] law, why [need he] take the trouble [to go to court]?[60]

Seemingly, from this detailed story in the Talmud emerge three opinions. Rabbi Chisda believes that one can never use force to retake an item, even if using the court system instead will lead to irreparable loss.[61] Alternatively, Rabbi Yehudah believes that one can only use force to retake an item if using the court system instead will lead to irreparable loss.[62] Finally, Rabbi Nachman believes that force can be used to retake an item even if using the court system will not lead to any loss.[63]

The Talmud elsewhere establishes that whenever there is a dispute between Rabbi Nachman and others concerning judiciary matters, the ruling follows Rabbi Nachman's opinion.[64] Consequently, almost all codifiers of Jewish law rely on the rule according to Rabbi Nachman, permitting the use of force even if using the court system will not lead to any loss.[65] Presumably, Jewish law is no different than American law, since "the privilege of an owner dispossessed of his chattel to recapture it by force . . . [is] recognized."[66]

B. Rabbi Nachman Reexamined

The opinion of Rabbi Nachman, however, is not as clear as it may seem. Closer introspection of the above Talmudic passage reveals that Rabbi Nachman only explicitly allowed force in the story about the water in the well. In that case, going to the courts would have caused the rightful owner irreparable loss of production in his field; there would be no more water in the well to irrigate the produce by the time the courts issued an injunction against the thief.[67] Although the courts would require the thief to pay for the stolen water, they would not have required him to pay for the incidental loss of the produce in the field.[68] However, when use of the courts would not lead to irreparable loss, Rabbi Nachman merely stated, "a man may take the law into his own hands for the protection of his interests."[69] Thus, without irreparable loss, no permission to use force to retake chattel is explicitly given.

This omission helps form the novel interpretation of Maimonides on self-help in this context. Maimonides writes:

A man may take the law into his own hands, if he had the power to do so, since he acts in conformity with the law and he is not obliged to take the trouble and go to court, even though he would lose nothing by the delay involved in court proceedings.[70]

In codifying our Talmudic passage, Maimonides not surprisingly follows the opinion of Rabbi Nachman, that "even though he would lose nothing by the delay involved in court proceedings," a person "may take the law into his own hands."[71] Yet, eerily absent from Maimonides is the privilege to use force to retake his item.[72] Thus, Maimonides apparently understood Rabbi Nachman's opinion as only allowing nonviolent self-help in cases where going to court will not lead to irreparable harm.[73]

C. Limitations

Despite Maimonides' novel understanding, the majority opinion in Jewish law interprets Rabbi Nachman as recognizing a privilege to use force to recapture chattel, even when using the courts will not lead to any irreparable loss.[74] As in American law, this privilege to use force is not carte blanche. After bringing the above opinions, the Talmud continues to debate these opinions through extensive analysis of eight scenarios where self-help is used.[75] The results of this discourse and the concomitant scholarly interpretations are numerous limitations on the opinion of Rabbi Nachman.[76]

1. Limitations Analogous to American Law

Similar to American law, Jewish law requires that force only be used by the person who is entitled to the item.[77] It is not enough that the self-helper believes that the item is rightfully his; he must be "certain" of this fact.[78] A mistaken belief will lead to the self-helper being liable for the force used.[79]

Additionally, Jewish law agrees with American law that if the item can be retrieved "without the use of force against the other," such force is "unprivileged."[80] The self-helper may only use force if there is no other peaceful way to retrieve the item. Likewise, a warning must be issued before force is used.[81]

Finally, force may only be used to recapture the taken item.[82] Once the item is safely in the self-helper's hands, the privilege no longer exists. Force as retribution or as future deterrent is equally forbidden.[83]

2. Dissimilarities to American Law

A few of the limitations in American law are not mentioned in Jewish law, presumably because they are not required for the use of force. Specifically, the need for "fresh pursuit" is notably omitted from the Jewish law sources on this privilege.[84] In all likelihood, Jewish law allows a self-helper to use force even after his ire has already diffused. Additionally, as there is no requirement to use force "reasonable under the circumstances," perhaps even deadly force or serious bodily harm would be privileged.[85] However, deadly force would only be privileged if it was the least amount of force necessary for the recapture — a highly unlikely scenario.

Lastly, many scholars think that Jewish law does not contain a "wrongful taking" limitation.[86] While it concurs with American law that a creditor cannot use force to collect collateral, the reason for this law is not because of a lack of "wrongful taking" by the debtor.[87] Rather, Jewish law only allows force to recapture the same item that was taken; money or collateral cannot be recaptured through the use of force.[88] Where the self-helper only recaptures the exact item taken, force may be used even if the perpetrator received the item without fraud or with a claim of right. Thus, force by a seller recapturing his own goods after a buyer defaults,[89] or force by a lender recapturing his item that was never returned would be privileged.[90]

D. Justifications
1. Maimonides

While Jewish law commentators provide numerous justifications for the self-helper's use of force to recapture chattel, it is important to reiterate Maimonides' contrary view, prohibiting force where going to court would not lead to irreparable loss.[91] Possibly, Maimonides finds no justification for force in this scenario, as the force is unnecessary, for going to court can recoup all the loss.[92] Maimonides' logic is very strong. If one is required to use the least violent approach, violence should never be privileged, as the option of using the courts is always the less violent approach!

Hence, justification for the majority view of Jewish law, that force can be used even when going to court would not lead to irreparable loss, must be identified.[93] Fortunately, two creative, distinct approaches for this justification have emerged.

2. First Approach: Reparable Loss as Irreparable Loss

The first approach explains the use of force with no irreparable loss in consonance with force by irreparable loss.[94] Since a perpetrator may flee the country or destroy the item, complete recourse through litigation is never assured.[95] Thus, every recapturing chattel scenario is one of potential irreparable loss.[96] Since force can definitely be used by irreparable loss, force can also be used where the reparability of the loss is in doubt.[97]

Another version of this same approach views the litigation costs and incidental losses associated with litigation, i.e., lost work, travel expenses etc., as irreparable loss.[98] In fact, even if this loss is not monetary, but merely the loss of inner peace due to the pressures and drama of litigation, it is considered irreparable loss.[99] Accordingly, a self-helper may use force to prevent this loss associated with litigation, just as he may use force to prevent bona fide irreparable monetary loss.[100]

3. Second Approach: Separate Right or Power

Significantly, a major difficulty of the first approach exists in its interpretation of the Talmudic passage quoted earlier. As the first approach views reparable loss simply as a doubtful irreparable loss or a non-monetary irreparable loss, the Talmud's distinction between "reparable loss" and "irreparable loss" is quite puzzling.[101] In truth, force can only be used by reparable loss because it has some irreparable loss quality.[102]

The second approach thus attempts to resolve this textual difficulty by permitting a self-helper to use force by reparable loss for its own, separate right or power. While the precise nature of this right or power remains vague, many compare this right to the power of the court to use force.[103] In viewing the self-helper as an extension of the court itself, the self-helper is no different than a judicial officer, empowered by the court to use force to enact justice.[104]

Others view this right as an inherent power in an individual with regard to one's own items.[105] This inherent power is premised on the secondary role of a court system in Jewish law.[106] For that reason, this power does not emanate from the courts, but rather from every individual's responsibility in "the administration of justice."[107]

Some proponents of this approach look outside the monetary dispute framework to justify the privilege to use force by reparable loss. Rather, the right to use force stems from the social responsibility of every individual to prevent others from doing bad deeds.[108] In other words, a self-helper can use force to recapture an item from a thief solely to prevent the thief from violating the prohibition of stealing.[109]

IV. Observations
A. First Observation: Justification Explains Limitation

As previously noted,[110] scholars explain the "fresh pursuit" requirement by the use of force to recapture chattel in American law by looking at the justification of this privilege. Since the justification for this privilege is based on the "frailties of human nature," this privilege logically only applies when the self-helper is still very upset over his loss. Further, the non-deadly force and "wrongful taking" requirements are easily understood in light of this justification.

Apparently, the lack of these limitations in Jewish law can be explained through Jewish law's unique justifications of this privilege. Not requiring "fresh pursuit," a "wrongful taking," nor non-deadly force makes perfect sense according to either of the two approaches used to justify the use of force in Jewish recapture law. According to the first approach, that the privilege to use force by reparable loss stems from its connection to irreparable loss, surely a "fresh pursuit" requirement would be ridiculous. Since force is privileged in order to prevent potential irreparable loss or definite non-monetary/incidental loss, it can be used any time. Whether there was a "wrongful taking" is further irrelevant, so long as there are potential irreparable losses at the current time.[111]

Similarly, according to the second approach, that the privilege to use force by reparable harm stems from a separate right or power, the lack of a "fresh pursuit" or "wrongful taking" limitation is reasonable. If viewed as an extension of the court system, courts can use their force whenever and on whatever they deem necessary. If viewed as an inherent power emanating from the individual, all that is essential is that the self-helper's ownership is being challenged.[112] Either way, the omission of "fresh pursuit" and "wrongful taking" requirements is not troubling.

B. Second Observation:
Inherent Good of the Individual

American law emphasizes an elaborate court system designed to prevent a "breach of the peace."[113] An individual's ability to use force can exist only through a special exception based on the "frailties of human nature."[114] In contrast, Jewish law favors the right of an individual, even to the detriment of the public welfare.[115]

"Self-help" is a good example of this outlook, as the omission of the "frailties of human nature"[116] justification reflects Jewish law's "fundamental trust in the individual."[117] By giving a self-helper the privilege to use force to recapture chattel, Jewish law assumes that the self-helper "would not take the law into his own hands unless it were justified and that, even then, he would act with restraint."[118]

V. Conclusion

Current events have brought self-help/self-defense laws to the public forum, sparking intense media discussion about their continued viability in modern society.[119] Further, "widespread publicity emphasizing the high cost of litigation" has set off much scholarly debate in the legal field surrounding the benefits and detriments of self-help remedies.[120] However, balancing the need for a strong court system with the need for protection of individual rights has long been the task of developed legal systems. Two legal systems that grapple with this balancing task are the American and Jewish legal systems, albeit with different results. Specifically with regard to recapturing chattels through the use of force, American law restricts the right of the self-helper more severely than Jewish law. The distinct justifications in each of these legal systems highlight the complex legal theories underlying this delicate balance. Thus, Reuben should think

carefully before hurling bolt cutters at Simon's head to retrieve his bicycle. It is not a simple decision.

Journal of International Law, Gonzaga University, May 15, 2013, www.law.gonzaga.edu
Reprinted with permission of the publisher

Endnotes

[1] Douglas Ivor Brandon, et al., *Special Project: Self-Help: Extrajudicial Rights, Privileges and Remedies in Contemporary American Society*, 37 Vand. L. Rev. 845, 850 (1984).

[2] *Id.*

[3] *Id; see generally* Gregg v.Georgia,428 U.S. 153 (1976).

[4] Brandon et al., *supra note 2*, at 850; *see also* René David, 11 Int'l Enc. Comp. L. 2-192 (1984).

[5] Craig Dolly, *The Electronic Self-Help Provisions of UCITA: A Virtual Repo Man?*, 33 J. Marshall L. Rev. 663, 668 (2000).

[6] Neil Hecht, Shimshon Ettinger, "Self-Help," v. 6, *Selected Topics in Jewish Law*, Open University of Israel Publishing House (1994) [published under the auspices of the Institute of Jewish Law, Boston University School of Law].

[7] Brandon, et al., *supra note 2*, at 849.

[8] Brandon, et al., *supra note 2*, at 849.

[9] Brandon, et al., *supra note 2*, at 849-50.

[10] Dolly, supra note 6, at 671. One area where self-help is still being debated is electronic self-help. *Id.* ("The use of self-help, specifically electronic self-help, has become a highly contested area").

[11] Brandon et al., *supra note 2*, at 850.

[12] W. Page Keeton et al, *Prosser & Keeton on Law of Torts*, § 22, at 137 (5th ed. 1984); *see also Restatement (Second) of Torts* § 100 (stating "[t]he use of force against another for the sole purpose of retaking possession of a chattel is privileged if . . . all the conditions stated in §§ 101-106 exist").

[13] *See* Richard A. Epstein, *The Theory and Practice of Self-Help*, 1 J.L. Econ. & Pol'y. 1, 29 (2005).

[14] W. Page Keeton et al, *supra note 13*, § 22, at 138; *see also Restatement (Second) of Torts* § 101-106. Importantly, where judicial remedy is unavailable, the necessity of these conditions is undeveloped in American law. *See Restatement (Second) of Torts* § 100 cmt. b; W. Page Keeton et al, *supra note 13*, § 22 n.7 ("Where these conditions are unfulfilled, it is unclear if the owner may still resort to self-help force to prevent destruction of the item or to prevent its removal from the jurisdiction and from legal recourse.").

[15] Brandon, et al., *supra note 2*, at 864.

[16] *Id.*; *see Restatement (Second) of Torts*: How Possession Obtained by Other § 101 (stating "[t]he use of reasonable force against another for the purpose of recaption is privileged if the other … has tortiously taken the chattel from the actor's possession without claim of right, or under claim of right but by force or other duress or fraud. . . .").

[17] *Restatement (Second) of Torts*: How Possession Obtained by Other § 101.

[18] W. Page Keeton et al, *supra note 13*, § 22, at 138; *see also Restatement (Second) of Torts*: How Possession Obtained by Other § 101 cmt. d, illus. 1 ("A finds B's automobile parked in the street. Knowing

it to be B's, he enters it and is about to drive away with it when B comes up. B is privileged to use force to retake the automobile").

[19] Viley O. Blackburn, Note, *The Right of Recaption of Chattels by Force*, 34 KY. L.J. 65, 65 (1945).

[20] *Restatement (Second) of Torts*: How Possession Obtained by Other § 101.

[21] *Restatement (Second) of Torts* § 101 cmt. c.

[22] W. Page Keeton et al, *supra* note 13, § 22, at 139; *see also* Kensinger Acceptance Corp. v. Davis, 269 S.W.2d 792, 794 (Ark. 1954).

[23] errromet Resources, Inc. v. Chemoil Corp., 5 F.3d 902, 904; *see also* *Restatement (Second) of Torts*: How Possession Obtained by Other § 101 cmt. d., illus. 4.

[24] People v. Reid, 69 N.Y.2d 469 (1987); People v. Green, 5 N.Y.3d 538 (2005).

[25] *Restatement (Second) of Torts*: Actor's Right to Possession of Chattel § 102.

[26] *Restatement (Second) of Torts*: Actor's Right to Possession of Chattel § 102 cmt. a.

[27] Brandon, et al., *supra* note 2, at 864; *see also Restatement (Second) of Torts*: Timeliness of Recaption § 103 ("The actor is not privileged to use force against another for the purpose of recaption unless he acts promptly after his dispossession or after his timely discovery of it.").

[28] W. Page Keeton et al, *supra* note 13, § 22, at 138.

[29] W. Page Keeton et al, *supra* note 13, § 22, at 138. With the widespread usage today of automobiles and airplanes, older case law is not that helpful.

[30] W. Page Keeton et al, *supra* note 13, § 22, at 138; *see also Restatement (Second) of Torts*: Timeliness of Recaption § 103, cmt. b, illus. 1-4 (allowing a leeway of a few days).

[31] *Restatement Second() of Torts*: Timeliness of Recaption § 103, cmt. a.

[32] *Id.*

[33] W. Page Keeton et al, *supra* note 13, § 22, at 138; *see also* Dyk v. DeYoung, 24 N.E. 520 (Ill. 1890).

[34] *Restatement (Second) of Torts*: Necessity of Demand § 104.

[35] W. Page Keeton et al, *supra* note 13, § 22, at 138.

[36] *Restatement (Second) of Torts*: Purpose of Actor § 105.

[37] Hatfield v. Gracen, 567 P.2d 546, 550 (Or. 1977).

[38] W. Page Keeton et al, *supra* note 13, § 22, at 138.

[39] W. Page Keeton et al, *supra* note 13, § 22, at 138; *see also Restatement (Second) of Torts*: Amount of Force Permissible § 106 (stating "[t]he use of force against another for the purpose of recaption is not privileged unless the means employed are (a) not in excess of those which the actor correctly or reasonably believes to be necessary to effect the reception, and (b) not intended or likely to cause death or serious bodily harm").

[40] *Restatement (Second) of Torts*: Amount of Force Permissible § 106, cmt. b.

[41] *Id.*

[42] Brandon, et al., *supra* note 2, at 864; *see also* Hodgeden v. Hubbard, 18 Vt. 504, 507 (1846).

[43] Brandon, et al., *supra* note 2, at 864.

[44] W. Page Keeton et al, *supra* note 13, § 22, at 138.

[45] *Restatement (Second) of Torts*: Amount of Force Permissible § 106, cmt. e.

[46] . Page Keeton et al, *supra* note 13, § 22, at 138.

[47] Brandon et al., *supra* note 2, at 863.

[48] *Id.; see also* Adam B. Badawi, *Self-Help and the Rules of Engagement,* 29 Yale J. on Reg. 1 (2012).

[49] Brandon, et al., *supra* note 2, at 863.

[50] Brandon, et al., *supra* note 2, at 863; Blackburn, *supra* note 20, at 65.

[51] Brandon, et al., *supra* note 2, at 865.

[52] Brandon, et al., *supra* note 2, at n.104.

[53] Brandon, et al., *supra* note 2, at 865.

[54] Brandon, et al., *supra* note 2, at 866; *see also* Blackburn, *supra* note 19, at 65.

[55] Brandon, et al., *supra* note 2, at 865.

[56] Brandon, et al., *supra* note 2, at n.106.

[57] The Babylonian Talmud: Baba Kamma, 27b-28a, at 143-49 (E.W. Kirzner, ed. & Isidore Epstein, trans., 1935) [hereinafter Baba Kamma] (Self-help in Jewish law is known in the Talmud by the Aramaic phrase "*Avid Inish Dina Linafshei,*" loosely translated as "doing justice for oneself by oneself.").

[58] Before such a foray, Michael J. Broyde offers some context to Jewish law generally:

[a] brief historical review will familiarize the new reader of Jewish law with its history and development. The Pentateuch (the five books of Moses, the Torah) is the elemental document of Jewish law and, according to Jewish legal theory, was revealed to Moses at Mount Sinai. The Prophets and Writings, the other two parts of the Hebrew Bible, were written over the next 700 years, and the Jewish canon was closed around the year 200 before the Common Era ("B.C.E."). The close of the canon until year 250 of the Common Era ("C.E.") is referred to as the era of the Tannaim, the redactors of Jewish law, whose period closed with the editing of the Mishnah by Rabbi Judah the Patriarch. The next five centuries were the epoch in which scholars called Amoraim ("those who recount" Jewish law) and Savoraim ("those who ponder" Jewish law) wrote and edited the two Talmuds (Babylonian and Jerusalem). The Babylonian Talmud is of greater legal significance than the Jerusalem Talmud and is a more complete work.

The post-Talmudic era is conventionally divided into three periods: (1) the era of the Geonim, scholars who lived in Babylonia until the mid-eleventh century; (2) the era of the Rishonim (the early authorities), who lived in North Africa, Spain, Franco-Germany, and Egypt until the end of the fourteenth century; and (3) the period of the Aharonim (the latter authorities), which encompasses all scholars of Jewish law from the fifteenth century up to this era. From the period of the mid-fourteenth century until the early seventeenth century, Jewish law underwent a period of codification, which led to the acceptance of the law code format of Rabbi Joseph Karo, called the *Shulhan Arukh,* as the basis for modern Jewish law. The *Shulhan Arukh* (and the *Arba'ah Turim* of Rabbi Jacob ben Asher, which preceded it) divided Jewish law into four separate areas: *Orah Hayyim* is devoted to daily, Sabbath, and holiday laws; *Even HaEzer* addresses family law, including financial aspects; *Hoshen Mishpat* codifies financial law; and *Yoreh Deah* contains dietary laws as well as other miscellaneous legal matter. Many significant scholars—themselves as important as Rabbi Karo in status and authority—wrote annotations to his code which made the work and its surrounding comments the modern touchstone of Jewish law. The most recent complete edition of the *Shulhan Arukh* (Vilna, 1896) contains no less than 113 separate commentaries on the text of Rabbi Karo. In addition, hundreds of other volumes of commentary have been published as self-standing works, a process that continues to this very day. Besides the law codes and commentaries, for the last 1200 years, Jewish law authorities have addressed specific questions of Jewish law in written responsa (in question and answer form). Collections of such responsa have been published, providing guidance not only to later authorities but also to the community at large. Finally, since the establishment of the State of Israel in 1948, the rabbinical courts of Israel have published their written opinions deciding cases on a variety of matters.

—Michael J. Broyde, *The Foundations of Law: A Jewish Law View of World Law*, 54 Emory L.J. 79, 97

[59] *See generally* Baba Kamma, *supra* note 58, at 27b, 143-45.

[60] Babylonian Talmud: Tractate Baba Kamma, Come-and-Hear. com, available at http://www.come-and-hear.com/babakamma/babakamma_27.html [hereinafter Come-and-Hear.com] (last visited Mar. 31, 2013).

[61] *See* Yisroel Zev Gustman, Bava Kama, BK Kuntrasai Shiurim 15 (understanding Rabbi Chisda as an opinion and not merely as a questioner).

[62] Come-and-Hear.com, *supra* note 61.

[63] Come-and-Hear.com, *supra* note 61.

[64] The Babylonian Talmud: Kethuboth I, 13a, at 68 (E.W. Kirzner, ed. & Isidore Epstein, trans., 1935).

[65] *See* Yechiel ben Asher, *Choshen Mishpat*, 15 Tur: 4:1 (Machon Yreschalayim, ed., 1994); Joseph ben Ephraim Karo, *Choshen Mishpat*, CM1 Shulchan Aruch 4:1 (Leshem, ed., 2004). The notable exception is Ephraim ben Shimshon, who follows the opinion of Rabbi Yehudah. *See* Rabbeinu Ephraim. His reasoning, that self-help through force is not a judiciary matter, is discussed later in this Article.

[66] W. Page Keeton et al, *supra* note 13, § 22, at 137.

[67] Shlomo Yitzhaki, Bava Kama 27b, 12 Rashi (Vagshal, ed. 1999)

[68] *See* Asher ben Yechiel, Bava Kama, Rosh, 27b (Vagshal, ed., 1999).

[69] Baba Kamma, *supra* note 58, at 27b, 144-45.

[70] Maimonides, *Laws of Sanhedrin, Mishneh Torah* 2:12, available at *Extraordinary Remedies: Extrajudicial Remedies*, Jewish Virtual Library, http://www.jewishvirtuallibrary.org/jsource/judaica/ejud_0002_0006_0_06189.html.

[71] *Id.*

[72] Vidal of Tolosa, *Laws of Slaves*, 10 *Maggid Mishneh* 3:7 (Frankel, ed., 1990) (quoting Shlomo Ben Avraham Hacohen, Maharshach). Importantly, Abraham diBotem, disagrees with this reading of Maimonides. Instead, he posits that Maimonides' addition of the phrase "if he had the power to do so" indicates that force could be used. *Laws of Sanhedrin, Lechem Mishneh* 2:12. This is also the understanding of Maimonides according to Joseph Karo. *Choshen Mishpat, Shulchan Aruch* 4:1.

[73] Vidal of Tolosa, *supra* note 73, 3:7 (quoting Shlomo Ben Avraham Hacohen, Maharshach). Further proof of Maimonides' opinion is gleaned from his statement in the Laws of Slaves, "When a servant whose master gave him a Canaanite maid-servant and whose ear was pierced does not desire to leave his master's domain when the Jubilee year arrives . . . his master . . . is permitted to strike him, because at that time, the servant becomes prohibited to have relations with a maid-servant." Maimonides, *Laws of Slaves, Mishneh Torah* 3:7, available at Chapter Three, Chabad.org (trans. Eliyahu Touger), http://www.chabad.org/library/article_cdo/aid/1363806/jewish/Chapter-Three.htm. Maimonides permits the owner to hit the slave "because at that time, the servant becomes prohibited to have relations with a maid-servant." Vidal of Tolosa, *supra* note 73,

3:7 (quoting Shlomo Ben Avraham Hacohen, Maharshach). If Maimonides allows one to "take the law into his own hands" through the use of force, he would have referenced the concept of self-help, instead of discussing prohibited relations. Vidal of Tolosa, *supra* note 73, 3:7.

[74] *See* Asher ben Yechiel, *supra* note 69, at 27b; Joseph Habiba, *Bava Kama*, 12 *Nimukei Yosef*, 27b (Vagshal, ed., 1999); *see also* Yechiel ben Asher, *supra* note 66, 4:1; Joseph ben Ephraim Karo, *Choshen Mishpat, Shulchan Aruch* 4:1.

[75] *See* Bava Kama, *supra* note 58, at 27b-28a, 143-49.

[76] Ettinger, *supra* note 7, at 14.

[77] *See* Asher ben Yechiel, *supra* note 69, at 27b.

[78] *See* Asher ben Yechiel, *supra* note 69, at 27b. According to many, he must be able to validate this certainty in a court. *See* Yisroel Zev Gustman, *supra* note 62, at15 (proving from here that the power to use force stems from the fact that the self-helper is an extension of the courts).

[79] Joseph ben Ephraim Karo, *supra* note 75, 4:1.

[80] *Restatement (Second) of Torts*: Amount of Force Permissible § 106, cmt. b; *see* Bava Kama, *supra* note 58, at 28a, 145-149.

[81] *See Otzar Miforshei Hatalmud* (Bava Kama 28a, n. 28) (stating a warning must be provided at the time the chattel is recovered).

[82] Joseph ben Ephraim Karo, *supra* note 75, 4:1.

[83] Ettinger, *supra* note 7, at 14.

[84] *See generally* Asher ben Yechiel, *supra* note 69, at 27b; Joseph Habiba, *supra* note 75, at 27b; Yechiel ben Asher, *supra* note 66, 4:1; Joseph ben Ephraim Karo, *supra* note 75, 4:1; *but see* Menachem Meiri, 5 Bava Kama 27b (*Zichron Yaakov*, ed., 1976) (implying a "fresh pursuit" requirement by stating that force can only be used before the item is actually taken from the self-helper's possession).

[85] *See* Joseph Habiba, *supra* note 75, at 27b (allowing the self-helper to hit the perpetrator "even one hundred times). The permissibility of using deadly force fits nicely with the second approach discussed later, that the power of the self-helper stems from an extension of the court system. Just like a court officer can mete out punishment of death, so too can a self-helper. *See generally* Yisroel Zev Gustman, *supra* note 62, at 15.

[86] Isaac ben Sheshet Perfet, 2 *Rivash* (Machon Yerushalayim, ed., 1993); Moses Isserles, *Choshen Mishpat* CM1 Rama 4:1 (Leshem, ed., 2004); *see also* Yehoshua Falk HaKohen, *Sefer Me'irat Einayim (Sma)(Choshen Mishpat* 4:1); *cf.* Joseph Colon Trabotto, *Maharik* (quoted in Rama, *Choshen Mishpat* 4:1).

[87] Asher ben Yechiel, *supra* note 69, at 27b; Joseph Habiba, *supra* note 75, at 27b.

[88] Isaac ben Sheshet Perfet, *supra* note 87; Moses Isserles, *supra* note 87, 4:1; *see also* Yehoshua Falk HaKohen, *Choshen Mishpat, Sma* 4:1; *cf.* Joseph Colon Trabotto, *Maharik* (quoted in *Choshen Mishpat*, Rama 4:1).

[89] Isaac ben Sheshet Perfet, *supra* note 87; Moses Isserles, *supra* note 87, 4:1; *see also* Yehoshua Falk HaKohen, *Choshen Mishpat, Sma* 4:1; *cf.* Joseph Colon Trabotto, *Maharik* (quoted in *Choshen Mishpat*, Rama 4:1).

[90] Yechiel Michel Epstein, *Choshen Mishpat*, Aruch Hashulchan 4:1.

[91] See *supra* text accompanying notes 69-72.

[92] *See generally* Yaakov Lorberbaum, CM1 *Nesivos Hamishpat* 4:1 (Leshem, ed., 2004) (using this logic as a proof against the use of force).

[93] See *supra* text accompanying notes 73-76.

94 *See generally* Yisroel Zev Gustman, *supra* note 62, at 15 (querying if reparable loss is similar to irreparable loss).

95 Yaakov Lorberbaum, *supra* note 93, 4:1.

96 Yaakov Lorberbaum, *supra* note 93, 4:1.

97 Yaakov Lorberbaum, *supra* note 93, 4:1. Accordingly, in the case of recapturing real property, where there is no potential for irreparable loss through fleeing or destruction, force would not be privileged.

98 Emanuel B. Quint & Neil S. Hecht, 2 Jewish Jurisprudence 94 (1986). The author of this Article thinks that the language of Asher ben Yechiel, Rosh (Bava Kama 27b), comports nicely with this interpretation.

99 *Id.*

100 *Id*

101 Moshe Gnizi, *Bava Kama, Moreshes Yaakov* 27b (Gnizi, ed., 1978).

102 *Id.*

103 *See* Asher ben Yechiel, *supra* note 69, at 27b; Joseph Habiba, *supra* note 75, at 27b.

104 Joseph Habiba, *supra* note 75, at 27b (comparing self-helper to a judicial officer); *see generally* Yisroel Zev Gustman, *supra* note 62, at 15 (querying the extent of this comparison and power).

105 *See* Yisroel Zev Gustman, *supra* note 62, at 15 (entertaining this approach). The author of this Article thinks that this understanding can be gleaned from the language of Asher ben Yechiel, Rosh (Bava Kama 27b), as well. *See also* Aryeh Leib Malin, *Siman* 75 (suggesting this interpretation within the view of Maimonides according to *Lechem Mishneh*).

106 *See* Ettinger, *supra* note 7, at 16.

107 *See* Ettinger, *supra* note 7, at 16.

108 Meir Auerbach, *Choshen Mishpat*, 2 Imrei Bina 9 (Belchotovksi, ed., 1900).

109 *Id.; but see* Elchonon Wasserman, *Bava Kama*, 2 Kovetz Biurim (E. S. Wasserman, ed. 1989) (doubting such an explanation based on Aryeh Leib Heller-Kahane, *Ketzos Hachoshen*, that there is no need to prevent the prohibition of stealing after the item is already stolen)

110 See *supra* text accompanying notes 56-58.

111 Similarly, deadly force may be allowed as well, as reparable loss is no different than irreparable loss.

112 Perhaps even deadly force can be used, as this relationship to one's item is very strong.

113 *See* Badawi, *supra* note 49.

114 *See supra* text accompanying notes 55-56.

115 *See* Ettinger, *supra* note 7, at 16.

116 *See supra* text accompanying notes 55-56.

117 *See supra* text accompanying notes 55-56.

118 This belief is especially seen in the second approach given as a justification. *See supra* text accompanying notes 100-108.

119 *See, e.g.,* Geoffrey Corn, *A Learning Opportunity in Trayvon Martin Case,* HOUS. CHRON., Apr. 21, 2012, http://www.chron.com/opinion/outlook/article/A-learning-opportunity-in-Trayvon-Martin-case-3498736.php; Eric Zorn, *Trayvon Martin and the Problematic Timeline,* Chi. Trib., Apr. 18, 2012, http://blogs.chicagotribune.com/news_columnists_ezorn/2012/04/trayvon-martin-and-the-problematic-timeline.html.

120 Brandon et al., *supra* note 2, at 925; *see also* Celia R. Taylor, *Self-Help in Contract Law*, 33 Wake Forest L. Rev., 839, 847 (1998).

Lesson

3

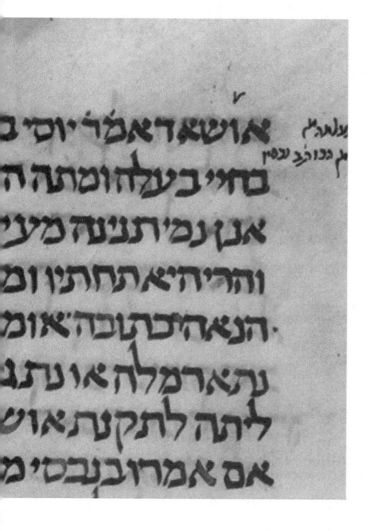

WINDFALL WRANGLES

DETERMINING OWNERSHIP FOR EXOTIC FINDS

Life yields all kinds of surprises. Sometimes they are the proverbial worm in the apple. But every so often we hear of someone who is blessed with a true windfall. However, when the weather is fair, everyone wants a share: it is common in such instances for multiple parties to claim a stake in the bonanza. In this lesson we discuss how to determine ownership when there are conflicting claims to life's valuable surprises.

CASE STUDY A

SOURCES: CHRISTINA CORRALES-TOY, "ISSAQUAH WOMAN FINDS A $600 SURPRISE IN MONTALCINO SEAFOOD," *THE ISSAQUAH PRESS,* FEBRUARY 22, 2016, WWW.THEEASTSIDE.NEWS/ISSAQUAH/ENTERTAINMENT/FOOD/ ISSAQUAH-WOMAN-FINDS-A-SURPRISE-IN-MONTALCINO-SEAFOOD-DISH/ ARTICLE_171E3D90-D9C3-11E5-A695-6BD4A1D5C550.HTML; "A WOMAN BIT DOWN ON A RARE PEARL WHILE EATING A MEAL OF CLAMS AND OTHER SEAFOOD AT AN ITALIAN RESTAURANT IN ISSAQUAH," *U.S. NEWS & WORLD REPORT,* FEBRUARY 24, 2016, WWW.USNEWS.COM/NEWS/OFFBEAT/ARTICLES/2016-02-24/ WOMAN-BITES-RARE-PEARL-WHILE-DINING-AT-ITALIAN-RESTAURANT

It was a chilly night in February 2016, but it was a special one for Lindsay Hasz from Issaquah, Washington, a city about twenty miles east of Seattle. It was a rare date night for Lindsay and her husband, Chris. "It's always a special occasion when we can find a babysitter," Lindsay joked.

They were dining on a seafood dish filled with clams and mussels at an Italian restaurant. As Lindsay began eating the clams, a bite into a hard, unknown substance stopped her in her tracks. "I knew it wasn't a shell because it didn't crack, and in fact, I thought I was going to break my tooth," she said. The culprit was a dark, black sphere.

Was it a pearl?

Lindsay took her find to gemologist Ted Irwin, president of the Northwest Geological Laboratory and director of the Northwest Geological Institute.

Irwin was initially skeptical because most often claims of finding valuable pearls in seafood turn out to be false.

But when he looked at it, he realized that she had a beautiful Quahog pearl, worth about $600. Irwin claimed that the chance of finding a natural, gem-quality pearl like the one Lindsay found is one in a couple million.

Lindsay wished to turn the pearl into a necklace thinking that this would be the optimal good luck charm. But she decided to first tell the restaurant owners, Fernando and Cindy Nardone, of her find.

POLL 1

To whom does the pearl belong?

1 Finder

2 Restaurant owners

3 Not sure

POLL 2

If the pearl were found on the restaurant floor and the owner could not be identified, who has a better claim?

1 Finder

2 Restaurant owners

3 Not sure

CASE STUDY B

In 1997, Pepsi Cola ran a promotion called the Globe Buck Contest. One bottle cap out of 565 million would have a winning mark worth a million dollars, paid out over a twenty-year period. In a famous March 1997 incident in Las Vegas, Judy Richardson Yeats and co-worker Sindy Allen went to court arguing over the true owner of the winning cap. Allen had the cap in her possession, but Yeats claimed that she was the one that bought the bottle and that Allen had inappropriately taken it from her.

Imagine the following scenario: Judy invites Sindy to her home for dinner and places a bottle of Pepsi at Sindy's plate. Sindy opens the bottle, inspects the bottle cap, and, lo and behold, it is the winning bottle cap.

POLL 3

To whom does the winning bottle cap belong?

1 Finder

2 Host

3 Not sure

CASE STUDY C

SOURCE: RABBI DAVID PARDO, *RESPONSA MICHTAM LEDAVID, YOREH DE'AH* 1

Reuben's daughter married Simeon. Reuben provided his daughter with clothing and ornaments as a dowry. Per the custom, he conveyed the dowry in a chest, and he gifted this chest to his daughter.

One day, Simeon was searching through the chest when he found small compartments, and behind them, small passageways that were hidden from the eye. Burrowing his hand into this concealed area, Simeon found a few coins that seemed to have fallen long ago into the passageways through the holes of the small compartments.

Simeon is an ethical man and wants to steer clear of anything close to theft. He asks whether he can keep these coins.

POLL 4

To whom do the coins belong?

1 Father

2 Daughter

3 Son-in-law

4 Not sure

TEXT 1

RABBI ADIN EVEN-ISRAEL (STEINSALTZ), *THE TALMUD: A REFERENCE GUIDE* (NEW YORK: RANDOM HOUSE, 1989), P. 254 (ⅱ)

Usually, *kinyan* refers to a mode of acquisition. After the act of *kinyan* has taken place, the object is legally the property of the buyer. Neither party can go back on the agreement, regardless of any change in the market values, or any unanticipated change in the article itself. Even if the object were to be destroyed while in the physical possession of the seller, the buyer would not be entitled to get his money back.

Various modes of acquisition confer ownership, depending on the nature of the object, such as *meshichah*—pulling the article; *mesirah*—transfer; *chazakah*—performing an act of taking possession; *hagbahah*—lifting up the article; *chalifin*—exchange or barter. . . . In general, money is not a valid *kinyan* for acquiring moveable property.

The word *kinyan* may also refer to taking possession of abandoned property (*hefker*).

RABBI ADIN EVEN-ISRAEL (STEINSALTZ)
1937–

Talmudist, author, and philosopher. Rabbi Even-Israel Steinsaltz is considered one of the foremost Jewish thinkers of the 20th century. Praised by *Time* magazine as a "once-in-a-millennium scholar," he has been awarded the Israel Prize for his contributions to Jewish study. He lives in Jerusalem and is the founder of the Israel Institute for Talmudic Publications, a society dedicated to the translation and elucidation of the Talmud.

TEXT 2

MAIMONIDES, *MISHNEH TORAH,* LAWS OF ACQUISITIONS AND GIFTS 2:12

הַמַּחֲזִיק בְּנִכְסֵי הַגֵּר וּבְהֶפְקֵר, וְהוּא אֵין דַּעְתּוֹ לִקְנוֹת, אַף עַל פִּי שֶׁבָּנָה
וְגָדַר, לֹא קָנָה.

If you encounter heirless or ownerless property, even if you take hold of it—and, in the case of land, even if you build upon it and fence it—if you do not have the intention to acquire it, it is not yours.

RABBI MOSHE BEN MAIMON (MAIMONIDES, RAMBAM) 1135–1204

Halachist, philosopher, author, and physician. Maimonides was born in Cordoba, Spain. After the conquest of Cordoba by the Almohads, he fled Spain and eventually settled in Cairo, Egypt. There, he became the leader of the Jewish community and served as court physician to the vizier of Egypt. He is most noted for authoring the *Mishneh Torah*, an encyclopedic arrangement of Jewish law, and for his philosophical work, *Guide for the Perplexed*. His rulings on Jewish law are integral to the formation of halachic consensus.

CHAVRUTA A

TEXT 3

TALMUD, BAVA METSI'A 11A

רָאָה אוֹתָן רָצִין אַחַר מְצִיאָה, אַחַר צְבִי שָׁבוּר, אַחַר גוֹזָלוֹת שֶׁלֹּא פָּרְחוּ,
וְאָמַר: זָכְתָה לִי שָׂדִי, זָכְתָה לוֹ.

הָיָה צְבִי רָץ כְּדַרְכּוֹ, אוֹ שֶׁהָיוּ גוֹזָלוֹת מַפְרִיחִין, וְאָמַר: זָכְתָה לִי שָׂדִי, לֹא
אָמַר כְּלוּם.

אָמַר רַב יְהוּדָה אָמַר שְׁמוּאֵל: וְהוּא שֶׁעוֹמֵד בְּצַד שָׂדֵהוּ.

וְתִקְנֵי לֵיהּ שָׂדֵהוּ! דְּאָמַר רַבִּי יוֹסֵי בְּרַבִּי חֲנִינָא: חֲצֵרוֹ שֶׁל אָדָם קוֹנָה לוֹ
שֶׁלֹּא מִדַּעְתּוֹ?

הָנֵי מִילֵּי בְּחָצֵר הַמִּשְׁתַּמֶּרֶת, אֲבָל חָצֵר שֶׁאֵינָה מִשְׁתַּמֶּרֶת, אִי עוֹמֵד בְּצַד
שָׂדֵהוּ אִין, אִי לֹא, לֹא.

If you see people running to take an ownerless item on your field—if it is an inanimate item, an immobilized deer, or an unfledged bird, and you say, "May my property acquire it for me," your property has acquired it for you.

If, however, the deer is running about normally and the bird has fledged, even if you say, "May my property acquire it for me," you have not acquired it.

Rav Yehudah (in the name of Shmuel) clarifies the first clause: The law only applies when the owner is standing next to the relevant field.

The Talmud questions the first clause: But shouldn't the field automatically acquire the item on behalf of its

BABYLONIAN TALMUD

A literary work of monumental proportions that draws upon the legal, spiritual, intellectual, ethical, and historical traditions of Judaism. The 37 tractates of the Babylonian Talmud contain the teachings of the Jewish sages from the period after the destruction of the 2nd Temple through the 5th century CE. It has served as the primary vehicle for the transmission of the Oral Law and the education of Jews over the centuries; it is the entry point for all subsequent legal, ethical, and theological Jewish scholarship.

owner without any other requirements? For Rabbi Yosei ben Chanina taught that a property acquires things on behalf of its owner even if the owner does not know that something is on the property. [Why then must an owner verbally express intent to acquire the item and be present at the side of the field?]

The Talmud answers: Rabbi Yosei's ruling only applies to a fenced property. The law with respect to an unfenced property is that it can only acquire an ownerless item if the owner is present alongside the relevant property [and expresses the desire to acquire the object]. If this does not transpire, the property owner does not acquire the ownerless item.

	OWNER **EXPRESSES** INTENT TO ACQUIRE **MOBILE** ITEM	OWNER DOES **NOT** EXPRESS INTENT TO ACQUIRE **MOBILE** ITEM	OWNER **EXPRESSES** INTENT TO ACQUIRE **IMMOBILE** ITEM	OWNER **DOES NOT** EXPRESS INTENT TO ACQUIRE **IMMOBILE** ITEM
Fenced property with owner **present**	✘	✘		
Fenced property with owner **not** present	✘	✘		
Unfenced property with owner **present**	✘	✘		
Unfenced property with owner **not present**	✘	✘		

POLL 5

Based on Text 3, if the pearl were found on the restaurant floor and the owner cannot be identified, who has a better claim?

1 Finder

2 Restaurant owners

3 Not sure

TEXT 4

TALMUD, BAVA METSI'A 25B–26A

> מָצָא בְגַל וּבְכוֹתֶל יָשָׁן, הֲרֵי אֵלוּ שֶׁלוֹ . . . מִפְּנֵי שֶׁיָכוֹל לוֹמַר לוֹ שֶׁל
> אֱמוֹרִיִים הֵן.
>
> אַטוּ אֱמוֹרִים מַצְנְעֵי יִשְׂרָאֵל לֹא מַצְנְעֵי?
>
> לֹא צְרִיכָא דְּשְׁתִיךְ טְפֵי.

If you find something of value buried under an antiquated heap of rubble or in an ancient wall [on someone else's secured property], it belongs to you. . . . This is because you can tell the owners of the property, "The article was left there by the ancient Amorites."

The Talmud asks: But do only Amorites hide objects? [Why can't the owners claim that they themselves, or their ancestors, hid it there?]

The Talmud answers: The law allowing the finder to keep the article only applies when the find is exceedingly rusty [and thus an obvious relic of ancient times].

QUESTIONS FOR DISCUSSION

1 If an Amorite sold a parcel of land, and after many subsequent sales it reaches my hand, why don't we say that each purchaser acquired the treasure by the same means and at the same time that the purchaser acquired the property in the first place?

2 Even if, for some reason, the means by which the purchaser bought the property cannot suffice to acquire the hidden treasure, why don't we say that the treasure's presence on the owner's secured property acquires it on behalf of the owner?

CHAVRUTA B

TEXT 5a

MORDECHAI, BAVA METSI'A 258 ⊕

וְלֹא שַׁיָּיךְ כְּהַאי גַּוְונָא לְמֵימַר חֲצֵרוֹ שֶׁל אָדָם קוֹנָה לוֹ שֶׁלֹּא מִדַּעְתּוֹ, וְזָכוּ בּוֹ הָרִאשׁוֹנִים שֶׁקְּנוּ הַכּוֹתֶל וְהַגַּל. דְּכֵיוָן דְּאֵין דָּבָר הַהוּא כִּשְׁאָר הַמְצִיאוֹת שֶׁפְּעָמִים הַוֵוי לָבָא, לֹא זָכָה בּוֹ.

כִּי כְּשֶׁקְנָאוֹ, לֹא הֶעֱלָה עַל לֵב לִקְנוֹת הַמַּטְמוֹן. הִלְכָּךְ, לֹא זָכָה אֶלָּא בַּדָּבָר שֶׁיִּרְצֶה לִקְנוֹת . . . אֲבָל בְּדָבָר שֶׁלֹּא הָיָה בְּדַעַת הַמּוֹכֵר לִמְכּוֹר וְלֹא דַעַת הַקּוֹנֶה לִקְנוֹת, לֹא קָנָה.

RABBI MORDECHAI BEN HILLEL CA. 1240–1298

Rabbi Mordechai was a disciple of Rabbi Meir (Maharam) of Rothenburg, as was his brother-in-law, Rabbi Meir Hakohen, author of *Hagahot Maimoniyot*. His work on the Talmud—published in most editions of the Talmud—includes a collection of *tosafot*, responsa, halachic decisions, and commentary. During the Rintfleisch massacres of 1298, Rabbi Mordechai was killed in Nuremberg, Germany, together with his wife (daughter of Rabbi Yechiel of Paris) and their five children.

The secured property cannot in this case acquire the article on behalf of the owner. This is because a secured property can only serve to acquire ownerless items that commonly appear on a property, not uncommon finds.

Why didn't the transaction of the land include all items on the property, including the hidden treasure? The answer is that during the time of the sale, the purchaser did not expect to acquire the treasure [because it is not a usual find], and one can only acquire that which one intends to acquire. . . . That which a buyer and seller did not have in mind cannot be part of the transaction.

TEXT **5b**

TOSAFOT, BAVA METSI'A 26A ⚏

וְאִם תֹּאמַר: וְלִיקְנֵי לֵיהּ חֲצֵירוֹ לְבַעַל הַגֵּל אוֹ לְבַעַל הַכּוֹתֶל?

וְיֵשׁ לוֹמַר: דְּאֵין חָצֵר קוֹנָה בְּדָבָר שֶׁיָּכוֹל לִהְיוֹת שֶׁלֹּא יִמְצָאֶנּוּ לְעוֹלָם, כְּמוֹ הָכָא שֶׁהוּא מוּצְנָע בְּעוֹבִי הַכּוֹתֶל.

> **TOSAFOT**
>
> A collection of French and German Talmudic commentaries written during the 12th and 13th centuries. Among the most famous authors of *Tosafot* are Rabbi Ya'akov Tam, Rabbi Shimshon ben Avraham of Sens, and Rabbi Yitschak ("the Ri"). Printed in almost all editions of the Talmud, these commentaries are fundamental to basic Talmudic study.

Why doesn't the secured property acquire the buried treasure for the owner?

The answer is that one's property does not acquire items that are hidden so well that they are unlikely to ever be found, such as in this case, where the treasure is concealed in a thick wall [or beneath rubble from antiquity].

QUESTIONS	ANSWER 1	ANSWER 2 (IF APPLICABLE)
Why don't we say that the acquisition device that transferred the property worked to transfer ownership of the treasure to the current landowner?		
Even if, for some reason, the means by which the purchaser bought the property cannot suffice to acquire the hidden treasure, why don't we say that the secured property acquired it for its owner?		

Learning Exercise 1

A meteorite falls into a fenced field, but the owners are away and unaware of this. Have they acquired the meteorite?

How would Mordechai and *Tosafot* rule in this case? Circle the correct choice.

MORDECHAI		TOSAFOT	
	Acquired		Acquired
	Not acquired		Not acquired

POLL 6

In Case Study C, if the father purchased the chest that unbeknownst to him had hidden coins, did he ever acquire the coins?

1 Yes

2 No

3 Not sure

TEXT **6**

RABBI DAVID PARDO, *RESPONSA MICHTAM LEDAVID, YOREH DE'AH* 1

אִם הַתֵּיבָה הַזֹּאת קְנָאָה חָמָיו שֶׁל זֶה מֵאִינִישׁ דְּעָלְמָא, לְכֻלְּהוּ פֵּירוּשֵׁי דְּלָעֵיל לֹא קָנָה הַמָּעוֹת הַלָּלוּ שֶׁהָיוּ טְמוּנִים וַעֲלוּמֵי עַיִן.

דְּאִילּוּ לְפֵירוּשׁ הַתּוֹסָפוֹת וְהָרָא"שׁ, הֲרֵי הָכֵי נַמֵּי יָכוֹל לִהְיוֹת שֶׁלֹּא יִמְצָאֵנוּ לְעוֹלָם הוֹאִיל וְלֹא הָיָה נִיכָּר אוֹתוֹ הַמָּבוֹא שֶׁאֲחוֹרֵי הַתֵּיבוֹת הַקְּטַנִים, וְדָמֵי לְמִצְּא בְּגַל כוּ'.

וּלְפֵירוּשׁ הַמָּרְדְּכַי נַמֵּי, הַךְ נַמֵּי דָּבָר שֶׁאֵינוֹ הֲוֶה הוּא, וּבְוַדַּאי כִּי כְּשֶׁקְּנָאָה וְלֹא יָדַע מֵאוֹתוֹ הַמָּבוֹא לֹא הֶעֱלָה עַל לִבּוֹ לִקְנוֹת הַמָּעוֹת.

RABBI DAVID PARDO
1718–1790

Halachic expert and liturgical poet. Rabbi Pardo served as the chief rabbi of Sarajevo, Bosnia and later moved to Jerusalem where he headed a yeshiva and served on the rabbinic court. A prolific writer, Rabbi Pardo is best known for his multivolume commentaries on *Tosefta* and *Sifrei*, and a supercommentary to Rashi's biblical commentary.

If Reuben bought this chest from a random person, all interpretations would agree that Reuben did not acquire these hidden coins.

According to *Tosafot,* it was very likely that he would never have found these coins because the passageways behind the small compartments were not noticeable. It is similar, then, to finding a treasure in an ancient heap of rubble [where the Talmud rules that the treasure belongs to the finder, which *Tosafot* explained to be so because the owner was not likely to find it].

According to Mordechai's interpretation we come to the same conclusion. Finding coins in a chest of this sort is highly unusual. Therefore, Reuben did not intend to acquire these coins when he acquired the chest.

POLL 7

In Case Study A (pearl found in seafood), did the restaurant owners ever own the pearl?

1 Yes

2 No

3 Not sure

POLL 8

In Case Study B (soda opened by guest), did the homeowner ever own the winning cap?

1 Yes

2 No

3 Not sure

TEXT 7a

MISHNAH, BAVA BATRA 4:9

וְלֹא אֶת הַבּוֹר וְלֹא אֶת הַגַּת וְלֹא אֶת הַשּׁוֹבָךְ, בֵּין חֲרֵבִין בֵּין יְשׁוּבִין . . . בַּמֶה דְבָרִים אֲמוּרִים בְּמוֹכֵר, אֲבָל בְּנוֹתֵן מַתָּנָה נוֹתֵן אֶת כּוּלָם.

When selling a field, if it contains a well, cistern, or dovecote, whether they are still in use or impaired, they are not included in the sale [unless the seller clearly stipulated that they are]. . . .

This is all said concerning a sale; but if one makes a gift of the field, the gift includes all of the field's contents.

MISHNAH

The first authoritative work of Jewish law that was codified in writing. The Mishnah contains the oral traditions that were passed down from teacher to student; it supplements, clarifies, and systematizes the commandments of the Torah. Due to the continual persecution of the Jewish people, it became increasingly difficult to guarantee that these traditions would not be forgotten. Rabbi Yehudah Hanasi therefore redacted the Mishnah at the end of the 2nd century. It serves as the foundation for the Talmud.

TEXT 7 b

RABBI SHMUEL BEN MEIR, BAVA BATRA 71A

וְטַעֲמָא מִשּׁוּם דְּנוֹתֵן בְּעַיִן יָפָה נוֹתֵן יוֹתֵר מִדַּאי, וַאֲפִילוּ מַאי דְּלֹא הֲוֵי בִּכְלָל שָׂדֶה, הוֹאִיל וְקָבוּעַ בְּתוֹךְ הַשָּׂדֶה.

וּמֵיהוּ אִם יֵשׁ מָעוֹת בַּשָּׂדֶה, אוֹ תְּבוּאָה תְּלוּשָׁה שֶׁאֵינָה צְרִיכָה לַקַּרְקַע, אוֹ כָּל דָּבָר שֶׁלֹּא הוּצְרַךְ לְתַנָּא דְּמַתְנִיתִין לְהַזְכִּיר וְלוֹמַר לֹא מָכַר, מִשּׁוּם דְּמִילְתָא דִּפְשִׁיטָא הוּא דְּאֵינוֹ בִּכְלָל שָׂדֶה כְּלָל, הַהִיא וַדַּאי לֹא קָנָה לָהּ מְקַבֵּל מַתָּנָה.

RABBI SHMUEL BEN MEIR (RASHBAM) 1085–1158

Talmudist and biblical commentator. Rashbam was born in Troyes, France, to Yocheved, the daughter of Rashi. Rashbam, a prominent member of the Tosafists, authored commentaries on the Pentateuch and the Talmud. Like his grandfather's, Rashbam's commentaries focus on the plain meaning of the Talmudic and biblical texts.

The reason for this is that a gift giver is usually more generous than a seller. Therefore, things that are not an essential part of the field will be a part of the gift so long as they are permanently fixed to the field.

However, if there is money or loose grain in the field, these are not part of the gift. The author of the Mishnah did not even need to say that they were not part of the sale, because that much is obvious. And unless stipulated otherwise, such things are not part of the gift.

Learning Exercise 2

Summarize your conclusions by indicating below who the legal owner is in each case.

CASE	LEGAL OWNER				
Pearl found by customer in seafood in restaurant		Customer		Restaurant owners
Pearl found by customer on restaurant floor		Customer		Restaurant owners
Winning Pepsi cap found by guest		Guest		Host
Coins found in gifted chest that was purchased by gift giver		Finder		Gift giver
Coins found in gifted chest that was inherited by gift giver		Finder		Gift giver

KEY POINTS

1 To effect the transfer of ownership—when purchasing an item, receiving a gift, or claiming an ownerless object—the acquirer must perform a designated *kinyan* (acquisition device). The acquirer must also intend that the *kinyan* trigger the transfer of ownership.

2 An ownerless immobile object that falls onto a fenced property belongs to the property owner, even if the property owner is unaware of this. Property owners assume that such items will remain there for their taking, and this mindset is sufficient intent to allow their properties to act as instruments of acquisition.

3 People do not expect that ownerless articles that land on their unfenced properties will remain there for their taking. This is why an unfenced property cannot acquire ownerless objects on behalf of the property owner, unless the property owner is present and expresses intent to acquire the item.

4 When a person acquires a property that contains a treasure that is buried under an ancient structure, the *kinyan* that transferred the property does not acquire the treasure for the owner. Similarly, the fact that the treasure sits on a secured property does not acquire the treasure for the owner.

5 This exception in the case of the hidden treasure is due to the fact that the buyer did not intend to acquire this hidden treasure. One way of explaining this is that a buyer does not intend to gain rare items that are not usually found on a property. Another way of explaining this is that a buyer does not intend to gain things that are unlikely to be found because of their state of concealment.

6 Once someone is established as the legitimate owner of an item, this person does not relinquish ownership by gifting or selling the item unintentionally.

7 From a mystical perspective, everything around us contains a concealed hidden treasure of spiritual power and purpose. Our job is to reveal this treasure by using all that is around us to pursue our mission in life by engaging in acts of goodness and kindness.

Continue your learning experience
ONLINE
Visit www.myJLI.com/dilemma3 for insightful and inspiring videos, articles, and readings on this topic.

Additional Readings

AN OVERVIEW OF THE COMMON LAW AND TALMUDIC APPROACHES TO LOST, MISLAID, AND ABANDONED PROPERTY

MENDY HALBERSTAM

Lost Property

Under the common law, the finder of lost property has title to the property as against the entire world except the true owner. This rule was established in the seminal case of *Armory v. Delamirie,* where the court held that a jewel found by a chimney sweep belonged to the chimney sweep since the original owner could not be found.[1] The *Armory* rule set forth two principles: (1) "[T]he finder . . . does not by such finding acquire an absolute property or ownership" in the lost item; and (2) Notwithstanding the above, the finder does have "such a property as will enable him to keep it against all but the rightful owner. . . ."[2] Thus, under the common law, a finder of any lost object has a property interest in that object, only it is one that can be superseded by that of the true owner. Indeed, under most current law, a true owner *never* loses legal title to their lost property. However, under the common law, a finder is under no obligation to affirmatively protect the true owner from the loss by picking up the item.[3] Additionally, the common law makes no distinction as to the nature of the lost item, or whether it had any identifying marks: as long as one finds an item that was lost and not simply mislaid,[4] the law was prepared to vest a property interest in the finder, with no affirmative obligations on his part with regard to using any identifying marks to seek out the owner.[5]

However, Talmudic law sees property ownership not as a utilitarian or pragmatic convention to assist in a functioning society, but as *a reality.* Therefore,

ownership rights are *never* terminated unless there is some mechanism to bring about that change.[6] The owner must actively relinquish ownership before someone else is able to take possession of it. Often, circumstances cause an owner to lose hope that he will ever be able to find the lost object. This is referred to in the Talmud as *ye'ush*—despair. As a result of such despair, a mental state of abandonment is created whereby the owner relinquishes possession. As a consequence of this abandonment, the finder of the lost object is able to take possession of it.[7] When this happens, the finder is vested with complete ownership rights, and the true owner can make no claim on the lost property.

Mislaid Property

Jewish law recognizes a fundamental distinction between lost property and mislaid property. While one who encounters lost property has an affirmative obligation to seek out the true owner, no such obligation is present for mislaid property. Indeed, one who encounters mislaid property not only *need not* pick it up, they are *prohibited* from picking up the property.[8] The rationale for this is obvious: if the property is placed in a particular place, the easiest way to ensure that the object is returned to its owner is to do nothing; the owner will return to retrieve his possession.[9]

The distinction between lost and mislaid property is recognized by the common law as well. Under the common law rule, the "finder" of the mislaid item must leave the item as a bailment with the person on whose property it was found, since the one who mislaid the property is most likely to remember where the item was placed, and return to that spot to retrieve his item.[10] Indeed, to intentionally place an item somewhere and forget to take it from where it was placed,

MENDY HALBERSTAM

An Associate in the Miami, Florida, office of Jackson Lewis P.C. He has extensive experience in both state and federal civil rights litigation matters.

"is not to lose it, in the sense in which the authorities referred to speak of lost property."[11]

The common law, like Jewish law, also looked to the place where the object was found as the crucial factor in determining whether an item was lost or mislaid. Thus, in *McAvoy v. Medina*, where the owner of a purse left it on the counter of a barber shop, the court awarded the shop owner possession until the owner would return.[12] In contrast, in the English case of *Bridges v. Hawkesworth* a visitor to a shop found a packet of money on the floor of the shop. The court in that case ultimately awarded possession to the finder and *not* to the possessor of the property.[13] The difference between the *Bridges* and *McAvoy* cases can likely be explained by reference to the *places* wherein each was found: in *Bridges*, the notes were found in a *public area* of the store, an area that was much like the street in the amount of foot traffic it had. Therefore, the notes were awarded to the finder since we assume that the owner will not think of returning to the store to find his money. *Per contra*, in *McAvoy* the purse seemed to have been intentionally placed on the store counter, where it was more likely that the true owner would return to retrieve the item. For that reason the court awarded the purse to the storekeeper as this was the most likely place to have the item eventually returned to the true owner.

In sum then, the common law would recognize this statement regarding the definitions of lost and mislaid property: "*Mislaid property* is that which is intentionally put in a certain place and later forgotten; property is *lost* when it is unintentionally separated from the dominion of its owner; and property is *abandoned* when the owner, intending to relinquish all rights to the property, leaves it free to be appropriated by any other person."[14] Because of this particular definition of lost, mislaid, and abandoned property, the common law establishes the rule for each shall be that "[A] finder of property acquires *no rights* in mislaid property, is entitled to *possession* of lost property against everyone except the true owner, and is entitled *to keep* abandoned property."[15]

Constructive Possession

The common law gave a landowner constructive possession of any chattel on his property.[16] Utilizing the principles above, this resulted in a property owner being entitled to any lost or abandoned item on his property, even if another person—for example an invitee—actually found that item first. Because the property owner already had constructive possession of the lost item from the minute he purchased the property, his possession will always override any subsequent possession (but not an earlier possession, i.e., he will still not have title against the true owner).

However, where an item is found in a public area within general private property, say the front area of a private store, constructive possession will not apply, as discussed earlier with regard to *Bridges v. Hawkesworth*. The public nature of such an area, and thus the lack of actual dominion over the public area, functionally precludes the property owner from claiming the area is his.[17] In fact, courts have expressly used this public/private principle to explain that even if U.S. courts were to follow the master-servant rule—a matter of great disagreement among the courts[18]—which principle gives the employer any lost items found by an employee during the course of employment, this would not apply where the lost item was found in a public place, an area wherein the employer has no controlling possession.[19]

This analysis of prior possession and constructive possession as establishing the prior possession of a property owner helps explain a number of classic English cases. For example, it explains why the property owner in *Hannah v. Peel*[20] who had never taken actual possession or exercised dominion over a home was *not* entitled to a brooch found by an officer.[21] It further explains why workers who found rings on the bottom of a pool of water were not entitled to keep the rings, even if the rings were deemed lost and not mislaid: because the property owner had prior constructive possession of the rings, he was entitled to keep them.[22] Finally, it explains why the owner of property in *Elwes v. Brigg Gas Co.*[23] was entitled to a prehistoric ship found on his property, and this, over the objections of the long-term lessee who had present possession of the property. The court in *Elwes* reasoned that the owner had constructive possession of the ship that preceded the present possession of the lessee.

Applying the holding in *Elwes*, U.S. courts have held that constructive possession will only work to give the landowner rights to a lost or abandoned property embedded in his property, not on it.[24] For property found on the property, but not attached to it, the owner will be entitled to it only if it is mislaid property, but not if it is lost or abandoned property.[25] However, some modern courts appear to apply the doctrine of constructive possession even to lost or abandoned property found on, not in, the property.[26]

Treasure Trove

At common law, money or bullion found in the earth, and where the facts indicate that it was there long enough for the intentionally buried items to have been abandoned,[27] was considered a treasure trove,[28] and belonged to the king. However, in U.S. jurisprudence, treasure trove does not belong to the government, but is treated like any other lost item, and may be categorized as either lost, mislaid, or abandoned, depending on the circumstances of the find. For example, the decision in *Corliss v. Wenner* refused to recognize the old doctrine of treasure trove which would have treated the property as lost and granted it to the finder, and instead held that all treasure trove property shall henceforth be considered *embedded property*, and thus held that the gold coins belonged to the property owner under the rule of constructive possession.[29] In *Benjamin v. Lindner Aviation, Inc.*,[30] the court held that money found in the wing of an airplane was obviously *mislaid*, not lost, since it was intentionally put there.[31] Further, it could not be deemed treasure trove, because the money had not been in the wing long enough to be classified as such.[32] However, according to *Benjamin*, if the money had been considered treasure trove, it would have gone to the finder, not to the owner of the premises, because that court held that the place wherein an item is found is immaterial (and thereby not following the cases that rely on an owner's constructive possession to give him rights to property found or abandoned *on* his property).[33] Finally, in *In re Seizure of $82,000 More or Less*,[34] the court held that money found in a

gas tank of a car seized by the government in a drug sting was *abandoned property* and not mislaid property.[35] The court distinguished *Benjamin*, explaining that the drug dealer who placed the money there had abandoned it as soon as police seized the car, since they could not get the money back without risking arrest.[36] Nonetheless, the court awarded the property to the car owners who had bought the car from the government because the mechanic-finder was an agent of the owners and had found it while working on their property.[37]

Comparing U.S. Common Law and Talmudic Principles

It is quite clear that *Corliss* and other modern courts will give all property found on or in property *to the property owner*. Only where an item may be found in a public or quasi-public place, might there be a distinction between lost, mislaid or abandoned property. This is clearly in contrast to the Talmudic view, at least with regard to treasure trove and embedded property,[38] where the Talmud almost always grants the items to the finder.[39] However, other cases, relying on the holding in *Elwes v. Brigg Gas Co.*, will only grant mislaid or embedded property to the landowner, but lost, abandoned, or treasure trove property—even if found on private property—will go to the finder. Accordingly, these courts would reach a result similar to that reached under Talmudic principles in treasure trove cases.[40]

Additionally, we have seen that courts are clearly split on the question of whether an employer is entitled to items found by an employee during the course of employment. On the one hand, *Ray v. Flower Hospital* found a "long line of cases where hotel chambermaids, bank janitors, bank tellers, grocery store bagboys and other employees have found property while in their employ, [and] virtually every case has charged the employee with the duty to turn the found property over to the employer."[41] On the other side, we have seen that *Kalyvakis v. The Olympia* held that the established trend in New York "tends to reject any master-servant exception to the law of finders."[42]

However, under well-established Talmudic principles, "[T]he hand of a worker is like the hand of his employer."[43] As such, an employee's find always belongs to the employer, as long as the find was made during and within the scope of his specified employment responsibilities.[44] Thus, the terms of employment would determine whether the Talmudic view accords with those U.S. courts that, like *Ray,* have applied agency principles to lost and abandoned items found by an employee.

You Be the Judge II (New York: Rohr Jewish Learning Institute, 2009), pp. 44–48

Endnotes

[1] *Armory v. Delamirie*, Kings Bench, 1722 (1 Strange 505).

[2] *Id.*

[3] However, under many statutory schemes, one who voluntarily decides to pick up a lost item must then bring the item to a designated place (usually the police) and the finder will only be given the lost item after some statutory time has elapsed. *See Benjamin v. Lindner Aviation, Inc.*, 534 N.W.2d 400 (Iowa 1995).

[4] Mislaid items will be discussed below.

[5] However, by voluntarily taking the lost item, the finder *is subject* to the obligations of a bailee. According to the modern view, the bailment requires the finder to exercise reasonable care with regard to the item. See Richard H. Helmholz, "Bailment Theories and the Liability of Bailees: The Elusive Uniform Standard of Reasonable Care," 41 *Kan. L. Rev.* 97 (1992).

[6] In other words, under the common law, property law was created not to reflect the realities of ownership, but instead to assist in the administration of a just and orderly society. See 11 Blackstone, *Commentaries on the Laws of England,* Book II, Ch. 1 ("[W]hen mankind increased in number, craft, and ambition, it became necessary to entertain conceptions of more permanent dominion. . . . Otherwise innumerable tumults must have arisen . . . while a variety of persons were trying to get the first occupation of the same thing. . . ."). Talmudic law, however, sees ownership in property as reflecting the absolute reality of ownership. Thus, even where recognizing ownership rights might offend our moral or societal sensibilities, the law will still protect those rights. This is also the reason Talmudic law recognizes a contract as a contract, even if the terms of that contract (e.g., contracting for a hitman) violate public policy and would otherwise be voidable under the common law. *See* Rest. 2d Contracts § 178. *See also* H. Patrick Glenn, Legal Traditions of the World 121 (2d ed. 2004).

[7] *See, generally,* Babylonian Talmud, Bava Metzia, 27a.

[8] *Code of Jewish Law, Choshen Mishpat* 260:9-10.

[9] *See* Rabbi Moshe Isserles, *Glosses to the Code of Jewish Law, Choshen Mishpat* 260:9.

[10] *See McAvoy v. Medina*, 93 Mass. (11 Allen) 548, (1866). *See also* Walter Wheeler Cook, "Ownership and Possession," *11 Encyclopedia of the Social Sciences* 521, 524 (1937) ("[I]t is obvious . . . that from the point of view of social policy the shopkeeper ought to be preferred to the customer, as in that event the article would be more likely to get back into the possession of the true owner.").

[11] *McAvoy, supra* note 10.

[12] *Id.*

[13] 7 Eng. Law & Eq. R. 424.

[14] *Paset v. Old Orchard Bank & Trust Co.*, 62 Ill. App. 3d 534, 537 (1978) (emphasis added).

[15] *Id.* (emphasis added).

[16] *See South Staffordshire Water Co. v. Sharman*, [1896] 2 Q. B. 44, 46-47 ("The possession of land carries with it in general, by our law, possession of everything which is attached to or under that land, and, in the absence of a better title elsewhere, the right to possess it also. And it makes no difference that the possessor is not aware of the thing's existence." citing Pollock and Wright's *An Essay on Possession in the Common Law at 41*.

[17] However, some see the decision in *Hawkesworth* as based on the fact that the item was found on top of the land, in contrast to inside the land. See *Hannah v. Peel*, [1945] K.B. 509, 521.

[18] Compare *Jackson v. Steinberg*, 200 P.2d 376, 378 (1948) (holding agency principles applicable to give lost item found by employee to employer); *Ray v. Flower Hosp.*, 439 N.E.2d 942, 945 (1981) ("In a long line of cases where hotel chambermaids, bank janitors, bank tellers, grocery store bagboys and other employees have found property while in their employ, virtually every case has charged the employee with the duty to turn the found property over to the employer for safekeeping [because] . . . the possession of the servant . . . [is] the possession of the [employer] and that, therefore, the element is wanting which would give the title to the servant as against the master. . . ."); *In re Seizure of $82,000 More or Less*, 119 F. Supp. 2d 1013, 1020 (W.D. Mo. 2000) (same) with *Kalyvakis v. The Olympia*, 181 F. Supp. 32, 36-37 (S.D.N.Y. 1960) (New York law "tends to reject any master-servant exception to the law of finders."); *Hamaker v. Blanchard*, 90 Pa. 377 (1879) *(same).*

[19] *See, e.g., Kalyvakis v. The Olympia*, 181 F. Supp. 32, 36-37, n.15 (S.D.N.Y. 1960) (granting employee-finder ownership of cash and explaining that "since it was found in a public place the finder would be entitled to it against all but the true owner," and further opining that English cases cited by employer "indicate significant differences from the case at bar in that the finding occurred in a private place as distinguished from a place open to the public.").

[20] *Hannah v. Peel,* [1945] K.B. 509.

[21] *Id.* at 520-21.

[22] *See South Staffordshire Water Co. v. Sharman*, [1896] 2 Q. B. 44.

[23] *Elwes v. Brigg Gas Co.*, 33 Ch. D. 562.

[24] *See, e.g., Corliss v. Wenner*, 34 P.3d 1100, 1104 (Idaho App. 2001) ("Possession of embedded property goes to owner of the land on which the property was found.").

[25] *Id.*

[26] *See id.* at 1106 (in order to discourage trespass, the court concludes that "We hold that the owner of the land has constructive possession of all personal property secreted in, *on or under his or her land.*"

[27] *See Ritz v. Selma United Methodist Church*, 467 N.W.2d 266, 269 (Iowa 1991). *See also Corliss, supra* note 25 ("Treasure trove carries with it the thought of antiquity, i.e., that the treasure has been concealed for so long as to indicate that the owner is probably dead or unknown.").

[28] *Treasure trove* derives from the Old French *tresor trove,* found treasure.

[29] See *Corliss*, 34 P.3d at 1105 ("[T]he modern trend . . . as illustrated by decisions of the state and federal courts, *is decidedly against*

recognizing the 'finders keepers' rule of treasure trove.") (emphasis added).

30 *Benjamin v. Lindner Aviation, Inc.*, 534 N.W.2d 400 (Iowa 1995).

31 *Id.* at 407.

32 *Id.* at 407-08.

33 *See id.* at 406 (citing *Zornes v. Bowen*, 274 N.W. 877, 879 [Iowa 1937]). *See also Weeks v. Hackett*, 71 A. 858, 860 (Me. 1908) ("In the absence of legislation upon the subject, the title to such property belongs to the finder as against all the world except the true owner and that ordinarily the place where it is found is immaterial.").

34 *In re Seizure of $82,000 More or Less*, 119 F. Supp. 2d 1013 (W.D. Mo. 2000).

35 *Id.* at 1018–19.

36 *Id.*

37 *Id.* at 1019.

38 But not mislaid property, as discussed earlier.

39 Talmud, Bava Metsi'a 25b–26a.

40 This is only in most cases, since Talmudic law does not make a distinction for embedded property, *per se*, that is, embedded property that does not appear to be mislaid.

41 See *supra* note 18.

42 *Supra* note 18.

43 Talmud, Bava Metsi'a 10a.

44 *Id.*

4

BETWEEN PROXIMATE AND REMOTE

IS ONE RESPONSIBLE FOR CAUSING AN INDIRECT LOSS?

Cause and effect succeed one another ad infinitum, and so the consequences of any given act can be deemed to be limitless. At what point do we consider the loss too remote and disconnected from the actions of a wrongdoer to hold him or her responsible? Is there a universal principle that can be applied consistently to all cases of indirect harm? In this lesson we examine the Talmud's distinctive approach to this area of law.

CASE STUDY A

SOURCE: RYAN W. MILLER, "TEENS USED POKÉMON GO APP TO LURE ROBBERY VICTIMS, POLICE SAY," *USA TODAY,* JULY 11, 2016, HTTP://WWW.USATODAY.COM/STORY/ TECH/2016/07/10/FOUR-SUSPECTS-ARRESTED-STRING-POKÉMON-GO-RELATED-ARMED-ROBBERIES/86922474/

Traveling across the land and engaging in the latest fad hasn't exactly worked out for all Pokémon Go users. Some have been robbed as a result of playing this game.

Four suspects were arrested when police in O'Fallon, Missouri responded to a report of an armed robbery early Sunday. The teens, whose ages range from 16 to 18, are suspected of committing about ten armed robberies in St. Louis and St. Charles counties in which they allegedly used the Pokémon app to bait victims.

The app, which allows users to interact virtually with Pokémon characters nearby in the real world, has a "Lure Module" that players can use to attract Pokémon characters to specific locations, called Pokéstops. By tapping the lure module, one has a good chance of attracting additional players to come collect these Pokémon characters.

"The way we believe the app was used is that you can add a beacon to a Pokéstop to lure more players," the O'Fallon Police Department wrote in a Facebook post. And when those additional players showed up, they were robbed at gunpoint of their valuables.

POLL 1

Should Nintendo be held liable for the robberies committed through the use of its game's features?

1 Yes

2 No

3 Not sure

CASE STUDY B

SOURCES: CARA MCGOOGAN, "POKÉMON GO MAKERS SUED FOR ENCOURAGING TRESPASSING," AUGUST 3, 2016, HTTP://WWW.TELEGRAPH.CO.UK/ TECHNOLOGY/2016/08/03/POKÉMON-GO-MAKERS-SUED-FOR-ENCOURAGING-TRESPASSING/; BEATRIZ COSTA-LIMA AND MARY HUDETZ, "THE 'POKÉMON GO' FILES," JULY 15, 2016, HTTP://WWW.INSURANCEJOURNAL.COM/NEWS/ NATIONAL/2016/07/15/420198.HTM; LAUREN KRAVETS, "MAN SAYS POKÉMON GO PLAYERS DAMAGED HIS PROPERTY," JULY 14, 2016, HTTP://KXAN.COM/2016/07/14/ NEIGHBOR-POKEMON-GO-HUNTERS-DAMAGED-PROPERTY/

A man in the United States is suing the makers of Pokémon Go on behalf of people whose properties are Gyms and Pokéstops in the augmented reality game, after he became frustrated with people trespassing on his private land.

The class action lawsuit is the first to be filed against the Pokémon Go makers, and is seeking damages that, while not specified, could be in excess of $5 million (£3.7 million) for a "flagrant disregard" for the impact of the game on real world places.

Jeffrey Marder, the New Jersey man who brought the case, claimed that at least five players had knocked on his door and asked to catch Pokémon in his backyard. The game superimposes creatures into the real world, which players must physically approach in order to catch.

"Defendants have shown a flagrant disregard for the foreseeable consequences of populating the real world with virtual Pokémon without seeking the permission of property owners," the lawsuit alleges.

While the players seeking to catch Pokémon characters in Marder's backyard were polite enough to knock on his door and ask permission, other players haven't been as considerate.

The Pflugerville, Texas police department posted a Facebook warning after officers spotted a man playing the game in a section of a police parking lot where the public isn't allowed. The player had to pass keep-out signs and climb over a fence to reach the area.

In Utah, Ethan Goodwin, 17, of Tremonton, was slapped with a trespassing ticket that he worries could cost him up to $200 after he and a couple of friends went on an early morning Pokémon chase at an abandoned grain silo. He managed to catch three creatures. "I wouldn't say it was worth it, but I would say I'm glad I have the Pokémon I have now," he joked.

But trespassing is only part of the problem. Some people have reported actual damage to their property perpetrated by Pokémon players.

Tavis Latham, a resident of Hutto, Texas, reported damage to his property to local police. He says he was trying to sleep at night when he heard someone banging on his fence. His backyard is adjacent to a park where there's a Pokéstop at the swing set. Peering through the window, Latham saw five to ten people in the park. He went outside to size up the situation when he noticed a hole in the fence. Latham believes one of the Pokémon players was responsible.

POLL 2

Should Nintendo be held liable for the trespassing, nuisance, and damages caused by Pokémon players?

1 Yes

2 No

3 Not sure

POLL 3

Should Nintendo be required to remove virtual Pokémon characters from private property upon the property owner's request?

1 Yes

2 No

3 Not sure

CASE STUDY C

SOURCES: RABBI SHLOMO BEN AVRAHAM HAKOHEN, *RESPONSA* 4:31; STEVEN FRIEDELL, "NOBODY'S PERFECT: PROXIMATE CAUSE IN AMERICAN AND JEWISH LAW," *HASTINGS INTERNATIONAL AND COMPARATIVE LAW REVIEW* 25:111, PP. 134–136

Filipe de Nis was born in Portugal around the year 1531. To the outside world, Filipe and his family lived as Christians. But Filipe had another name, Shlomo Marcos, and at home, he observed Shabbat and other Jewish rituals. A few decades earlier, in 1497, all Jews living in Portugal were forced to convert and Shlomo's parents were among them.

Shlomo became a wealthy merchant, and around the year 1580, he moved to Venice with his two brothers. Still living within the grasp of the Catholic Church, they were forced to continue to live outwardly as Christians. One brother departed shortly after their arrival for the Middle East but left behind a son, Ya'akov.

They were planning to immigrate to the Ottoman Empire to escape the clutches of the Inquisition and live openly as Jews. Shlomo's wife and two children had already gone to live in the Jewish ghetto in Dubrovnik, on the Adriatic Sea. Shlomo and his nephew, Ya'akov, were still in Venice, and Shlomo arranged for Ya'akov to be circumcised in secret by a mohel named Jose Naar. Shlomo himself was circumcised in secret as well by a mohel named Dr. Benarogios.

At dawn on October 12, 1585, the Venetian Inquisition arrested Shlomo for practicing Judaism in secret. After more than nine months of imprisonment, Shlomo informed the inquisitors on July 29, 1586 that Benarogios and Naar had circumcised him and his nephew, respectively. Eventually, Shlomo was released from prison but was required to post a substantial bail.

On August 20, 1586, the Inquisition publicly posted a summons for Benarogios and Naar, giving them nine days to appear before the tribunal. On November 20, 1586, the Inquisition banished both of them from Venice, on pain of death, for failure to respond to the summons.

Benarogios, or representatives acting on his behalf, sought compensation from Shlomo in rabbinic court for the losses incurred in having to flee Venice for the Ottoman Empire. These included his losses from selling his home and furnishings at reduced prices, the travel expenses for him and his family, and the loss of income and financial support he was receiving from the Venetian Jewish community.

POLL 4

Should Shlomo be obligated to compensate Benarogios for his losses?

1 Yes

2 No

3 Not sure

CHAVRUTA A

TEXT 1

TALMUD, BAVA BATRA 22B

מַרְחִיקִין אֶת הַסּוּלָם מִן הַשּׁוֹבָךְ אַרְבַּע אַמּוֹת כְּדֵי שֶׁלֹּא תְּקַפּוֹץ הַנְּמִיָּיה . . .
הָא גְּרָמָא הוּא?
אָמַר רַב טוֹבִי בַּר מַתְנָה: זֹאת אוֹמֶרֶת גְּרָמָא בְּנִיזָקִין אָסוּר.

One may not place a ladder [even on one's own property if it will be] four cubits from a neighbor's dovecote, because a marten might use the ladder to access the dovecote. . . .

The Talmud asks: But even if this were to happen, it would only be a *gerama*—an indirect cause rather than a direct act of damage. Why then must one abide by this rule?

Rav Tovi bar Matnah explained: This ruling informs us that it is forbidden to cause damage, even indirectly.

BABYLONIAN TALMUD

A literary work of monumental proportions that draws upon the legal, spiritual, intellectual, ethical, and historical traditions of Judaism. The 37 tractates of the Babylonian Talmud contain the teachings of the Jewish sages from the period after the destruction of the 2nd Temple through the 5th century CE. It has served as the primary vehicle for the transmission of the Oral Law and the education of Jews over the centuries; it is the entry point for all subsequent legal, ethical, and theological Jewish scholarship.

TEXT 2

MISHNAH, BAVA KAMA 6:4 (icon)

הַשּׁוֹלֵחַ אֶת הַבְּעֵרָה בְּיַד חֵרֵשׁ שׁוֹטֶה וְקָטָן, פָּטוּר בְּדִינֵי אָדָם וְחַיָּיב בְּדִינֵי שָׁמַיִם.

שָׁלַח בְּיַד פִּקֵּחַ, הַפִּקֵּחַ חַיָּיב.

If one sends a flaming torch in the hands of a mentally incompetent adult or minor, the sender will not be liable to compensate a third person who suffered a loss from the fire. However, the sender is held liable by the laws of Heaven [even if he didn't instruct the messenger to cause harm].

If, however, one sends a flaming torch in the hands of a mentally competent person, [even if he instructs him to cause damage to another], it will be the competent person who is liable [to pay damages in a court of law].

MISHNAH

The first authoritative work of Jewish law that was codified in writing. The Mishnah contains the oral traditions that were passed down from teacher to student; it supplements, clarifies, and systematizes the commandments of the Torah. Due to the continual persecution of the Jewish people, it became increasingly difficult to guarantee that these traditions would not be forgotten. Rabbi Yehudah Hanasi therefore redacted the Mishnah at the end of the 2nd century. It serves as the foundation for the Talmud.

TEXT 3

MAIMONIDES, *MISHNEH TORAH*, LAWS OF TESTIMONY 17:7

הַשּׂוֹכֵר עֵדֵי שֶׁקֶר לְהָעִיד לַחֲבֵירוֹ, פָּטוּר מִדִּינֵי אָדָם וְחַיָּיב בְּדִינֵי שָׁמַיִם.

If one hires false witnesses to testify on behalf of a friend [and the friend cannot be found to return what he was awarded on account of this testimony], the hirer is not liable to compensate the victim for the loss [because the loss he caused was indirect]. But the hirer is held liable by the laws of Heaven.

RABBI MOSHE BEN MAIMON (MAIMONIDES, RAMBAM) 1135–1204

Halachist, philosopher, author, and physician. Maimonides was born in Cordoba, Spain. After the conquest of Cordoba by the Almohads, he fled Spain and eventually settled in Cairo, Egypt. There, he became the leader of the Jewish community and served as court physician to the vizier of Egypt. He is most noted for authoring the *Mishneh Torah*, an encyclopedic arrangement of Jewish law, and for his philosophical work, *Guide for the Perplexed*. His rulings on Jewish law are integral to the formation of halachic consensus.

TEXT 4

RABBI SHLOMO BEN ADERET, *RESPONSA* 1:1052

דְּכָל גַּרְמָא בִּנְזָקִין מְחַיְּיבִין אֶת הַגּוֹרֵם לְסַלְּקָהּ.

In all cases of *gerama* (indirect damage), the court will oblige one to remove the cause of harm.

RABBI SHLOMO BEN ADERET 1235–1310

Medieval Halachist, Talmudist, and philosopher. Rashba was born in Barcelona, Spain, and was a student of Nachmanides and Rabbi Yonah of Gerona. He was known as *El Rab d'España* ("the Rabbi of Spain") because of his fame as a rabbinical authority. More than 3,000 of his responsa are extant, dealing with varied questions on Halachah and religious philosophy, addressed to him from Spain, Portugal, Italy, France, Germany, and even from Asia Minor. Among his numerous students were the Ritva, Rabbeinu Bechaye, and the Re'ah.

QUESTIONS FOR DISCUSSION

According to Talmudic law . . .

1 Before the fact, is it forbidden to indirectly cause a loss to another?

2 Before the fact, will a court intervene to stop someone from causing an indirect loss to another?

3 After the fact, is someone who causes an indirect loss going to be held liable in a court of law?

4 After the fact, is someone who causes an indirect loss going to be held liable by the laws of Heaven?

5 Are there cases when an indirect actor will not carry any liability at all? Why?

TEXT 5

LEVITICUS 19:14–18

> וְלִפְנֵי עִוֵּר לֹא תִתֵּן מִכְשֹׁל, וְיָרֵאתָ מֵאֱלֹקֶיךָ אֲנִי ה'. . .
>
> לֹא תֵלֵךְ רָכִיל בְּעַמֶּיךָ, לֹא תַעֲמֹד עַל דַּם רֵעֶךָ, אֲנִי ה'. . .
>
> וְאָהַבְתָּ לְרֵעֲךָ כָּמוֹךָ, אֲנִי ה'.

You shall not place a stumbling block before a blind person; you shall fear your God. I am the Lord. . . .

You shall not go around as a gossipmonger among your people. You shall not stand by [the shedding of] your neighbor's blood. I am the Lord. . . .

You shall love your neighbor as yourself. I am the Lord.

TEXT 6a

TALMUD, BAVA METSI'A 37A

> אָמַר לִשְׁנַיִם: גָּזַלְתִּי לְאֶחָד מִכֶּם מָנֶה, וְאֵינִי יוֹדֵעַ אֵיזֶה מִכֶּם . . . נוֹתֵן לָזֶה
> מָנֶה וְלָזֶה מָנֶה.
>
> וּרְמִינְהִי: גָּזַל אֶחָד מֵחֲמִשָּׁה וְאֵינוֹ יוֹדֵעַ אֵיזֶה מֵהֶן גָּזַל, זֶה אוֹמֵר אוֹתִי גָּזַל
> וְזֶה אוֹמֵר אוֹתִי גָּזַל - מַנִּיחַ גְּזֵילָה בֵּינֵיהֶם וּמִסְתַּלֵּק . . .
>
> הָתָם דְּקָא תָּבְעִי לֵיהּ, הָכָא - בְּבָא לָצֵאת יְדֵי שָׁמַיִם.

If someone says to two people, "I stole money from one of you but I do not recall whom" . . . the thief gives to each of them the full sum.

The Talmud asks: But haven't we learned otherwise? "If someone admits to stealing money from one of five people but cannot recall from whom, and each of the five claims to be the victim—the thief discharges his legal obligation by holding on to the sum until the matter is clarified." . . .

The Talmud answers the contradiction: The latter case is when the thief is sued [and only wishes to do what is required by the court]. The former case refers to someone who says, "I want to fulfill my Heavenly obligations."

TEXT **6**b

RASHI, AD LOC.

מֵאֵלָיו בָּא לִימָלֵךְ מַה יַּעֲשֶׂה וְלֹא יֵעָנֵשׁ, דְּהַשְׁתָּא וַדַּאי אַמְרִינָן יְדֵי שָׁמַיִם לֹא יָצָאתָ עַד שֶׁתִּתֵּן לִשְׁנֵיהֶם, שֶׁאִם תְּהֵא מוּנַחַת עַד שֶׁיָּבֹא אֵלִיָּהוּ, נִמְצָא הַנִּגְזָל מַפְסִיד עַל יָדְךָ.

RABBI SHLOMO YITZCHAKI (RASHI) 1040–1105

Most noted biblical and Talmudic commentator. Born in Troyes, France, Rashi studied in the famed *yeshivot* of Mainz and Worms. His commentaries on the Pentateuch and the Talmud, which focus on the straightforward meaning of the text, appear in virtually every edition of the Talmud and Bible.

This person comes voluntarily and asks how to make amends in order to avoid divine punishment. In such a case, it is obvious that both people must be compensated completely. For if the matter remains as adjudicated by the court—where the disputed sum remains in limbo until evidence is produced—the effect will be that the thief will have caused the victim a loss.

TEXT 7

RABBI ZALMAN NECHEMIAH GOLDBERG, *AFIKEI YEHUDAH,* P. 263

גְּרָמָא בִּנְזָקִין חַיָּיב בְּדִינֵי שָׁמַיִם וְלֹא בְּדִינֵי אָדָם, שֶׁהַתּוֹרָה הִגְבִּילָה כֹּחַ בֵּית דִּין שֶׁלֹּא לְחַיֵּיב בִּגְרָמָא כְּדֵי שֶׁלֹּא יָבוֹאוּ לְחַיֵּיב גַּם בִּגְרָמָא רְחוֹקָה.

One is liable for indirectly causing a loss under the laws of Heaven but exempt in the earthly court. The Torah restricted the power of the earthly court, not allowing it to demand compensation for any indirect losses, lest it come to also oblige compensation for very remote causes.

RABBI ZALMAN NECHEMIAH GOLDBERG
1932–

Rabbinic judge and halachic authority. Born in the former Soviet Union, Rabbi Goldberg immigrated as a child to Israel. He lectures widely on Jewish law, is editor-in-chief of the *Talmudic Encyclopedia,* and served on the rabbinic High Court in Jerusalem. He is renowned as one of the foremost halachic decisors of today.

TEXT 8

RABBI YOM TOV ASEVILLI, KIDUSHIN 42B

וְהַשׁוֹלֵחַ פָּטוּר לְגַמְרֵי, וַאֲפִילוּ מִדִּינֵי שָׁמַיִם, כֵּיוָן שֶׁכְּבָר נִשְׁתַּלֵּם הַנִּיזָק מִן הַפִּיקֵחַ. מַה שֶּׁאֵין כֵּן בְּשׂוֹכֵר עֵדֵי שֶׁקֶר, שֶׁפָּטוּר מִדִּינֵי אָדָם וְחַיָּיב בְּדִינֵי שָׁמַיִם, דְּלָא אִשְׁתַּלֵּים נִיזָק מִנְּזָקֵיהּ.

The one who gives a flaming torch to a competent person is completely exempt, even by Heavenly standards, because the competent person will pay restitution [and thus the torch giver will not have caused any enduring loss]. On the other hand, with regard to the case where someone hires false witnesses, the court is unable to get the beneficiary of the false testimony to repay the wrongful award. This is why the hirer, while not liable to pay restitution, is liable under the laws of Heaven.

RABBI YOMTOV ASEVILLI
(RITVA) CA. 1250–1330

Spanish rabbi and Talmudist. Ritva was born in Seville. He is mostly known for his Talmudic commentary, which is extremely clear, and to this day, remains most frequently quoted and used.

TEXT 9

TALMUD, BAVA KAMA 98A–B

אָמַר רַבָּה: הַשּׂוֹרֵף שְׁטָרוֹ שֶׁל חֲבֵירוֹ פָּטוּר, דְּאָמַר לֵיהּ נְיָירָא קְלָאִי מִינָּךְ ...

אָמַר אַמֵּימַר: מַאן דְּדָאִין דִּינָא דְּגַרְמִי מַגְבֵּי בֵּיהּ דְּמֵי שְׁטָרָא מְעַלְּיָא.

Rabah said: "One who burns a creditor's loan document is not liable to pay the entire uncollectable loan, for the offender can say, 'I burned mere paper.'" . . .

Ameimar said, "Those courts that penalize cases of *garmi* (indirect loss) will make the offender compensate for the full value of the loan."

TEXT 10

RABBI YITSCHAK BEN AVRAHAM, *TOSAFOT,* BAVA BATRA 22B

וְנִרְאֶה לְרִיצְבָּ"א: דְּדִינָא דְּגַרְמִי הֲוֵי מִטַּעַם קְנָס ... וּלְכַךְ כָּל הֶיזֵק הַמָּצוּי וְרָגִיל לָבֹא, קָנְסוּ חֲכָמִים. וְטַעַם דְּקָנְסוּ, שֶׁלֹּא יְהֵא כָּל אֶחָד הוֹלֵךְ וּמַזִיק לַחֲבֵירוֹ בְּעַיִן.

Rabbi Yitschak ben Avraham (Ritsba) explained: When the Talmud held some cases of indirect loss to be liable, these were [not rulings of compensation mandated by the Torah but] rabbinic fines. . . . The sages imposed such fines in cases of indirect loss that were common enough, so that people would not go about destroying people's property indirectly.

RABBI YITSCHAK BEN AVRAHAM (RITSBA)
D. CA. 1210

An important member of the *Tosafot* school of Talmudic learning that flourished in France during the 12th and 13th centuries. Rabbi Yitschak was a leading student of Rabbi Yitschak Hazaken (Ri) who headed an academy in Dampierre, France. His teachings are preserved in the various *Tosafot* collections of Talmudic commentary.

TEXT 11

RABBI YECHIEL MICHEL EPSTEIN, *ARUCH HASHULCHAN, CHOSHEN MISHPAT* 386:20

> דְּכֵיוָן דְּרָאוּ חֲכָמֵינוּ זִכְרוֹנָם לִבְרָכָה לִקְנוֹס בְּמִילֵי דִּשְׁכִיחִי, וְלְסִימָן זֶה
> קָרְאוּ גַּרְמִי, וְלָכֵן בְּכָל גְּרָמָא גַּם כֵּן, אִם לְפִי רְאוֹת עֵינֵי בֵּית דִּין נַעֲשָׂה
> שְׁכִיחַ וְרָגִיל, חַיָּיב לְשַׁלֵּם מִשׁוּם קְנָס.

The Talmudic sages saw fit to issue fines for cases of indirect loss that they considered to be common, referring to these cases by the word *garmi*. And we ought to apply this to other instances of indirect loss. If a court determines a given act that causes an indirect loss to be common enough, it should penalize the wrongdoer to compensate the victim.

RABBI YECHIEL MICHEL HALEVI EPSTEIN
1829–1908

Noted author on Jewish law. Rabbi Epstein lived in Czarist Lithuania and was chief rabbi of Novozybkov, a town near Minsk, and later, of Navahrudak, where he served until his death. A prolific writer, his primary work is *Aruch Hashulchan,* an expanded and reworked code of Jewish law.

TEXT 12

TALMUD, SHABBAT 10A

> כָּל דַּיָּין שֶׁדָּן דִּין אֱמֶת לַאֲמִיתּוֹ . . . מַעֲלֶה עָלָיו הַכָּתוּב כְּאִילוּ נַעֲשָׂה שׁוּתָּף
> לְהַקָּדוֹשׁ בָּרוּךְ הוּא בְּמַעֲשֵׂה בְּרֵאשִׁית.

Any judge who adjudicates a case to its ultimate truth . . . is considered by Scripture to have partnered with God in the act of Creation.

Figure 4.1

Indirect Cause in the Talmud

1	It is forbidden to indirectly cause damage to another.
2	The court intervenes to stop someone from causing indirect damage.
3	After the fact, those who caused indirect damage are not liable to pay compensation in a court of law.
4	Those who caused indirect damage are liable to pay compensation under the laws of Heaven.
5	The court is authorized to penalize wrongdoers in cases of indirect harm if, without such penalization, these acts would commonly be exploited by wrongdoers.

POLL 5

Does Nintendo carry any degree of liability for the robberies committed through the use of its game's features?

1 Yes

2 No

3 Not sure

POLL 6

Should Nintendo be held liable for the damages caused by trespassing Pokémon players?

1 Yes

2 No

3 Not sure

POLL 7

Should Shlomo be obligated to compensate Benarogios for his losses?

1 Yes

2 No

3 Not sure

TEXT 13

RABBI SHLOMO BEN AVRAHAM HAKOHEN, *RESPONSA* 4:31

אֵינוֹ עוֹלֶה עַל הַדַּעַת שֶׁאִם הָיָה אוֹמֵר "אָדָם אֶחָד מֵאַשְׁכְּנַז אוֹ מִתּוֹגַרְמָה עָבַר עָלַי וּמַלְנִי" שֶׁהָיוּ מַאֲמִינִים אוֹתוֹ, שֶׁכֵּיָן שֶׁהָיָה בְּמָקוֹם שֶׁיֵּשׁ מוֹהֲלִים מֻחְזָקִים, שֶׁהִמְתִּין לִימוֹל עַד שֶׁיַּעֲבוֹר אִישׁ נָכְרִי מֵאֶרֶץ אַחֶרֶת אֲשֶׁר לֹא הֻחְזַק אֶצְלוֹ לְבָקִי וּמוּמְחֶה לָמוּל אֲנָשִׁים גְּדוֹלִים כָּמוֹהוּ. וּבְוַדַּאי לֹא הָיוּ פּוֹטְרִין אוֹתוֹ, עַד שֶׁיֹּאמַר לָהֶם מִי מֵאַנְשֵׁי הָעִיר מָלוֹ, וְאִם לֹא יַגִּיד יְמִיתוּהוּ.

RABBI SHLOMO BEN AVRAHAM HAKOHEN (MAHARSHACH) CA. 1520–1601

Rabbi Shlomo was born in Serrai, Greece, near Salonika. He served as rabbi in Bitol, in present-day Yugoslavia, and eventually of the Castile congregation in Salonika. He was famed for his halachic decisions.

I cannot imagine that if he would have said, "A passer-by from Germany or the Ottoman Empire circumcised me," that they would have believed him. There were numerous notable and professional circumcisers in Venice, so it would have made no sense that he would wait for an unknown foreigner to pass through town to get his circumcision. Surely, they would have never freed him until he would have disclosed which Venetian Jew had circumcised him. And if he had not divulged this information, they would have killed him.

KEY POINTS

1 It is forbidden to cause a loss to another, even indirectly.

2 The court is tasked with neutralizing indirect causes of harm.

3 God holds us accountable for any loss that we cause to another person, even indirectly, until the victim is compensated.

4 A court will not enforce compensation in cases of indirect loss. One reason for this rule is that it is extremely difficult, if at all possible, to determine a principled line of demarcation between proximate causes and remote causes that can be applied consistently in all cases.

5 Rabbinic courts are empowered to act for the benefit of society. If unscrupulous people will commonly take advantage of the lack of liability and go about causing people indirect losses, the courts will penalize such behavior and require the offenders to remunerate their victims.

6 Jewish courts have two distinct duties and operate on two levels. The first is to administer God's true justice on Earth. This calls for firm rules and restrained judges to ensure that the absolute truth is always met. The second role is to prevent chaos in society and to promote peace. This latter role calls for more flexibility and ingenuity in order to ensure the best possible outcomes for society.

Continue your learning experience

ONLINE

Visit www.myJLI.com/dilemma4 for insightful and inspiring videos, articles, and readings on this topic.

Appendix

TEXT **14**

STEVEN FRIEDELL, "NOBODY'S PERFECT: PROXIMATE CAUSE IN AMERICAN AND JEWISH LAW," *HASTINGS INTERNATIONAL AND COMPARATIVE LAW REVIEW* 25:111, PP. 112–113

American courts generally analyze proximate cause by using a foreseeability test and/or a direct connection test. . . . The foreseeability test requires the fact finder to determine if the defendant should have reasonably foreseen the type of harm that occurred. The direct connection test asks the fact finder to decide whether the harm complained of was a direct consequence of the defendant's wrongful act. As part of this test, some courts will ask the jury to determine if the damage followed in an "unbroken sequence, without an intervening efficient cause," from the defendant's negligent act.

STEVEN F. FRIEDELL

Professor of law, Rutgers University. Friedell is an expert in federal income tax law, maritime law, and Jewish law; he has served on the Maritime Law and Jewish Law committees of the Association of American Law Schools. A member of the American Law Institute, he has spoken widely on tort law, admiralty, and Jewish law.

TEXT **15**a

STEVEN FRIEDELL, IBID., PP. 113–116

The foreseeability test and direct connection tests are open-ended.

The foreseeability test can be used by both sides and can justify any result. . . . Some courts have stretched the foreseeability concept to impose liability in some fairly far-fetched cases; other courts have been more restrained. The resulting conflict in the cases demonstrates that the courts are making use of the same words [to] mean whatever they are desired to mean. . . .

The direct consequences test is also highly plastic. Consequences can be "direct" even when there is a substantial interval of space or time. . . . By contrast, consequences can be "indirect" even when the connection to the defendant's misconduct is plain.

TEXT **15**b

STEVEN FRIEDELL, IBID., PP. 141–142

American scholars have voiced . . . criticisms of the proximate cause doctrine. Henry Edgerton wrote that the word proximate "is so ambiguous that it is almost impossible to use it consistently." A nineteenth-century lawyer, Nicholas St. John Green, wrote: "When a court says a damage is remote, it does not flow naturally, it is not proximate; all they mean, and all they can mean, is that under all the circumstances they think the plaintiff should not recover. They did not arrive at that conclusion themselves by reasoning with those phrases, and by making use of them in their decision they do not render that decision clearer to others. The employment of such phrases has never solved one legal difficulty."

TEXT 16a

MAIMONIDES, *MISHNEH TORAH,* LAWS OF DAMAGE TO PROPERTY 8:13 ⊞

אֵין הַנְּזָקִין מִשְׁתַּלְּמִין . . . אֶלָּא בִּרְאָיָה בְּרוּרָה וּבְעֵדִים הַכְּשֵׁרִים לְהָעִיד.

We do not award damages for a tort . . . without clear evidence and valid witnesses.

TEXT 16b

MAIMONIDES, IBID., LAWS OF SANHEDRIN 24:6 ⊞

יֵשׁ לַדַּיָּין תָּמִיד לְהַפְקִיר מָמוֹן שֶׁיֵּשׁ לוֹ בְּעָלִים, וּמְאַבֵּד וְנוֹתֵן כְּפִי מַה שֶׁיֵּרְאֶה לִגְדּוֹר פִּרְצוֹת הַדָּת וּלְחַזֵּק הַבֶּדֶק, אוֹ לִקְנוֹס אַלָּם זֶה.

At all times, a court has the prerogative to declare something belonging to someone as ownerless and to either destroy it or give it to whomever—this in order to close societal breaches or to penalize a criminal.

Additional Readings

NOBODY'S PERFECT
PROXIMATE CAUSE IN AMERICAN AND JEWISH LAW

STEVEN F. FRIEDELL

Introduction

Although it may seem counterintuitive, wrongdoers are not liable for most of the damage they cause. The law leaves most of the burden of torts on the victims because it would be neither just nor practical to hold culpable defendants liable for all the harm they cause.[1] To do otherwise would expose a wrongdoer to liability to an indefinite number of people for an indefinite amount of time. The difficult task for any legal system is to define the criteria that determine the limits of liability and to prescribe the procedures for applying those criteria. This Article will compare the doctrine of proximate cause used in American courts with a set of doctrines that have been worked out over the centuries in Jewish law.

Although they differ, the rules in both legal systems are open-ended, permitting almost any result in any particular case. The problem is more severe in American law because juries decide many proximate cause questions and jury instructions on proximate cause are confusing. The instructions give the jury, which is ignorant of precedent, no real guidance on how to decide the scope of liability issue. By contrast, Jewish law uses trained professionals to judge cases, and these judges are familiar with the precedents and the need to achieve justice in each case. The open-ended nature of the Jewish legal rules on indirect damages

STEVEN F. FRIEDELL

Professor of law, Rutgers University, Camden, N.J. Friedell is expert in federal income tax law, maritime law, and Jewish law; he has served on Maritime Law and Jewish Law committees of the Association of American Law Schools. A member of the American Law Institute, he has spoken widely on tort law, admiralty, and Jewish law.

empowers judges to make decisions that will justly deal with the particular facts of each case.

This Article will explore the problem in both systems and suggest ways in which the American system can be reformed. Part I will discuss the proximate cause rules in American law. Part II will cover the Talmudic sources on indirect damage, and Part III will focus on the three most influential approaches of medieval commentators. We will see that the medieval approaches neither explain the Talmudic examples satisfactorily nor predict future outcomes with certainty. Part IV will focus on a case that arose out of the Venetian Inquisition in the late Sixteenth Century. We will see how two rabbis reached different results even though they used the same approach to the problem of indirect damages. The last part of the Article will look at some of the lessons that can be drawn from a comparison of Jewish and American law on the issue of proximate cause.

I. The Proximate Cause Tests of American Law

American courts generally analyze proximate cause by using a foreseeability test and/or a direct connection test.[2] For a time, a few courts asked juries to decide if the injuries were the "natural or necessary" consequences of the defendant's acts.[3] The foreseeability test requires the fact finder to determine if the defendant should have reasonably foreseen the type of harm that occurred.[4] The direct connection test asks the fact finder to decide whether the harm complained of was a direct consequence of the defendant's wrongful act.[5] As part of this test, some courts will ask the jury to determine if the damage followed in an "unbroken sequence, without an intervening efficient cause," from the defendant's negligent act.[6]

The foreseeability and direct connection tests are open-ended. The foreseeability test can be used by both sides and can justify any result. If viewed at a high level of abstraction, almost any consequence can be deemed foreseeable. However, if one focuses on the particular facts of a case, almost nothing is foreseeable.[7] For example, no one would expect that failure to maintain a railroad right-of-way would cause a man to get his peg leg stuck in the hole such that he would break his good leg while trying to extricate a car from the mud. However, the risk of physical injury to one stuck in a hole is foreseeable.[8] Some courts have stretched the foreseeability concept to impose liability in some fairly far-fetched cases;[9] other courts have been more restrained.[10] The resulting conflict in the cases demonstrates that the courts "are making use of the same words [to] mean whatever they are desired to mean."[11]

One effort to solve the problem is to hold a defendant liable if the harm was within the risk that the defendant negligently created.[12] For example, if the defendant gives a loaded gun to a young child, and the child drops it on her foot, the defendant is not liable.[13] One can say that the defendant was not negligent with respect to that risk of the child dropping the gun. Alternatively, one can argue that the injury did not flow from the aspect of the defendant's conduct that made it wrongful.[14] Although helpful in some cases, this approach shifts the difficulty from the uncertainty over the meaning of "foreseeability" to the equally difficult task of defining what is meant by "risk."[15] As the *Restatement (Third) of Torts* observes, the concept of risk is flexible and can be understood in both a broad and narrow sense.[16] Indeed the Restatement asserts that courts should use a hindsight approach to determining the correct risk. It says:

If an event appears to have been normal, not unusual, and closely related to the danger created by the actor's original conduct, it is regarded as within the scope of the risk even though, strictly speaking, it would not have been expected by a reasonable man in the actor's place.[17]

According to the Restatement, the risk created by a speeding driver includes the chance that a person hit by the car and forced to use crutches will suffer further injury when she falls later even though the driver could not reasonably foresee this particular risk.[18] Nor would one say that a driver who speeds is negligent with respect to this particular risk.

Because of its flexibility, the harm-within-the-risk approach is often useless in predicting a case's outcome. For example, suppose a railroad wrongfully delays the shipment of goods and an unusual flood destroys the goods while in the railroad's terminal. Are we to say that flooding was not within the risk created by the negligent delay?[19] Or can we look more broadly at the risks created and recognize that delays in shipment prolong the risk of loss or injury to the goods from a variety of causes?[20] The harm-within-the-risk approach cannot answer these questions. Professor Dobbs summarizes the problem by saying, "It is not usually possible to say that only one description of the risk is the right one, so the question calls for judgment."[21] The judgment that is required is not a further application of the test of foreseeability. It is the application of something else—at best some policy choice[22] but perhaps a gut feeling, sympathy, or even prejudice. Whatever it is, judges and juries are determining the liability issue based on that "something else," not on the principle of foreseeability. It is particularly galling when juries make the judgment because typical jury instructions not only offer no guidance as to how to make that judgment, they do not even inform the jury that a judgment of that kind is required.

The direct consequences test is also highly plastic. Consequences can be "direct" even when there is a substantial interval of space or time. For example, when a spark from a railroad engine set fire to some grass next to the rail, which then spread across the road, burned 200 yards of stubble and destroyed a house at the end of the field, the damage was nonetheless held to be direct.[23] By contrast, consequences can be "indirect" even when the connection to the defendant's misconduct is plain. For example, a court held that a lumber company that sold defective lumber to the plaintiff's employer was not liable for the plaintiff's injuries when the scaffolding collapsed where the lumber company and the plaintiff's employer were aware that the lumber was defective and not suitable for its intended use.[24]

The efforts that have been used to explain these two cases are unsatisfactory. It is said that the damage in the fire case was direct because the railroad's negligence operated on conditions and forces that existed at the time, and that no new forces came into operation.[25] By contrast, the court exonerating the lumber company said that the knowledge of the plaintiff's employer broke the chain of causation between the injuries and the alleged negligence of the lumber company.[26] Neither argument is compelling. By turning the arguments around one could exonerate the railroad by reasoning that the 200 yards of stubble, and certainly the road that the fire had to cross, broke the chain of causation. In the scaffold case one could argue that the employer's willingness to use defective lumber was a condition that existed at the time of the negligent sale by the lumber company.

The direct consequences test is further complicated when courts introduce the notion that an "independent efficient cause" will exonerate the defendant. For example, in *Loftin v. McCrainie*,[27] railroad employees negligently allowed some wild steers to escape from a cattle car and did not attempt to retake them until the next morning. As the defendant's agents were chasing the steers down a street, some automobile drivers blew their horns, which excited the steers. One of the steers charged into the plaintiff, causing her injuries. The court said that the blowing of the horns was not an independent efficient cause but was set in motion by the original wrongful act. It reasoned that the blowing of the horns might have been an intervening independent cause had the defendant's employees been in complete control of the steers.[28] The court's interpretation was strained and artificial. The motorists blew their horns to try to clear the road of the steers. This was arguably a new force, not one existing at the time of the original negligence. The court apparently thought the result was just because the defendant was negligent and the plaintiff was "absolutely faultless."[29]

At first blush, Professor Beale's suggestion that there is no proximate cause when a defendant's conduct had "come to rest in a position of apparent safety"[30] helps explain the court's hypothetical in *Loftin*. If the railroad's agents had regained control of the steers, they would have been in a "position of apparent safety" so that any honking by other drivers would be a new cause that would break the chain of causation. However, this explanation offers little more than a description of the result reached. We could also say that the steers, even if under control, were still in a position of danger because they were near traffic and one could anticipate that drivers would honk their horns. As Professor Beale observed, the "apparent safety" test boils down to a foreseeability issue.[31] The steers would have been apparently safe if there was no foreseeable risk that they would cause harm. Consequently, this test suffers from the same kind of weakness observed above concerning the foreseeability test.

Either despite these difficulties or because of them, the courts have established categorical rules that deprive the jury of any say in resolving many proximate cause issues. For example, the "egg-shell skull" rule dictates that a negligent defendant who causes some foreseeable personal injury to another is liable for all personal injuries to that victim no matter how unlikely.[32] As a result, a victim of a minor traffic accident who becomes psychotic as a result of the collision can recover from the negligent motorist.[33] Another settled rule is the "danger invites rescue" doctrine, which holds that the negligent actor is generally liable for the physical injuries to a rescuer.[34] Similarly, courts will hold negligent defendants who injure others liable for the results of subsequent medical treatment even if the doctor or nurse has been negligent.[35] By contrast, many courts hold that neither a state nor a parole board is liable for injuries inflicted by a prisoner released on parole.[36] In all of these situations courts are in effect saying, "Proximate cause is generally a question of fact for the jury to decide but in this case the matter is so clear that it must be decided by the court as a matter of law." Only cases that do not fall within some well-recognized category are left to the jury.[37]

One might find the subject of proximate cause perplexing because of the inconsistencies between the categorical rules. For example, it seems highly unlikely that a minor car accident would cause one of the passengers to become psychotic. It seems much more probable that releasing a convicted felon on parole would expose the public to future harm. Yet the law allows recovery in the former case but not the latter one.[38] These inconsistencies can be justified. A driver's insurance can be expected to compensate the victims of automobile crashes even when the injuries are unusual. Given the social policy of encouraging widespread use of the automobile with all of its inherent dangers, one can tolerate a small increase in insurance premiums to compensate victims who suffer unusual consequences. By contrast, there is an overall public good in releasing individuals from prison who appear ready to behave as productive members of society. Exposing parole board members to liability would likely discourage them from allowing early release.

A more serious problem occurs when judges give the proximate cause issue to the jury. Justice demands that the jury receive instructions that are clear and that accurately state the factors to consider in reaching a decision. The typical jury instruction on proximate cause does neither of these things. A typical instruction is as follows:

Negligence is a legal cause of [loss] [injury] [or] [damage] if it directly and in natural and continuous sequence produces or contributes substantially to producing such [loss] [injury] [or] [damage], so that it can reasonably be said that, but for the negligence, the [loss] [injury] [or] [damage] would not have occurred.[39]

We should either instruct the jury that it should weigh a list of factors[40] or that it should use its common sense in limiting the liability of a negligent actor who has caused damage. The standard jury instruction does neither of these things. We instead give jurors an instruction on "natural and continuous sequence" that can only hope to confuse them.[41] Neither these two phrases nor a fuller description of the foreseeability and the direct causation tests are capable in themselves of allowing juries to reach reasoned outcomes.[42]

II. Indirect Liability in Talmudic Law

It would be helpful to contrast the proximate cause problem in American law with a similar problem in Jewish law.[43] Over the past 2000 years, the Jewish legal system has developed several approaches for limiting liability for indirect harm. These approaches differ from the American doctrines but have some parallel features. Of particular importance, the Jewish legal rules on indirect damages are open-ended. These rules work well in Jewish law, however, because they provide rabbinical courts with flexibility to do justice

in individual cases. The legal rules' lack of determinacy is not as great a problem in Jewish law. That system lacks juries so that learned judges can exercise judgment in applying the rules. Also Judaism has a legal and religious culture that is well suited to a process of *ad hoc* adjudication.

The Babylonian Talmud contains many pronouncements on indirect damages. Sometimes the Talmud refers to a case of this type as *gerama*, a word meaning "cause." At other times it uses the expression *dina d'garmei*, meaning "the law of causes." At other times the Talmud uses no term at all. The Talmud sets out no system for explaining the results. The following set of Talmudic statements as collected by the medieval Tosafot[44] gives a sense of the range of the cases:

- If A threw an object from the top of the roof that would have landed on a cushion, but B removed the cushion while the object was in mid-air, B would not be liable.[45] Further, even if A removed the cushion (by pulling on a rope when the object was in mid-air), A would not be liable.[46]
- If a person brought fruits into another's courtyard without permission, and an animal ate them and was injured by them, he is exempt.[47] Similarly, if one put poison before another's animal and the animal ate it and died, he would be exempt under the laws of man but liable under the laws of Heaven.[48]
- A person who puts a torch in the hand of a deaf-mute, imbecile or minor would be exempt under the laws of man for damage caused.[49]
- If one made a breach in a fence in front of another's animal, allowing it to escape and do damage, he is exempt under the laws of man.[50]
- If one bends down another's stalk in front of a fire so that the stalk is destroyed, he is exempt under the laws of man.[51]
- If one does work with the waters of purification thus disqualifying them from their intended use, he is exempt under the laws of man.[52]
- If a person fanned a fire that was also fanned by the wind, and the fire caused damage, he is exempt.[53]
- If one frightened another, he is exempt under the laws of man. It is considered as though the injured person frightened himself.[54]

- If one incited a dog or snake to bite another, he is exempt.[55]

Another example of exemption for indirect damage, one not given by the Tosafot, is the case of a person who bribes witnesses to testify falsely. Even though he indirectly causes a loss to the affected party, he is considered liable only under the laws of Heaven.[56] A similar ruling applies to a witness who refuses to testify and thereby causes a loss to one of the parties.[57]

The Talmud did allow recovery for some types of indirect damage. As summarized by the Tosafot, liability was imposed in the following cases:

- If a person pointed out another's field to bandits, the person pointing it out is liable.[58]
- If a money changer recommends a coin as being good but it turns out to be bad, he would be liable unless he were an expert and the mistake involved a new type of coin that had just been issued.[59]
- Jewish law prohibited the planting of two different crops in the same field. If a fence of a vineyard near a field of crops has been broken through, the crop owner may tell the vineyard owner to repair it; if it is broken through again, he may tell him again to repair it. If the owner of the vineyard abandons the broken fence and renders the produce proscribed because the two different crops are planted too closely together, then he is liable.[60]
- If a judge decides a case incorrectly, he is liable according to Rabbi Meir even if he did not physically transfer the money or object in dispute from one party to another.[61]
- If one burns another's notes of indebtedness, he is liable.[62]
- If one sells a note of indebtedness to another and then waives the debt, thus causing a loss to the new owner of the note, he is liable.[63]

The Talmud suggests that there were disagreements about at least some of these statements.[64] For example, if a defendant destroyed another's note of indebtedness, some rabbis would hold the defendant liable for only the value of the paper whereas others would hold the defendant liable for the amount of the note.[65] Indeed some of the leading post-Talmudic codifiers

like Maimonides imposed liability even in the face of Talmudic dicta to the contrary.[66]

An important feature of the Talmudic rules is that the Talmud does not clearly indicate the criteria to be used to determine whether to impose liability for indirect damage. The closest one can come to such an explanation is in the discussion about the Mishnaic exemption for one who gives a lit fire to a deaf-mute, imbecile or minor. Two Palestinian sages disagreed over the scope of this exemption. Resh Lakish held that the exemption only applied if one handed over a flickering coal that was soon to go out. Rabbi Yohanan would have exempted even one who handed over a coal already in flames. Rabbi Yohanan would have imposed liability had the defendant given tinder, shavings, and a fire to the deaf-mute or other legally incompetent individual because "then his act was certainly the cause."[67] Resh Lakish explained his ruling by saying that damage is "certain" when he handed over a lit fire.[68] We may conclude that Resh Lakish and Rabbi Yohanan held the same standard—that liability for indirect damage would be imposed only if the damage was certain to occur. They differed only in the application of that principle to the case at hand.[69]

It does not follow, however, that the Talmud contained a general rule that liability for indirect damage turned on a determination of whether the damage was "certain" to happen. The difficulty arises from Resh Lakish's view that fire is a separate heading of liability from that caused by a person.[70] We therefore cannot know if he would have applied his concept of "certainty" to all cases of damage caused by a person. Moreover we cannot know if other Talmudic rabbis subscribed to the "certainty" requirement. Nonetheless, many post-Talmudic rabbis made the certainty of damage a prerequisite for liability.[71] Other rabbis did not impose this requirement.[72]

Another feature of the Talmudic law of indirect damage was that a defendant who was exempt under the laws of man might be liable under the laws of Heaven. This meant not only that God might seek to punish the defendant in some way, either in this life or in the world to come, but also that a rabbinic court could enjoin the defendant from acting in a manner that would continue to cause the indirect harm.[73] A rabbinic court could thus protect people from all sorts of environmental harms—smoke, noxious odors, leaking privies—that caused indirect harm. Moreover, a rabbinic court's determination that a defendant was liable under the laws of Heaven would likely carry great moral force in a small, closely knit religious community. It might induce the defendant to pay for some or all of the harm caused. Further, rabbinic courts and Jewish communities had the power to develop additional rules of liability if necessary to preserve order in the community.[74]

III. Medieval Interpretation of the Talmudic Rules

In the post-Talmudic period, rabbis took a variety of approaches to explain the Talmud's many statements on the law of indirect damage. Three approaches were most influential: the Ri as elaborated by the Rosh, the view of the Ritzvah, and the analysis by Nahmanides. We will look at each of their approaches in turn and will consider the shortcomings of each as a method of resolving the problem of liability for indirect harm.

A. The Ri and the Rosh

The Ri, Rabbi Isaac ben Samuel of Dampierre (died c. 1185),[75] was one of the most famous Tosafists, a group of scholars in France and Germany who sought to reconcile apparent contradictions in the Talmudic text. According to the Ri, a defendant is liable for indirect harm only if two requirements are satisfied: the defendant must himself do the injury to the property of another and the injury must occur at the time of the deed.[76] All other indirect damages are not compensable. The Ri used two terms to describe the different types of indirect damage. A defendant was liable for damage that was termed *garme*; he was exempt for damage that was termed *gerama*.

As pointed out by the Tosafot,[77] the Ri's explanation could not account for all of the Talmudic cases. Under Jewish law a non-ordained judge could be liable for making a mistaken ruling. The Mishnah[78] held that if a non-ordained judge declared ritually unclean produce to be ritually clean, and the owner himself mixed them with his other produce, the judge is liable.[79] Under Jewish law, if one mixes ritually clean produce with ritually unclean produce, the entire mixture becomes unclean. The judge's ruling would cause a financial loss since ritually clean produce has a higher value. The Ri could not account for this

Mishnaic holding. The judge did not touch the property, and the damage did not occur at the time he declared it ritually clean.[80]

Despite this difficulty, the Ri's approach was given a major boost when it was adopted by the Rosh, Rabbi Asher ben Jehiel (c. 1257-1327). The Rosh added one important factor borrowed from the Talmud. In order to be liable, the damage must be certain to occur (*bari hezeka*).[81] He explained that if a person incited another's dog to bite, the damage would be *gerama* and the defendant would be exempt because it was possible that the dog would not bite.[82] By contrast, if one informs a gentile robber about a Jew's property, the informer is liable for the subsequent theft since the Talmud regards it as certain (*vadai*) that the robber would not have mercy on a Jew's property. The Ri's test, augmented by the Rosh's gloss, became the standard approach to limiting liability until the middle of the seventeenth century.

In his Talmudic commentaries, the Rosh limited liability severely by his strict interpretation of the three prerequisites of liability. According to the Rosh, the first requirement—action against the thing damaged—is not satisfied when a person removes the cushions underneath a thrown object. The person removing the cushions did nothing to the object itself. As for immediacy, the Rosh said that when one removes cushions from underneath an object thrown from a roof, he is exempt because "when he removed them, the object was not yet broken; [it only broke] when it hit the ground."[83] Similarly, immediacy is lacking where one incited another's dog to bite a third party because the dog bite did not occur until later.[84] The Rosh also strictly defined the concept of certainty. When one incites another's dog to bite, the damage is not certain.[85] The dog might have ignored the defendant. Thus, even though the defendant intended the dog-bite, the damage is considered *gerama*.

The Rosh's formulation seems strict. If someone other than the defendant caused damage, or if the defendant's action somewhat preceded the damage, or if there was some uncertainty about whether the damage would occur, the Rosh's test would preclude liability.

Sometimes the Rosh applied his strict approach in practice. In one responsum, the Rosh exempted a man who was alleged to have aided his sister in taking her husband's belongings. It was alleged that the wife had thrown them out of the window and the defendant then helped his sister move them to another place. The defendant did not take the goods for himself. Because the wife had already stolen the goods, the Rosh reasoned, the defendant merely prevented the husband from pursuing his stolen property. Because the defendant did not damage the property, the injury was *gerama* and the defendant was exempt from liability.[86]

But in other cases, the Rosh was more willing to impose liability for indirect damage. In one responsum, Reuben produced a document purporting to be a release by Simon. A rabbinical court had upheld the validity of the release. The witnesses who signed the release later admitted that they had signed falsely, explaining that they had done what Reuben asked after he had gotten them drunk. The Rosh ruled that the release must be given effect since a rabbinical court had already approved it, but that the witnesses were liable. The damage they caused was *garme* because all three of the Ri's requirements were satisfied. The witnesses had done the damage to Simon's assets, the damage was certain to occur, and the damage occurred to Simon at the moment they signed the document.[87] The Rosh did not apply the requirements of *garme* as strictly as he might have. The witnesses were not a direct cause of any loss to Simon. Reuben still had to present the release in court and have it approved by that court. One could argue that the loss occurred later and that it was not certain to occur since Reuben might have had a change of heart.

In another case, a person bound another's animal and left it in the sun to die. In finding that there was liability the Rosh wrote, "He himself did the damage to the other's property by binding his animal, it is *bari hezeka* because he will certainly die, and the damage begins immediately and progressively gets worse."[88] The Rosh regarded the defendant as doing damage to the animal even though the animal died by exposure to the sun. He also regarded the damage as certain even though it was possible someone might have rescued the animal, and the Rosh regarded the death as immediate even though only some of the damage occurred when the defendant acted.[89]

The Rosh's responsa suggest that he intended the criteria for liability to be applied flexibly. The Rosh's own difficulty with applying his criteria to actual cases suggests that the rules themselves will not determine the outcome.

B. The Ritzvah

The Ritzvah, Rabbi Isaac ben Abraham, who lived in the twelfth century, agreed with the Ri that there were two types of indirect damage—*garme*, for which one was liable, and *gerama*, for which one was exempt. But he rejected the Ri's criteria. Instead, based on the Jerusalem Talmud,[90] the Ritzvah insisted that the liability imposed in *garme* cases was a rabbinic fine meant to deter others from causing similar damage. As is true of other rabbinic fines, liability is imposed when the type of injury is "common and ordinarily happens."[91] According to the Ritzvah the only reason that liability is not imposed in *gerama* cases is that the injuries are not common or ordinary. It matters not whether the injury occurred at the same time as the wrongful act or whether the defendant inflicted the harm directly on the object injured. The Ritzvah's approach was widely adopted in the thirteenth century.[92] Afterwards it took a back seat to the Ri's approach, but it enjoyed a strong revival in the seventeenth century.[93]

At first blush, the Ritzvah's approach seems to be easier to apply than the Ri-Rosh three-part test. A judge is only required to know whether the damage is a type that occurs commonly and frequently. But that raises several difficulties. For example, how often must damage occur before it is frequent or common? In making that determination, how is the court to characterize the damage? A broad definition will more likely lead to a finding that the damage is common. A narrower definition, more tailored to the facts of the case, will more likely lead to a finding that the damage was uncommon. Further, can damage that was at one time common become uncommon at a later time? Finally, can a court take into account the seriousness of the damage or the ease with which it could have been prevented in making that determination? In sum, there is substantial uncertainty about how to apply the Ritzvah's test. It leaves the court with substantial flexibility.

A striking example is a case decided by Rabbi Menahem Mendel Krochmal (c. 1601-1666) who was chief rabbi of Moravia.[94] A non-Jew stole a silver ritual object from a Christian church and sold it to a Jew, who re-sold it to another Jew who was the defendant in the case. The non-Jewish thief was caught, and he told his captors that he sold the object to a Jew but that he was unable to identify him. The Jewish community, under pressure from the church, paid for the stolen object and sought reimbursement from the defendant (the first fence was too poor to reimburse the community). The defendant argued that even the first fence would not be liable since the thief could not recognize him. Rabbi Krochmal dismissed this argument by writing:

> Since the power [of the church] is strong, [the damage] is common and certain to occur. That is so because they usually bring the thief among the Jews so that he can say which one bought the stolen item, even if it is not true, for their mouths have spoken lies as has happened many times due to our many sins. Thus, one who commits this violation is called a pursuer and one who causes danger to the public. Therefore it is obvious that he must pay the community for all of its damage.

Rabbi Krochmal went on to hold that the defendant was liable because the first fence would not have bought the stolen church items if he knew that he would be unable to resell them. Drawing on a Talmudic proverb,[95] Rabbi Krochmal said that it takes both a mouse and a mouse hole to steal a piece of cheese. The defendant therefore was a "pursuer" who endangered the Jewish community. Further, he reasoned that even if the damage were merely indirect, it would still be proper to force the defendant to pay. He invoked the rule that in case of *gerama* the court can force the defendant to prevent future harm.[96] Here, he reasoned that the harm had not yet occurred because the thief did not identify the fence. The damage would have been much worse had the fence been identified.

Rabbi Krochmal did not mechanically apply the Ritzvah's test. Although he states that events like this had occurred many times, his determination that the damage was "common" seems to have been influenced by the potential for serious repercussions against the Jewish community. Rabbi Krochmal distinguished a case where the Maharalbah[97] held that a fence was not liable when, on account of his illegal activities, a government official arrested innocent Jews and forced them to pay ransom. Rabbi Krochmal reasoned that fencing Christian ritual objects was more serious than an ordinary act of fencing stolen property. According to Rabbi Krochmal, the case before him differed from that before the Maharalbah in that the Jewish fence damaged the public and the matter was common.

In reaching his decision, Rabbi Krochmal characterized fencing of ordinary stolen property as different from fencing church property. It is not clear why that characterization should be made or that it supported his conclusion. One could just as well characterize both cases simply as examples of receiving stolen property. But even if they were to be differentiated, in the Maharalbah's case a government official actually arrested a number of innocent Jews; in Rabbi Krochmal's case the church and the Jewish community settled the matter without any arrests or violence. Moreover, it would seem that fencing of ordinary stolen property would be far more common than fencing of church items. Nonetheless, Rabbi Krochmal was apparently aware of a great potential for mischief in the case before him. If Jews were known to fence stolen church ritual items, there would be enormous potential for religious hatred and serious violence. The church's claim was not merely for loss of valuable goods but for insult to Christianity.

Rabbi Krochmal's responsum shows that the Ritzvah's test does not dictate any particular result. It leaves open the issue of how to characterize the loss and allows flexibility in determining whether the type of loss is common. Far from dictating any particular outcome, the Ritzvah's test is a tool that a judge must use wisely to reach a needed result.

C. Nahmanides

Nahmanides, also known as Rabbi Moses ben Nahman or the Ramban (c. 1194-1270), wrote a treatise on the subject of indirect damages where he concluded:

> Take hold of the following general rule. Every cause which results in injury where it is impossible for the injury not to occur and where it is not dependent on another's will—but when he caused it the injury occurred or would occur in the future—in such cases Rabbi Meir imposed liability. In the Gemarah[98] this is called certain injury [*bari hezekah*].[99]

According to Nahmanides, the plaintiff must satisfy only two elements: the defendant must be a cause of the injury and the injury must occur of necessity. Neither immediacy nor direct contact with the thing injured is required.[100] Unlike some other authorities, Nahmanides thought that there was liability even for unintentional injuries, even in cases where the defendant was completely without fault.[101] He recognized an exception for informers who were forced to reveal the location of another's assets.[102]

Nahmanides's approach is closer to the Ri's than to the Ritzvah's.[103] It rejects the notion that liability is imposed as a fine. Nahmanides emphasized that the doctrine is called *dina d'garme*, "the *law* of *garme*," not "the *fine* of *garme*."[104] Although Nahmanides disagreed with the Ri on the resolution of certain important issues,[105] his rejection of the Ritzvah's approach served to bolster the Ri's view. In fact, later authorities like Rabbi Joseph Caro said that Nahmanides had adopted the Ri's view.[106]

The difficulty with Nahmanides's approach is ascertaining how certain the injury must be. Nahmanides exempts the person who hires others to testify falsely.[107] He also exempts a person who breaks another's fence so that animals escape and cause damage.[108] In these cases he regards the damage as uncertain to occur. The witnesses could have chosen not to testify and the animals might not have escaped or caused damage. However, he would impose liability on an informer who reveals another's valuables to a robber. In that case the damage is regarded as if it occurred when the informer told the robbers.[109] Similarly, a judge who renders a verdict in error is liable even though the party he held liable pays the judgment later.[110] The damage is regarded as having occurred at the moment he imposed the verdict. These cases are hard to distinguish. Robbers might possibly have a change of heart; those who win lawsuits through a judge's error might forego collection. It is hard to say how the damage in those two cases is regarded as more "certain" than the false testimony of witnesses who were paid or the escape of animals through a broken fence.[111] Given this tension, Nahmanides's approach can be relied upon by any plaintiff or defendant.

In short, all of the medieval approaches we have studied are indeterminate. They are imperfect explanations of the Talmudic cases and leave us uncertain as to their application in future cases. This uncertainty is illustrated by an actual case that is described in the next section.

IV. An Analysis of a Case from the Venetian Inquisition

By the late sixteenth century, the approach taken by the Ri and the Rosh dominated rabbinic analysis of the indirect damage problem. Two major figures of this period, the Maharam of Lublin[112] and the Maharshakh,[113] were called upon to help resolve a difficult case that arose out of the Venetian Inquisition. Their responsa dramatically show that the test they were using was indeterminate.

A. The Facts

The two responsa[114] provide a brief outline of what happened but provide no names or dates. More detailed information is available from the records of the Venetian Inquisition[115] that were published a few years ago. The following account emerges from these three sources.

Filipe de Nis, who had the Jewish name of Solomon Marcos, was born in Portugal around 1531 to two Conversos.[116] He became a wealthy merchant and later went to Venice with his two brothers around 1580. They had travelled from Portugal to Flanders and then to Venice. One brother departed shortly thereafter for the Levant but left behind a son, Jacob, and the other brother died a few years later. Filipe, Jacob and the other members of the household lived in an expensive house outside the ghetto. To the outside world, Filipe and his family lived as Christians. But inside their home, they observed the Jewish Sabbath and other Jewish customs and rituals.

The Nis family was planning to immigrate to the Ottoman empire where they could live openly as Jews. Filipe's wife and two children had gone to live in the Jewish ghetto in Dubrovnik. His nephew, while still in Venice, had been circumcised by a mohel[117] named Jose Naar. One Easter when Filipe fell sick, he called for another mohel, named Dr. Benarogios, to circumcise him.

At dawn on October 12, 1585, the Inquisition arrested Filipe. The Inquisitors found that he was circumcised and practicing as a Jew. After more than nine months of imprisonment, Filipe informed the Inquisitors on July 29, 1586 that Benarogios and Naar had circumcised him and his nephew, respectively.[118] On August 20, 1586, the Inquisition publicly posted a summons to Benarogios and Naar, giving them nine days to appear.[119] On November 20, 1586, the Inquisition banished them from Venice, on pain of death, for failure to respond to the summons.[120]

Filipe wrote letters to his wife and persuaded her to return to Venice and be reconciled to Christianity. The Inquisition sentenced Filipe to forced residence in Venice. He was released from prison but was required to post a substantial bail. Seven months after his wife and children returned to Venice and were reconciled to Christianity, Filipe requested that the bail be returned to him.[121] We do not know if the Inquisition returned the bail to Filipe. We also do not know if he remained in Venice.

Benarogios sought compensation in a rabbinic court for his various losses in having to flee Venice for the Ottoman Empire. These included his expenses in leaving Venice such as the losses from selling his home and furnishings at reduced prices, the expense of bringing his wife and young children to him, and the loss of income and financial support of the community. He filed suit, apparently *ex parte*.[122] The questioner asked the Maharam of Lublin: "If God should cause us to acquire jurisdiction over the informer's assets," would the informer be liable for these losses "if the mohel can clearly show what he lost." Apparently Benarogios hoped that a rabbinic decree would allow him to levy against wares belonging to Filipe de Nis.

We will now see how the Maharshakh and the Maharam of Lublin used the law of indirect damages to resolve the issue of liability in this case.

B. The Maharshakh
The Maharshakh saw two fatal objections, one procedural and one substantive, to holding Filipe liable.[123] The procedural objection was that in the absence of witnesses who could testify about the amount of Benarogios's losses, his complaint must fail. The substantive objection was that Filipe caused only indirect injury based on the rule of *gerama*. The Maharshakh reasoned that Filipe did not inform the Inquisitors about any of the mohel's assets, but only informed them about the mohel himself. Although the court

could not issue a judgment against Filipe, the Maharshakh wrote that Filipe would need to pay Benarogios for his losses if he hoped to atone for his sin of converting to Christianity.

The Maharshakh did not explain in this responsum why the damages were indirect or *gerama*. In other responsa he showed that he followed the approach of the Ri and the Rosh.[124] As variously stated by the Maharshakh, a defendant is liable for damages that are sufficiently direct under the rule of *dina d'garme* if (1) the defendant himself does the damage to the plaintiff's property, (2) the damages are certain to occur, and (3) the damages occur immediately when the defendant performs his act. It would appear that the mohel's damages failed to meet any of these three requirements. First, Filipe did not take away any property belonging to Benarogios. Instead, Benarogios spent money on his own to avoid capture and to bring his family out of Venice. Second, the damages were not certain to occur as it was possible that the Inquisition would have arrested the plaintiff. Third, the damages did not occur immediately when the defendant informed the Inquisitors but rather some time later.

As we will see, the Maharam of Lublin responded to these objections.

C. The Maharam of Lublin
The Maharam of Lublin first responded to the procedural difficulty of lack of competent testimony. Relying on a responsum of the Maharil,[125] the Maharam of Lublin ruled that a rabbinic enactment allowed the victim of an informer to recover damages although the victim had no witnesses who could testify about the amount of his losses.

The Maharam of Lublin had to extend the Maharil's holding. Benarogios, unlike the victim in the Maharil's responsum, had not been arrested. The Maharam reasoned that when Filipe de Nis revealed the mohel's identity to the Inquisition, it was as if Benarogios were arrested at that moment. Consequently, a court should regard any money spent by Benarogios to escape as if it were spent to be released from capture.

Having swept aside the procedural objection, the Maharam of Lublin turned to the substantive issue of whether the damage to the mohel was a case of *gerama* or *garme*. The Maharam, like the Maharshakh, followed the Ri and the Rosh, but he reached different results. The Maharam of Lublin distinguished three different types of damage suffered by the mohel: (1) the expenses of the mohel's escape from Venice, (2) the expense of bringing his family out of Venice, and (3) the loss of employment suffered by the mohel.

The Maharam of Lublin determined that the mohel could recover his expenses in escaping from Italy. Since Benarogios had in effect been arrested at the moment Felipe informed the Inquisition, his damages were regarded as if they were expenses to escape arrest. The Maharam quoted the Mordekhai who said, "When one hands over another's body to gentiles it is as if he directly handed his money over."[126]

The Maharam of Lublin did not allow Benarogios to recover his expenses in bringing his wife and family to him. These expenses did not occur immediately when the informer acted and therefore failed to satisfy at least one of the Ri's requirements.[127] However, the Maharam of Lublin determined that Benarogios could recover damages for his lost work. He ruled that these losses were similar to the lost earnings a worker suffers if locked in a room and unable to work. Damages for lost earnings are generally recoverable when a defendant intentionally, knowingly, or recklessly injures a defendant's body or directly prevents a person from working.[128] The key to allowing recovery for the mohel's lost earnings was again the Maharam of Lublin's view that Filipe de Nis had directly injured the mohel when he informed on him. If the informing was a direct injury to the mohel, then it was as if Filipe had at that moment prevented the mohel from obtaining his livelihood.

The Maharam of Lublin imposed a major limitation on Benarogios's ability to recover. He wrote that the above reasoning was conditioned on the assumption that Filipe de Nis could have saved himself without revealing the mohel's name. For example, perhaps Filipe could have convinced the Inquisition that a foreigner who had since left Venice had circumcised him. However, if the informer had to reveal the mohel's name, then no compensation was due.

We may summarize the differences between the Maharam of Lublin and the Maharshakh as follows: the Maharam of Lublin would impose liability for Benarogios's expenses of leaving Italy and for his lost employment but only if Filipe de Nis did not act under compulsion. The Maharam of Lublin regarded these elements of damage as garme. He also would allow Benarogios to take an oath as to the amount of his losses and recover on that basis even without competent witnesses. The Maharshakh regarded all of the damage as gerama and therefore uncollectible even if Filipe did not act under duress. Also, he would not allow Benarogios to recover these damages unless he had competent witnesses who could verify the amount of the loss. The Maharshakh, however, concluded that to atone for his wrongs, Filipe must pay whatever damages he has caused the mohel, even if he acted under duress.

D. *Gerama, Garme* and the Converso's Dilemma

The opinions of the Maharam of Lublin and the Maharshakh show that even when two rabbis use the same basic approach to deciding whether liability extends to indirect liability, they may come to different conclusions. The Maharam of Lublin imposed liability because of his extension of earlier rulings and concepts. The Maharshakh was not so willing.

The Maharshakh's strict application of the Ri's approach is particularly striking since he was willing in another responsum[129] to stretch the requirements. The questioner in that responsum asked the Maharshakh if Simon was liable for losses to Reuben caused by Simon's mistaken return of a document to a gentile merchant that enabled the merchant to collect a debt from Reuben for a second time. The Maharshakh answered that Simon was liable. Simon was deemed to meet all the Ri's requirements: (1) he himself damaged Reuben by returning the document to the merchant, (2) the damage was deemed to be immediate because it was analogous to the case of one who destroys another's note thereby causing loss to the creditor, and (3) it was obvious that return of the document to the merchant would cause loss to Reuben because one could assume that the gentile merchant would be unsympathetic to a Jew. In reaching this result the Maharshakh disputed the authenticity of a contrary responsum attributed to the Rashba even though Rabbi Joseph Caro had quoted that responsum in his authoritative commentary.[130]

Given that the Maharshakh was willing to use the Ri's test in a flexible manner, why was he unwilling to be more flexible in the mohel's case? Although he does not allude to it, one possibility is that Benarogios undertook a severe risk in circumcising a Converso. The risk was not only that the circumcision could endanger himself and the Converso, but that it would also endanger the Jewish community as a whole. Rabbis and Jewish communal organizations had long recognized the danger and forbade the circumcision of gentiles who sought to convert to Judaism if it was prohibited by the non-Jewish authorities.[131] Presumably this prohibition applied also to the circumcision of Conversos because the non-Jewish authorities regarded them as Christians and were especially sensitive to preventing them from resuming Jewish practices. Jews took the matter so seriously that if a mohel violated this prohibition, Jewish law permitted other Jews to reveal the name of the mohel to the gentile authorities if it would save the community from harm.[132]

Another factor that may have influenced the Maharshakh was the predicament faced by Filipe de Nis. Two religions claimed him as one of their own. What one religion might view as an act of piety the other religion would view as betrayal. Further, since he was a second-generation Converso, he did not choose the awful situation in which he found himself. He was in peril from the moment of his birth.

Although we cannot be sure of the Maharshakh's reasoning, he appears to have used the rules of indirect injury in a flexible manner. He adapted them to the needs of each case. The rules themselves did not decide these cases for indeed the Maharam of Lublin applied the same rules and reached different results.

V. Comparison of Jewish and American law

Jewish and American legal systems have developed parallel approaches to the problem of limiting liability for indirect harm. The Ri and the Rosh required that damage be immediate, direct and certain to occur. This is similar in some respects to the idea that proximate cause limits liability to the direct consequences of the defendant's wrongful act. The Ritzvah's approach—limiting liability to damage that is common and usual—is similar to the foreseeability test. Nahmanides' approach of requiring necessity has its parallel in early descriptions of proximate cause, limiting damages to those harms that necessarily resulted from the defendant's conduct.[133]

The experience of Jewish law teaches that these approaches to limiting liability are all indeterminate. Their genius and true value rests on their ability to change and adapt to the needs of individual cases. In the hands of a skillful and wise judge they can be used to correct perceived injustices or prevent further harm to the community.

Early on, rabbis recognized the difficulty of formulating a universal test for the scope of liability. The Tosafot recognized that the Ri's test was not capable of explaining all of the Talmudic cases.[134] In the thirteenth century, the Mordekhai wrote that he could not understand the Ri's distinctions.[135] Some 300 years later Rabbi Mordecai ben Abraham Jaffe wrote, "It is not entrusted to every man to be able to reckon which are cases of *garmi* and which are *gerama*. Rather the sages of blessed memory reckoned them by themselves and said that these are cases of *garmi* for which one is liable."[136] American scholars have voiced similar criticisms of the proximate cause doctrine. Henry Edgerton wrote that the word *proximate* "is so ambiguous that it is almost impossible to use it consistently."[137] A nineteenth-century lawyer, Nicholas St. John Green, wrote:

> When a court says this damage is remote, it does not flow naturally, it is not proximate; all they mean, and all they can mean, is, that under all the circumstances they think the plaintiff should not recover. They did not arrive at that conclusion themselves by reasoning with those phrases, and by making use of them in their decision they do not render that decision clearer to others. The employment of such phrases has never solved one single difficulty....[138]

The proximate cause doctrine in American law has two problems. One is that courts impose liability in some cases where damage is less foreseeable or less direct than other cases where it does not impose liability. The second issue is that we give little guidance to juries in their determination of the proximate cause question.

As this Article has shown, the first problem can be resolved by understanding the policy factors that courts implicitly consider when they determine the proximate cause issue as a matter of law. The second problem is more serious.[139] The difficulty with assigning the matter to the jury is that the jury instructions do not clearly tell the jury what is expected of them. The standard jury instruction is so bad that even the judges giving it have no clear idea what it means.

One might think that the difficulties we have been discussing would be more serious in the context of Jewish law. Since Judaism views the law as an expression of God's will, one might think that Jewish courts would have a greater concern for finding predictable rules. There are several reasons why this is not so. Rabbinic courts approach their task with the utmost seriousness. Not only are they charged with interpreting and applying God's revealed law, but they consider themselves responsible for the maintenance of the world by correct application of that law and are accountable for the destruction of the world if they pervert the law.[140] This seriousness with which rabbinic judges approach their task does not translate into a demand for fixed, inflexible rules. There are several reasons for this. Partly out of concern for the seriousness of making an incorrect decision, Jewish law emphasizes compromise as a better way of resolving disputes. The court not only encourages the parties to settle their dispute, but also seeks authority from the parties to resolve the dispute by imposing a compromise rather than by applying the strict law.[141] Jewish law also lacks a concept of *stare decisis*. Each rabbinic judge is obligated to determine the law for himself. Prior decisions and other writing sources must be consulted, but in the end each judge remains bound to make his own determination of the correctness of prior rulings. The Talmudic dictum is that "a judge only has what his eyes see."[142] Consistent with this view, there is no appellate process in Jewish law.[143] Moreover, because Jewish law is a religious system, courts are mindful of the parties' obligations not only to each other but also to God. As we have seen, in many instances of indirect damage the defendant is exempt only according to the laws of man but is obligated under the laws of Heaven.[144] Consequently, even when a defendant would be exempt for indirect damage, he might find himself under moral pressure backed up by possible social sanctions for failing to compensate the victim. Jewish law also recognizes that sometimes compensation would be required as

a religious act of atonement even if not legally required.[145] Further, Jewish law allows courts to enjoin defendants who engage in activities that threaten to bring about continued indirect damage.[146] The cumulative effect of all these rules and practices has been to entrust rabbinic courts with a broad level of discretion, trusting in the rabbis' training and wisdom to arrive at a just result.

It would be asking too much to expect a set of instructions that would educate the jury about all of the policy factors that it ought to consider. Even law students after a semester of study have difficulty understanding and applying these concepts. The jurors, however, have a lifetime of experience and hopefully a measure of common sense. What is needed is an instruction telling them how to use that experience and common sense in resolving the proximate cause problem.

New York courts have improved on the instructions used in other states. Their basic instruction on proximate cause reads, "An act or omission is regarded as a cause of an injury if it was a substantial factor in bringing about the injury, that is, *if it had such an effect in producing the injury that reasonable people would regard it as a cause of the injury.*"[147] Unfortunately the instruction combines the issue of proximate cause and cause-in-fact. It uses the word "cause" to mean both cause-in-fact and "one at fault." However, it may indicate to jurors the notion that they are not to hold someone liable unless reasonable people would conclude that they should be held liable. It would be better to instruct the jury as follows:

> *The law does not impose liability on a negligent actor for all damage that results from the negligent act. The law does this to avoid making negligent actors liable to an indefinite number of people for an indefinite amount of time and for an indefinite amount of money. If you find that the defendant was negligent and was a cause-in-fact of the injury, you should impose liability if reasonable people would regard liability in this case to be just and fair.*

Taken as a whole, the Jewish legal system was comfortable having rules on indirect damages that contained a high level of uncertainty. The American legal system is different. It chooses jurors not for their advanced learning and wisdom, but because it hopes they reflect the common sense judgment of the people. If we give jurors the proper tools to do their job, the system is likely to work well enough.

Hastings International and Comparative Law Review, 25:1, (Spring 2002)
Reprinted with permission of the publisher

Endnotes

[1] *See, e.g., In re* Kinsman Transit Co., 388 F.2d 821, 824 (2d Cir. 1968) (Kinsmann II) ("Numerous principles have been suggested to determine the point at which a defendant should no longer be held legally responsible for damage caused "in fact' by his negligence.... Such limiting principles must exist in any system of jurisprudence for cause and effect succeed one another with the same certainty that night follows day and the consequences of the simplest act may be traced over an ever-widening canvas with the passage of time.") One limitation, akin to the doctrine of proximate cause, is that a person who violates a statute is not liable for resulting injuries unless the plaintiff was within the class of persons that the statute was designed to protect and unless the injuries were the type that the statute was designed to prevent. The law occasionally makes exceptions to this rule, but these exceptions can be justified by particular policies and goals that are unique to the circumstances. For example, in *Kernan v. American Dredging Co.*, 355 U.S. 426 (1958), the Court held that violation of a Coast Guard regulation that was intended to prevent collisions constituted negligence per se even though no collision occurred. A seaman died when the tug carried a torch too close to the water such that it ignited highly inflammable vapors. The Court imposed liability in part out of a recognition that seamen are not covered by worker's compensation and that industrial employers owe a special responsibility to their workers.

[2] *E.g.*, Pattern Jury Instructions: Fifth Circuit, Civil Cases § 4.6 (for injuries caused by unseaworthiness, proximate cause requires a showing that the injury was "a direct result or a reasonably probable consequence"); Florida Standard Jury Instructions in Civil Cases 5.1(a) ("legal cause" defined in terms of "directly and in natural and continuous sequence"); Illinois Pattern Jury Instructions - Civil No. 15.01 (1995) ("natural or probable sequence").

[3] Ryan v. N.Y. Cent. R.R. Co., 35 N.Y. 210, 311 (1866); Thomas v. Winchester, 6 N.Y. 397, 402 (1852). *See also* Hoag & Alger v. Lake Shore & Mich. S. R.R. Co., 85 Pa. 293 (1877) ("natural, foreseen, and necessary").

[4] Dan Dobbs, The Law of Torts 447 (2000). *See also* 1 N.Y. Pattern Jury Instructions - Civil No. 2:72 (3d ed. 2000) (defining intervening causes for which defendant is liable in terms of whether a reasonably prudent person "would have foreseen an act of the kind committed by [a third person] would be a probable result of the defendant's negligence").

[5] *See, E.g.*, Pattern Instructions for Kansas (PIK) No. 5.01 (1966) ("direct, unbroken sequence"). By 1975 the Kansas Committee on Pattern Jury Instructions recommended that "no instruction be given defining causation." PIK 5.01 (1975 Supp.). However, the instruction on intervening cause asks jurors to determine "whether the causal connection between the party responsible for the first cause and the injury was broken by the intervention of a new, independent cause which acting alone would have been sufficient to have caused the injury." PIK 5.03 (1975 Supp.).

[6] Dellwo v. Pearson, 107 N.W.2d 859 (Minn. 1961). *But see* Wartnick v. Moss & Barnett, 490 N.W.2d 108 (Minn. 1992) (concluding defendant not liable for effects of a intervening cause which was not reasonably foreseeable by the original wrongdoer).

[7] *See* Patrick J. Kelley, *Restating Duty, Breach, and Proximate Cause in Negligence Law: Descriptive Theory and the Rule of Law*, 54 Vand. L. Rev. 1039, 1046 (2001) ("Both "foreseeability' and "public policy' work beautifully as explanations of judicial decisions because they are both so open-ended they can be used to explain any decision, even decisions directly opposed to each other.") *See also* Clarence Morris & C. Robert Morris, Jr., Morris on Torts 165-66 (2d ed. 1980).

[8] *See* Hines v. Morrow, 236 S.W. 183 (Tex. Civ. App. 1922).

[9] *See, E.g.*, Chicago, Rock Island & Pac. Ry. Co. v. Goodson, 242 F.2d 203 (5th Cir. 1957) (holding defendant liable for explosion when it allowed water to back up onto another's land; the water allowed some oil in a pit to rise so that it came in contact with a hot exhaust pipe).

[10] *E.g.*, Wood v. Pa. R.R. Co., 177 Pa. 306 (1896) (unforeseeable that when a speeding vehicle hits a person, the person's body would fly off at an angle and strike another person); Ryan v. N.Y. Cent. R.R. Co., 35 N.Y. 210 (1866) (unforeseeable that fire would spread beyond first building).

[11] *See* W. Page Keeton, Prosser and Keeton on the Law of Torts 300 (5th ed. 1984).

[12] *E.g.*, Socony-Vacuum Oil Co. v. Marshall, 222 F.2d 604 (1st Cir. 1955). *See also* Restatement (Third) of Torts § 29 (Prelim. Draft No. 3, 2001).

[13] Restatement (Second) of Torts § 281(b) cmt. f, illus. 3 (1965). *See* Kelley, *supra* note 7, at 1065-66. In the latest draft of the Restatement, the example now is that the defendant gave a shotgun to a 9-year old. *See* Restatement (Third) of Torts § 29 cmt. f, illus. 2 (Prelim. Draft No. 3, 2001).

[14] 2 Fowler Harper & Fleming James, Jr., The Law of Torts 1138 (1956).

[15] Restatement (Second) of Torts § 281(b) cmt. g (1965). *See also* Keeton, *supra* note 11, at 283.

[16] Restatement (Second) of Torts § 281(b) cmt. g (1965).

[17] *Id.*

[18] *Id.*

[19] *See* Dobbs, *supra* note 4, at 476 (noting railroad's delay "was negligent, but not because of the danger of flooding").

[20] *See* Green-Wheeler Shoe Co. v. Chicago, Rock Island & Pac. Ry. Co., 106 N.W. 498, 500 (Iowa 1906) ("Defendant should have foreseen, as any reasonable person could foresee, that the negligent delay would extend the time during which the goods would be liable in the hands of the carrier to be overtaken by some such casualty, and would therefore increase the peril that the goods should be thus lost to the shipper.") In admiralty cases, an unreasonable delay constitutes a violation of the carrier's duty to care for the cargo. Sedco, Inc. v. S.S. Strathewe, 800 F.2d 27, 32 (2d Cir. 1986). This strips the carrier of the exemptions such as Act of God. *See* Atl. Mut. Ins. Co. v. Poseidon Schiffahrt, 313 F.2d 872 (7th Cir. 1963) (concluding unreasonable delay makes carrier insurer of goods). *See* Michael Sturley, 2A Benedict on Admiralty § 123, at 12-19 (2000). *See also*

Smith v. U.S. Shipping Emergency Fleet Corp., 2 F.2d 390 (S.D.N.Y. 1924), *modified* 26 F.2d 337 (2d Cir. 1928) (noting risk of cargo loss increased by extended route "simply because the risk would be prolonged").

[21] Dobbs, *supra* note 4, at 469.

[22] One concern that may have motivated the courts in the cases on negligent delay was that the delay deprived the cargo owner of its insurance. *See* 1 Robert Hutchinson, A Treatise on the Law of Carriers § 307 (3d ed. 1906). *See generally* Steven F. Friedell, *The Deviating Ship*, 32 Hastings L.J. 1535, 1543 (1981).

[23] Smith v. London & S.W. Ry. [1870] 6 L.R.-P.C. 14.

[24] Stultz v. Benson Lumber Co., 59 P.2d 100, 104 (Cal. 1936).

[25] *See* Keeton, *supra* note 11, at 294.

[26] *Id.* at 693. *See also* Pittsburg Reduction Co. v. Horton, 113 S.W. 647 (Ark. 1908). In that case the court exonerated a company that discarded an unexploded dynamite cap near a public school, which subsequently injured a boy. One boy, Charlie, brought the cap home and played with it. His mother, who did not know what it contained, would pick it up when he finished playing with it. With her permission, Charlie brought the cap to school a week later where he traded it to another boy, Jack, who was severely injured when the cap exploded. Although the defendant was negligent, and its negligence was plainly a cause-in-fact of the injury, the court held Charlie's mother's actions "broke the causal connection" between the company's negligence and the injury. *Id.* at 649. For a similar case, see *Carter v. Towne*, 103 Mass. 507 (1870), where the court held that a mother's custody of gunpowder meant that the person who sold it to her nine year-old son was not a direct cause of his subsequent injuries.

[27] 47 So. 2d 298 (Fla. 1950).

[28] *Id.* at 302.

[29] *Id.*

[30] Joseph H. Beale, *The Proximate Consequences of an Act*, 33 Harv. L. Rev. 633, 651 (1920). *See also* Keeton, *supra* note 11, at 278.

[31] Beale, *supra* note 30, at 652. *See also* First Springfield Bank & Trust v. Galman, 702 N.E.2d 1002, 1007 (Ill. App. Ct. 1998) (in deciding whether something is a condition or a cause the court considers the kind of hazard created, its gravity, its relation in time and space to the injury, and foreseeability).

[32] *E.g.,* Koehler v. Waukesha Milk Co., 208 N.W. 901 (Wis. 1926) (woman died from infection after she cut her finger on a broken milk bottle); Spade v. Lynn & Boston R.R., 52 N.E. 747, 748 (Mass. 1899) (plaintiff can recover for emotional harm even if greater than that normally expected).

[33] Steinhauser v. Hertz Corp., 421 F.2d 1169, 1173 (2d Cir. 1970).

[34] Wagner v. Int'l Ry. Co., 133 N.E. 437, 438 (N.Y. 1921).

[35] *See* Keeton, *supra* note 11, at 309.

[36] *E.g.,* Jenks v. Ohio Dep't of Youth Serv., 66 Ohio Misc. 2d 115 (Ct. Cl. 1993) (finding of fact); Johnson v. State, 841 P.2d 1254 (Wash. Ct. App. 1992); Kiger v. State, 802 P.2d 1248 (Mont. 1990); Rivers v. State, 328 A.2d 398 (Vt. 1974). Cf. Fleming v. State, 41 Cal. Rptr. 2d 63 (Cal. Ct. App. 1995) (failure to arrest parolee for leaving state without permission was not proximate cause of murder committed out of state); Hartley v. State, 698 P.2d 77 (Wash. 1985) (failure to revoke habitual traffic offender's driver's license was not legal cause of personal injuries and fatalities caused by driver). *But see* Grimm v. Ariz. Bd. of Pardons & Paroles, 564 P.2d 1227 (Ariz. 1977) (parole board liable for gross negligence and recklessness).

[37] Kelley, *supra* note 7, at 1054.

[38] *See* text, *supra* notes 33 and 36.

[39] Florida Standard Jury Instructions in Civil Cases 5.1(a) (2001). As one author commented on a similar instruction, "Difficult though it may be for the average juror to understand this definition, it is standard." Graham Douthwaite, Jury Instructions on Damages in Tort Cases 153 (2d ed. 1988). California courts used to give a similar instruction. BAJI No. 3.75 (7th ed. 1986). The California Supreme Court disapproved of this instruction in *Mitchell v. Gonzales*, 819 P.2d 872 (Cal. 1991). The new instruction defines "cause of injury" as "a substantial factor in bringing about the injury, damage, loss or harm. BAJI No. 3.76 (8th ed. 1994). This confuses the cause-in-fact issue with the issue of scope of liability. Adding to the confusion, the California instructions define a concurring cause as one "that was operative at the moment of injury." *Id.* No. 3.77.

[40] *See, e.g.,* Jane Stapleton, *Legal Cause: Cause-in-Fact and the Scope of Liability for Consequences*, 54 Vand. L. Rev. 941, 1007-09 (2001) (listing multiple factors).

[41] *E.g.,* Illinois Pattern Jury Instructions - Civil No. 15.01 (1995). Colorado defines "cause" in the same terms. However, it drops the word "proximate." Colorado Jury Instructions, 4th - Civil No. 9.26 (2000). *See* Restatement (Third) of Torts § 29, reporter's notes to cmt. e, at 214 (Preliminary Draft No. 3, 2001). For other examples of confusing instructions see *supra* note 2. The term "proximate" is also likely to confuse jurors, many of whom think it means "approximate" or some other fabrication. *See Mitchell*, 819 P.2d at 877-78 (citing Robert Charrow & Veda Charrow, *Making Legal Language Understandable: A Psycholinguistic Study of Jury Instructions*, 79 Colum. L. Rev. 1306, 1353 (1979)).

[42] *See* Dobbs, *supra* note 4, at 447. *See* William Prosser, *Proximate Cause in California*, 38 Calif. L. Rev. 394, 424 (1950) ("There are probably few judges who would undertake to say just what [the old California jury instruction on proximate cause] means, and fewer still who would expect it to mean anything whatever to a jury."). Some have concluded that the proximate cause problem is better analyzed as a problem of duty to be resolved by the judge instead of the jury. *See* Leon Green, Rationale of Proximate Cause (1927).

[43] For other discussions of the problem of liability for indirect damage in Jewish law, see Irwin Haut, *Causation in Jewish Law*, 3 Nat'l Jewish L. Rev. 1 (1988) and Irwin Haut, *Causation in Jewish Law - Part II*, 4 Nat'l Jewish L. Rev. 9 (1989); Shalom Albeck, *Gerama and Garme*, *in* 7 Encyclopaedia Judaica 430 (1972). *See also* Irene Merker Rosenberg, Yale Rosenberg & Bentzion Turin, *Murder by Gruma: Causation in Homicide Cases under Jewish Law*, 80 B.U. L. Rev. 1017 (2000).

[44] B. Bava Batra 22b. The word "tosafot" means "supplements or additions. The collection of these commentaries and dialectical remarks were written in the twelfth to fourteenth centuries in France and Germany and are printed alongside the Talmudic text.

[45] B. Bava Kamma 47b.

[46] The Provincial scholars Meiri and R. Jonathan Ha-kohen of Lunel added the idea that the one throwing the object pulled on a rope. Meiri, *B. Bava Kamma* 26b; Perush Rabbenu Yehonatan, *B. Bava Kamma* 26. *Id.*

[47] *Id.*

[48] *Id.*

[49] B. Bava Kamma 59b.

[50] B. Bava Kamma 55b.

[51] *Id.* The Talmud limits this rule so that it applies to two kinds of situations. One is where the fire is spread by an unusual wind. The other is where the defendant covers an object with the stalk. Under the law there is generally no liability for damage by fire to goods

that are covered. Therefore the defendant has prevented the owner of the covered object from recovering from the one who set the fire. *B. Bava Kamma* 56a.

52 *Id.*

53 *B. Bava Kamma* 60a.

54 *B. Kiddushin* 24b.

55 *B. Bava Kamma* 23b.

56 *B. Bava Kamma* 55b.

57 *Id.*

58 *B. Bava Kamma* 116b.

59 *B Bava Kamma* 99b.

60 *B. Bava Kamma* 100a-b.

61 *B. Sanhedrin* 33a-b.

62 *B. Bava Kamma* 99b. Burning the note only causes indirect damage to the creditor as presentation of the note is not necessary for collection of the debt.

63 *B. Bava Kamma* 89a.

64 Some rabbis were known to impose liability in cases of *garme*. *B. Bava Kamma* 98b.

65 *B. Bava Kamma* 98b.

66 *See* Maimonides, *H. Hovel U-Mazik* 7:7; *H. Nizkei Mammon* 14:7. *See also* Rif, *B. Bava Kamma* 11b-12a (suggesting the law did not support the view that one who removes the pillows is exempt for damage to objects thrown from the roof).

67 *B. Bava Kamma* 59b-60a. Rabbi Yohanan uses the Hebrew term *vadai* to describe the certainty with which his actions caused the damage.

68 *B. Bava Kamma* 9b; 22b. Resh Lakish uses the Aramaic term *bari hezeikah*.

69 Rabbi Lichtenstein suggests a different analysis. He emphasizes that only Resh Lakish uses the term *bari hezeka*h (the damage is certain). According to him, Resh Lakish did not mean that damage was certain but only that there was a high risk of damage. This high level of risk would suffice to make the fire the equivalent of the defendant's ox. A person is liable for damage done by his ox even though damage is not certain to occur. Shi'rei Harav Aharon Lichtenstein, Dinei D'Garmi 116 (1999/2000).

70 *B. Bava Kamma* 22a.

71 *See infra* text accompanying notes 81 and 99.

72 *See infra* text accompanying note 90.

73 *B. Bava Batra* 22b.

74 *B. Yevamot* 90b; *B. Sanhedrin* 46a.

75 *See* 9 *Encyclopaedia Judaica* 31 (1972).

76 *B. Bava Batra* 22b.

77 *Id.*

78 The Mishnah is part of the Babylonian Talmud that was completed around 200 A.D. It formed the basis for the discussions in the Babylonian and Palestinian academies. Those discussions are reflected in the Gemarah, which was compiled in Babylonia about 300 years later. A different and independent work known as the Jerusalem Talmud was completed around the year 400. This was also based on the Mishnah.

79 *B. Bava Batra* 100a (quoting *Mishnah, Bekhorot* 4:4).

80 This is based on an interpretation of *B. Bekhorot* 28b. The Gemarah first suggests that the Mishnah interpretation is according to Rabbi Meir who judged cases of *garme*. But Rabbi Ilai then explained in the name of Rav that the Mishnah, in saying "he mixed them with his produce," is to be understood to mean that the *judge* mixed them with the *owner's* produce. *Rashi, B. Bekhorot* 28b. The implication is that, according to Rabbi Meir, the judge would be liable even if the owner mixed them with his own produce pursuant to the judge's decision. See Rabbi Nissim Chaim Moses Mizrachi (d. 1749), *Responsa Admat Kodesh* 1, *Hoshen Mishpat* 69. Because Jewish law usually follows the view of Rabbi Meir, it is important to establish what he held.

81 *Rosh, B. Bava Batra* 2:17. *See also Rosh, B. Bava Kamma* 9:13.

82 *Rosh, B. Bava Batra* 2:17.

83 *Id.*

84 *Id.*

85 *Id.*

86 *Responsa Rosh* 64:1. The Rosh analogized the case to one where a person breaks down a fence allowing animals to escape. He would be exempt for the loss of the animals. *See* text, *supra* note 50. Although the Talmud holds that the one breaking down the fence would be liable under the laws of Heaven, the Rosh held that such liability applied to the damage to the fence but not to the animal. *See also Responsa Rosh* 95:1 (if one stole another's land but did not plow it or plant on it, or if one stole a house but did not use it, the damage to the owner from not being able to use his property is only *gerama*). In another responsum the Rosh ruled that a Jewish community, a *kahal*, was not liable for indirect losses it caused Reuben. Reuben had given a personal note to a non-Jew to cover a debt owed by the *kahal*. The non-Jew took in pledge some notes that Reuben had received from other non-Jews. Reuben pleaded several times with the *kahal* to redeem his notes, but they refused, and even ignored a judgment that Reuben obtained in a rabbinic court. Reuben then redeemed the notes himself, but they had become worthless due to the delay. The Rosh distinguished the case from the rule that one who burns another's notes is liable, because here the *kahal* did nothing at all to the notes themselves. Indeed, the *kahal* was completely passive, and therefore the damage was merely *garama*. This was therefore analogous to removing the cushions while an object is in mid-air. The person removing the cushions is exempt because he did not do anything to the falling object itself. *Responsa Rosh* 101:10.

87 *Responsa Rosh* 58:6.

88 *Rosh, Sanhedrin* 9:2.

89 In another responsum, Reuben left a barrel in a public way and placed a rock on top of it to keep it from rolling. Simon removed the rock when Reuben was not present, saying that the rock belonged to him. The next day Reuben found that his barrel had broken. Reuben sued Simon for damages, and Simon claimed that he had replaced the rock with another. The Rosh ruled that if Simon would take an oath to support his version of the events, then he would be exempt. But the Rosh specifically ruled that this was not a case of *gerama* because the barrel was certain to roll if it lacked a support. Simon would have been liable had he not substituted another rock as he claimed. *Responsa Rosh* 101:3. The Rosh did not discuss the other requirements of *garme*—direct injury to the object and immediate injury. But the Rosh apparently did not insist that Simon actually touch the barrel or that the damage occur immediately when he removed the stone. But see R. Moses Alshekh (c. 1507-1593), *Responsa Mahram Alshekh* 134 (saying that the damage in this case occurred "immediately").

90 The Jerusalem Talmud records the view that a fine is imposed on those who tear another's note of indebtedness. *P. Shevuot* 6:6. *See also P. Kilaim* 7:3 (Rabbi Meir imposed a fine on a man who suffered his vine to overshadow his fellow's growing grain, which rendered it forfeit). The Jerusalem Talmud is a separate work from the Babylonian Talmud and is not considered authoritative when its rulings conflict with the Babylonian Talmud.

[91] *B. Bava Batra* 22b.

[92] *E.g.,* the Maharam of Rothenburg, Rabbi Meir ben Baruch (c. 1215-1293), *Responsa Maharam of Rothenburg* 4:460 (Prague ed.); Rabbi Yakar ben Samuel Ha-levi (thirteenth century, Cologne and Mainz), *Responsa Rosh* 101:1 (the liability of the informer is on account of a rabbinic fine); Rabbi Moses ben Jacob of Coucy, *Sefer Mitzvot Gadol, Mitzvot Asseh* 70. *But see Responsa Maharam of Rothenburg* 4:1013 (Prague ed.) (damage must be immediate).

[93] Shabbetai ben Meir Ha-kohen, better known as the Shakh (1621-1662), adopted this approach in his highly influential commentary on the Shulhan Arukh. *See* Shakh, *Shulhan Arukh, Hoshen Mishpat* § 381.

[94] *Responsa Zemach Zedek* 36.

[95] *B. Gittin* 45a.

[96] See *supra* text accompanying note 73.

[97] Rabbi Levi ben Habib (c. 1483-1545 Jerusalem), *Responsa Maharalbah* 5.

[98] The term Gemarah refers to that part of the Talmud that reflects the discussions of the academies on the Mishnah. *See supra* note 78.

[99] Moshe Hirshler, Hiddushei Haramban, Kuntres Dina De*garme* 127 (Moshe Hirshler ed., 1969/1970).

[100] A responsum that had been attributed to Nahmanides but which is now believed to be written by the Rashba says that to be *garme* the damage must be done by the defendant's act to the body of the thing injured. *Responsa Rashba* (attributed to Nahmanides 240).

[101] Hirshler, *supra* note 99, at 121.

[102] *Id.* at 123.

[103] He rejected the Ritzvah's use of the Jerusalem Talmud for support. *See supra* note 90. Nahmanides asserted that the Jerusalem Talmud quotes rabbis who imposed fines in particular cases of indirect damage because they did not hold that there was generally a rule of liability in those cases. Hirshler, *supra* note 99, at 122.

[104] *Id.* at 118.

[105] For example, according to Nahmanides one who removes cushions is liable for the breakage of falling objects. Hirshler, *supra* note 99, at 132. According the Ri, this is a case of *gerama*. *See supra* note 81.

[106] *Responsa Avkat Rokhel* 89. *See also* Solomon Luria (1510-1565), Yam Shel Shelomo, *B. Bava Kamma* 9:26 (supporting the Ri's view and quoting Nahmanides to refute the Ritzvah).

[107] Hirshler, *supra* note 99, at 129.

[108] *Id.* at 126-27.

[109] *Id.* at 130.

[110] *Id.* at 126.

[111] Another difficulty with Nahmanides's approach is his position that one who "prepares damage" is never liable. *Id.* at 131. Nahmanides thus explains that a person who sets poisonous food before an animal is not liable for the death or injury of the animal. *Id.* Nahmanides's conclusion is too broad. The informer and the judge who rule erroneously are both liable even though they merely created the conditions where others took away the plaintiff's property. *Id.*

[112] The Maharam of Lublin, Rabbi Meir ben Gedaliah, occasionally referred to simply as the Maharam, lived from 1558 to 1616 in Lublin, Cracow, and Lemberg.

[113] The Maharshakh, Rabbi Solomon ben Abraham Ha-kohen, lived from about 1520 to about 1601 primarily in Salonika.

[114] *Responsa Maharam of Lublin* 61:4; *Responsa Maharshakh* 31. For a more detailed account of the facts as reported in these sources, see Steven F. Friedell, *The Maharam of Lublin and the Maharshakh on*

the Tort Liability of an Informer, *in* A. Enker & S. Deutch, Studies in Jewish Law 279 (1998) (in Hebrew).

There is no doubt that the Inquisition records and the Maharshakh's responsum deal with the same case. The Maharshakh's responsum says that the events occurred in Venice, and the Venetian Inquisition records contain only one case involving a mohel. Also, both of these sources indicate that the defendant was circumcised by someone other than the mohel who circumcised the defendant's brother's son. The Maharam of Lublin's responsum is more general, and there is a possibility that he dealt with a similar but different case. It tells us that the events occurred in "Italy" and it recounts the circumcision only of the defendant. However, it is likely that the Maharam of Lublin was describing the same case that came before the Maharshakh. Events of this kind were rare. Indeed, there is no known case of a similar denunciation. The questions addressed to each rabbi present only arguments on behalf of the mohel, and the two rabbis addressed the same issues. This suggests that the case was brought *ex parte*. Moreover, in both responsa, the questions posed used the same expression, *makhaneh yisrael*, to describe a ghetto. The Maharam's responsum describes the ghetto where the Converso did not reside; the Maharshakh's responsum describes the ghetto in Dubrovnik. Although the term was common in Biblical literature as a description of the Israelite camp in the desert and in rabbinic literature as the area outside the Temple but inside the walls of Jerusalem, its occurrence in these two responsa as a description of a ghetto may be unique and would suggest that the two questions were written by the same author. Other scholars agree that the two rabbis addressed the same case. *See* H. J. Zimmels, Die Marranen in der Rabbinischen Literatur 151 (1932); Judah Rosenthal, *Le-Korot Ha-Yehudim be-Polin Le-or Shut Ha-Maharam Mi-Lublin*, 31 Sinai 311, 330 (1952).

[115] *See* 7 Pier Cesare Ioly Zorattini, Processi Del S. Uffizio Di Venezia Contro Ebrei E Giudaizzanti 77-171 (1989) [hereinafter Processi]. For descriptions of the proceedings against the Jews based on the Venetian records, see Brian Pullan, The Jews of Europe and the Inquisition of Venice 1550-1670 (1983); Pier Cesare Ioly Zorattini, The Inquisition and the Jews in Sixteenth Century Venice, Proceedings of the Seventh World Congress of Jewish Studies 83 (1981); Cecil Roth, *Les Marranes a Venise*, 89 Revue des Etudes Juives 20 (1930). The Venetian Inquisition was more humane than others and did not sentence any Conversos to death. On two occasions it banished Jews from Venice on pain of death if they should return. One of these banishments was in this case, against Benarogios and Naar should they return to Venice. *See* Zorattini, *supra*, at 83, 86. But those arrested by the Venetian Inquisition faced long terms of imprisonment and the possibility of torture. *See* Pullan, *supra*, at 132-37.

[116] *See* Processi, *supra* note 115, at 131. A Converso is someone who had been forced to convert to Christianity or is the descendant of such a person. Many Conversos secretly observed some Jewish practices.

[117] A mohel is someone who performs a ritual circumcision. Such circumcisions are normally performed when an infant is eight days old or when a non-Jew converts to Judaism. But a person who is born Jewish has an obligation to be circumcised as an adult if infant circumcision was not performed.

[118] Processi, *supra* note 115, at 137.

[119] *Id.*

[120] *Id.* at 150-51.

[121] *Id.* at 165-67.

122 The Maharshakh assumed that Nis was before the court. He wrote, "It appears from the question that the informer now resides outside the place where he was forced to convert and that he has now returned to the true and just faith, for otherwise what would be the purpose of knowing if the law makes him liable."
Jewish law requires that testimony normally be received only in the presence of the opposing party. But an exception is made in cases of an informer because of the danger that the informer will cause further damage. *See Responsa Rivash* 237; *Responsa Rosh* 17:1; Shulhan Arukh, H.M. 388:14. These sources refer to the taking of testimony, not to the filing of suit, but the need for secrecy extends to the entire proceeding. *See* Moses Isserles (c. 1525-1572), *Darkhei Moshe, Tur H.M.* 388:15. Although Jewish law normally required that testimony not be given until after the defendant's answer, courts were allowed to deviate from this procedure. *Responsa Rivash* 234.
Unlike the Maharshakh, the Maharam of Lublin does not address the question of atonement. The Maharam of Lublin would likely have addressed this issue had the informer been before the Bet Din, as he often prescribed measures for repenting even when no damages were legally due, as was common at that period. *See, e.g., Responsa Maharam of Lublin* 43, 44.

123 As indicated earlier, neither the Maharshakh nor the Maharam of Lublin used the actual names of the parties, referring to Dr. Benarogios as "the mohel" and to Felipe de Nis as either "the converso" or "the informer."

124 *See Responsa Maharshakh* 1:27, 53, 54.

125 Rabbi Jacob ben Moses Moellin (c. 1360-1427), *Responsa Mahari Moellin* 86.

126 *Mordekhai, B. Bava Kamma,* 9:114. The Mordekhai analogized the cost to medical expenses that are collectible and are deemed to be caused directly by the defendant.

127 See *supra* text accompanying note 76.

128 The Maharam of Lublin cites as authority Mordekhai, *B. Bava Kamma* 9:114. The rule is stated as follows in the Shulhan Arukh:
If he put him into a room, locked the door on him, and prevented him from doing his work, he only pays for his loss of time. But if he was already in the room, and he locked him in so that he could not exit, it is *gerama benizkin* and he is exempt under the laws of man. *Shulhan Arukh, Hoshen Mishpat* 420:11. The distinction was derived from the Rosh, *B. Bava Kamma* 8:3. In the first example the defendant performed an act upon the body of the plaintiff; in the second example he did not. Ephrayim ben Aaron Navon, Mahaneh Efrayim, Sekhirut 18 (1738).

129 *Responsa Maharshakh* 1:27.

130 Bet Yosef, *Commentary to the Talmud, Hoshen Mishpat* 386 (quoting *Responsa Rashba* 3:76).

131 *See Mordekhai, Yevamot* 4:41; *Responsa Maharah Or Zarua* 142. The Responsa Maharah Or Zarua, like the Mordekhai, dates from the thirteenth century. *Cf. Solomon Luria, Yam Shel Shelomo, B. Yevamot* 4:49 (warning against converting gentiles to Judaism because of the grave offense to the gentile government). *See* Solomon Ibn Verga (15-16th centuries), *Shevet Yehudah* 64 (some Marranos are circumcised in hiding, and there are some who circumcise themselves out of fear of having it being revealed); Reuven Bonfil, *New Information on Rabbi Menaham Azariah da Fano and His Age, in* Studies in the History of Jewish Society 98 (1980) (in his notebook listing circumcisions, mohel concealed names of the Conversos that he circumcised).

132 *Responsa Maharah Or Zarua* 142; Hillel ben Naphtali Zevi, Bet Hillel, Yoreh Deah 267 (c. 1615-1690).

133 *See supra* text accompanying note 3.

134 *See supra* text accompanying note 77.

135 *Mordekhai, B. Bava Kamma* 119.

136 *Levush, Hoshen Mishpat* 386. Rabbi Jaffe lived from about 1515-1612.

137 Henry W. Edgerton, *Legal Cause,* 72 U. Pa. L. Rev. 211, 213 (1924).

138 Nicholas St. John Green, *Torts under French Law,* 8 Am. L. Rev. 508, 519 (1874).

139 *See, e.g.,* Kelley, *supra* note 7, at 1063.

140 *See* Yehiel ben Asher (c. 1270-1340), *Tur, Hoshen Mishpat* 1. The Tur is one of the foremost codes of Jewish law, a precursor to the Shulhan Arukh. It is significant that its author placed this description of the judge's responsibility at the beginning of the section on civil law.

141 *See* Shulhan Arukh *Hoshen Mishpat* 12:20. *See generally* Steven F. Friedell, *The "Different Voice" in Jewish Law: Some Parallels to a Feminist Jurisprudence,* 67 Ind. L. J. 915, 920 (1992).

142 *B. Bava Batra* 131a.

143 Even in modern day Israel where an appellate system has been instituted for rabbinic courts, some maintain that the decisions of the appellate court are binding only on the parties to the case but not on the lower court judges. *See* 4 Menachem Elon, Jewish Law 1810-1818 (1994).

144 *See* text, *supra* notes 48-52, 54, 56-57.

145 *See* text, *supra* notes 122, 124.

146 *See* text, *supra* note 73.

147 1 N.Y. Pattern Jury Instructions – Civil No. 2:70 (3d ed. 2000) (emphasis added.).

Lesson

5

MAKING THE RIGHT TURN

ENGINEERING ETHICS INTO DRIVERLESS VEHICLES

The advent of the self-driving car promises to significantly reduce the 1.25 million traffic deaths that occur each year worldwide by removing their primary cause—human error. However, this technology poses some ethical dilemmas inasmuch as these machines will have to make decisions regarding whom to save or protect in the event of a collision. Those creating the vehicle's algorithm will literally decide who shall live and who shall die. This lesson aims to apply ancient Talmudic considerations to this very modern problem.

CASE STUDY A

A traveling autonomous vehicle suddenly notices a pedestrian ahead. By its calculation, the pedestrian cannot get out of the way and will die if struck. The only thing the vehicle can do to avoid hitting the pedestrian is to make an immediate turn. However, there is a brick wall on both sides of the road, and hitting it would kill the car's passenger.

POLL 1

What would be the most moral way to program the AV? To protect the . . .

1 Passenger

2 Pedestrian

3 Not sure

CASE STUDY **B**

A traveling autonomous vehicle suddenly notices a steel construction barrier ahead. Hitting it would kill the passenger. The only thing the vehicle can do to avoid hitting the barrier is to make an immediate turn, but on both sides there is one pedestrian who would be killed by the vehicle.

POLL 2

What would be the most moral way to program the AV? To protect the . . .

1 Passenger

2 Pedestrian

3 Not sure

POLL 3

What if one potential victim is a seventeen-year-old with a bright future and the second potential victim is an elderly person who is in bad health?

1 My answers stay the same.

2 My answers change.

POLL 4

What if there are multiple passengers in the car versus one pedestrian, or multiple pedestrians versus one passenger?

1 My answers stay the same.

2 My answers change.

POLL 5

If one AV were programmed to save the greater number of lives, even at the expense of the passenger, and another were programmed to put the passenger first, which would you be more likely to buy?

1 The one that saves the most lives

2 The one that protects its riders

3 No difference

TEXT 1

PHILIPPA FOOT, "THE PROBLEM OF ABORTION AND THE DOCTRINE OF THE DOUBLE EFFECT," *OXFORD REVIEW* 5 (1967)

Suppose that a judge or magistrate is faced with rioters demanding that a culprit be found for a certain crime and threatening otherwise to take their own bloody revenge on a particular section of the community. The real culprit being unknown, the judge sees himself as able to prevent the bloodshed only by framing some innocent person and having him executed.

Beside this example is placed another in which a pilot whose airplane is about to crash is deciding whether to steer from a more to a less inhabited area. To make the parallel as close as possible it may rather be supposed that he is the driver of a runaway tram which he can only steer from one narrow track on to another; five men are working on one track and one man on the other; anyone on the track he enters is bound to be killed. In the case of the riots the mob have five hostages, so that in both the exchange is supposed to be one man's life for the lives of five.

The question is why we should say, without hesitation, that the driver should steer for the less occupied track, while most of us would be appalled at the idea that the innocent man could be framed.

It may be suggested that the special feature of the latter case is that it involves the corruption of justice, and this

PHILIPPA FOOT
1920–2010

Philosopher and ethicist. Born and raised in England, Foot graduated with a degree in philosophy from Somerville College, Oxford, where she later became a lecturer and senior research fellow. She authored many essays in the field of ethics and was one of the founders of contemporary virtue ethics, inspired by the ethics of Aristotle. Foot is best known for introducing the ethical thought experiment known as the Trolley Problem, which has generated an extensive amount of literature and debate.

is, of course, very important indeed. But if we remove that special feature, supposing that some private individual is to kill an innocent person and pass him off as the criminal, we still find ourselves horrified by the idea.

QUESTION FOR DISCUSSION

Is there a coherent philosophical principle that can explain this seeming inconsistency?

Figure 5.1

The Questions

1	How should AV programmers direct vehicles to respond in the aforementioned case studies?
2	Assume that you are about to purchase an AV and have the option to decide between two vehicles, one whose algorithm is more passenger-protective than the other. Would it be ethical to choose whichever you prefer, or must you purchase a particular one?
3	Assume that the only vehicle available is one that runs contrary to what is deemed to be the most ethical algorithm. Are you allowed to purchase this AV?

CHAVRUTA A

TEXT 2

TALMUD, BAVA METSI'A 62A 👥

שְׁנַיִם שֶׁהָיוּ מְהַלְכִין בַּדֶּרֶךְ, וּבְיַד אֶחָד מֵהֶן קִיתוֹן שֶׁל מַיִם, אִם שׁוֹתִין שְׁנֵיהֶם מֵתִים, וְאִם שׁוֹתֶה אֶחָד מֵהֶן, מַגִּיעַ לַיִשּׁוּב.

דָּרַשׁ בֶּן פְּטוּרָא: מוּטָב שֶׁיִּשְׁתּוּ שְׁנֵיהֶם וְיָמוּתוּ, וְאַל יִרְאֶה אֶחָד מֵהֶם בְּמִיתָתוֹ שֶׁל חֲבֵירוֹ.

עַד שֶׁבָּא רַבִּי עֲקִיבָא וְלִימֵּד: "וְחֵי אָחִיךָ עִמָּךְ" (וַיִּקְרָא כה, לו) - חַיֶּיךָ קוֹדְמִים לְחַיֵּי חֲבֵירָךְ.

Two people are traveling [in a desert], and one of them has a flask of water. If both drink from it, they will both die. If only one of them drinks, this person will be able to make it to the next village.

Ben Petura taught, "It is preferable that both drink and die, as opposed to one witnessing the death of the other."

But then Rabbi Akiva came and cited the following verse: "Let your brother live *with* you" (LEVITICUS 25:36). The wording implies that your life takes precedence over the life of another.

BABYLONIAN TALMUD

A literary work of monumental proportions that draws upon the legal, spiritual, intellectual, ethical, and historical traditions of Judaism. The 37 tractates of the Babylonian Talmud contain the teachings of the Jewish sages from the period after the destruction of the 2nd Temple through the 5th century CE. It has served as the primary vehicle for the transmission of the Oral Law and the education of Jews over the centuries; it is the entry point for all subsequent legal, ethical, and theological Jewish scholarship.

BEN PETURA

Ben Petura is quoted once in all of Talmudic literature, in connection with the question of two lost people who only have enough water to sustain one of them. Nothing is really known about this sage, but it is evident that he lived prior to Rabbi Akiva (ca. 50–137 CE).

RABBI AKIVA
CA. 50–137 CE

Third-generation Mishnaic sage (*tana*). Rabbi Akiva was born in Israel when it was under Roman rule. He was initially unlearned in Torah, and his unlikely path toward excellence in Torah study—which he began at the age of 40 because of the encouragement of his wife, Rochel—has been widely retold by Jews for generations. After the failure of the Bar Kochba revolt, in which Rabbi Akiva played a central role, the Romans banned the study of Torah, and Rabbi Akiva was executed for teaching Torah publicly. He is one of the most beloved and important scholars in Jewish history.

QUESTION FOR DISCUSSION

Can this passage be brought to bear on any of our case studies?

	APPLICA-BLE OR NOT APPLICABLE?	IF APPLICA-BLE, HOW WOULD BEN PETURA RULE?	IF APPLICA-BLE, HOW WOULD RABBI AKIVA RULE?
Case A			
Case B			

TEXT 3

LEVITICUS 25:35–36 ⊕

וְכִי יָמוּךְ אָחִיךְ וּמָטָה יָדוֹ עִמָּךְ וְהֶחֱזַקְתָּ בּוֹ גֵּר וְתוֹשָׁב וָחַי עִמָּךְ.
אַל תִּקַּח מֵאִתּוֹ נֶשֶׁךְ וְתַרְבִּית וְיָרֵאתָ מֵאֱלֹקֶיךָ וְחֵי אָחִיךָ עִמָּךְ.

When your brother becomes destitute and his hand falters beside you, you shall support him [whether] a convert or a resident, so that he can live with you.

You shall not take interest from him. Fear your God, and let your brother live with you.

CHAVRUTA B

TEXT 4

TALMUD, PESACHIM 25A–B

בְּכָל מִתְרַפְּאִין, חוּץ מֵעֲבוֹדָה זָרָה, וְגִילּוּי עֲרָיוֹת, וּשְׁפִיכוּת דָּמִים . . . וּשְׁפִיכוּת דָּמִים גּוּפֵיהּ מְנָלָן?

סְבָרָא הוּא. כִּי הַהוּא דְּאָתָא לְקַמֵּיהּ דְּרָבָא. אָמַר לֵיהּ: מָרֵי דוּרַאי אָמַר לִי זִיל קַטְלֵיהּ לִפְלַנְיָא וְאִי לֹא קָטְלִינָא לָךְ. אָמַר לֵיהּ: לִיקְטְלוּךְ וְלָא תִּיקְטוֹל. מַאי חָזֵית דְּדָמָא דִּידָךְ סוּמָק טְפֵי, דִּילְמָא דָּמָא דְּהַהוּא גַּבְרָא סוּמָק טְפֵי.

One may violate any of the Torah prohibitions to cure a [life-threatening] disease, except for the prohibitions of idolatry, forbidden sexual relations, and murder. . . .

How do we know that this is so for murder?

It's a matter of common sense, as demonstrated by the following story: A man once came before Rava and said: "The ruler of my city has told me, 'Go kill that particular person, and if you do not, I will kill you.'" Rava said to him: "Let him kill you rather than you kill the innocent person. For what makes you think that your blood is redder? Maybe the blood of that person is redder!"

ABBA BEN YOSEF (RAVA)
CA. 280–352

Fourth-generation Talmudic sage (*amora*), referred to in the Talmud as Rava (short for Rabbi Abba). Rava is one of the most oft-cited rabbis of the Talmud. He lived in Machoza, Babylonia. He was famous for his debates with his study-partner, Abaye; their debates are considered classic examples of Talmudic dialectical logic. Out of hundreds of their recorded disputes, the law was decided according to Rava's opinion in all but six cases.

QUESTION FOR DISCUSSION

Can this passage be brought to bear on any of our case studies?

	APPLICABLE OR NOT APPLICABLE?	HOW WOULD RAVA RULE?	DOES AGE OR QUALITY OF LIFE MAKE ANY DIFFERENCE?
Case A			
Case B			

TEXT 5

RABBI ASHER BEN YECHIEL, KETUVOT 1:4

מַשְׁמַע, הָא בַּעֲבוֹדַת כּוֹכָבִים, כְּגוֹן אִם כָּפְפוּ קוֹמָתוֹ לְהִשְׁתַּחֲווֹת לַעֲבוֹדַת
כּוֹכָבִים, אוֹ בִּשְׁפִיכוּת דָּמִים, כְּגוֹן שֶׁהִכּוּהוּ בְּגוּפוֹ עַל אָדָם אַחֵר וַהֲרָגוּהוּ,
כֵּיוָן שֶׁאֵינוֹ עוֹשֶׂה מַעֲשֶׂה כְּלָל, אֶלָּא אֲחֵרִים עוֹשִׂים בּוֹ מַעֲשֶׂה, אֵינוֹ
מְחוּיָּב לִמְסוֹר אֶת עַצְמוֹ.

RABBI ASHER BEN YECHIEL (ROSH) 1250–1328

Rabbi, author, and Talmudist, he is widely known by the acronym "Rosh." Rabbi Asher was a native of Germany, where he was a prominent disciple and successor of Rabbi Meir (Maharam) of Rothenburg. Due to the persecution and massacres of German Jewry under Emperor Rudolph I, Rabbi Asher was forced to flee, and in 1305, he arrived in Toledo, Spain. He is best known for his halachic commentary on the Talmud. Rabbi Asher was the father of Rabbi Ya'akov, the author of the *Arba'ah Turim*.

In the case of idolatry, if they physically force you to bow to an idol, or in the case of murder, if they use your body to hit and kill someone else—in these instances, you need not sacrifice your life. You will not have committed an act in these cases; others will have done so through you.

CASE STUDY C

A driver suddenly notices ten pedestrians ahead. By the driver's calculation, the pedestrians cannot get out of the way and will die if they are struck. The only thing the driver can do to avoid hitting the ten pedestrians is to make an immediate turn. But on either side there is one pedestrian who would be killed by the vehicle. The driver will be relatively safe either way.

POLL 6

Can Text 4 be used to justify choosing the course of action that saves the most lives?

1 Yes

2 No

3 Not sure

TEXT 6a

II SAMUEL 20:1–21 ⓘ

וְשָׁם נִקְרָא אִישׁ בְּלִיַּעַל, וּשְׁמוֹ שֶׁבַע בֶּן בִּכְרִי אִישׁ יְמִינִי, וַיִּתְקַע בַּשֹּׁפָר
וַיֹּאמֶר, אֵין לָנוּ חֵלֶק בְּדָוִד וְלֹא נַחֲלָה לָנוּ בְּבֶן יִשַׁי . . .

וַיַּעַל כָּל אִישׁ יִשְׂרָאֵל מֵאַחֲרֵי דָוִד אַחֲרֵי שֶׁבַע בֶּן בִּכְרִי, וְאִישׁ יְהוּדָה דָּבְקוּ
בְמַלְכָּם מִן הַיַּרְדֵּן וְעַד יְרוּשָׁלָם . . .

וַיֵּצְאוּ אַחֲרָיו אַנְשֵׁי יוֹאָב, וְהַכְּרֵתִי וְהַפְּלֵתִי, וְכָל הַגִּבֹּרִים, וַיֵּצְאוּ מִירוּשָׁלַם
לִרְדֹּף אַחֲרֵי שֶׁבַע בֶּן בִּכְרִי . . . וַיָּבֹאוּ וַיָּצֻרוּ עָלָיו בְּאָבֵלָה בֵּית הַמַּעֲכָה . . .

וַתִּקְרָא אִשָּׁה חֲכָמָה מִן הָעִיר, שִׁמְעוּ שִׁמְעוּ, אִמְרוּ נָא אֶל יוֹאָב, קְרַב עַד
הֵנָּה וַאֲדַבְּרָה אֵלֶיךָ.

וַיִּקְרַב אֵלֶיהָ, וַתֹּאמֶר הָאִשָּׁה, הַאַתָּה יוֹאָב, וַיֹּאמֶר אָנִי, וַתֹּאמֶר לוֹ שְׁמַע
דִּבְרֵי אֲמָתֶךָ, וַיֹּאמֶר שֹׁמֵעַ אָנֹכִי.

וַתֹּאמֶר לֵאמֹר, דַּבֵּר יְדַבְּרוּ בָרִאשֹׁנָה לֵאמֹר, שָׁאֹל יִשְׁאֲלוּ בְּאָבֵל וְכֵן הֵתַמּוּ.
אָנֹכִי שְׁלֻמֵי אֱמוּנֵי יִשְׂרָאֵל, אַתָּה מְבַקֵּשׁ לְהָמִית עִיר וְאֵם בְּיִשְׂרָאֵל, לָמָּה
תְבַלַּע נַחֲלַת ה'.

וַיַּעַן יוֹאָב וַיֹּאמַר, חָלִילָה חָלִילָה לִי אִם אֲבַלַּע וְאִם אַשְׁחִית. לֹא כֵן הַדָּבָר
כִּי אִישׁ מֵהַר אֶפְרַיִם שֶׁבַע בֶּן בִּכְרִי שְׁמוֹ נָשָׂא יָדוֹ בַּמֶּלֶךְ בְּדָוִד, תְּנוּ אֹתוֹ
לְבַדּוֹ, וְאֵלְכָה מֵעַל הָעִיר.

There happened to be there a wicked man whose name was Sheva ben Bichri, from the tribe of Benjamin. He blew a shofar and declared, "We have no portion with David, neither have we an inheritance in the son of Jesse." . . .

So all the men of Israel deserted David to follow Sheva ben Bichri. But the men of Judah stayed by their king all the way from the Jordan to Jerusalem. . . .

Joab's men went after Sheva with the archers, slingers, and all the warriors. . . . They came and besieged Sheva at Abel of Bet-Ma'acha. . . .

A wise woman called out from within the city, "Listen, listen! Tell Joab to come close so that I may speak to him."

He came near and she said, "Are you Joab?"

He said, "I am."

She said to him, "Hear the words of your servant."

"I am listening," he said.

She said, "Surely you should have spoken first peacefully. Had you inquired about peace of the people of Abel, they would have made peace. I am of those who are peaceful and faithful to Israel. Why do you seek to destroy a major city in Israel? Why should you swallow up the inheritance of God?"

Joab answered, "Far be it, far be it from me that I should swallow up or destroy. The matter is not so. Rather, a man of the hills of Ephraim named Sheva ben Bichri has lifted his hand against the king, against David. Give us just him and I will depart from the city."

TEXT 6b

JERUSALEM TALMUD, TERUMOT 8:4 🔊

סִיעוֹת בְּנֵי אָדָם שֶׁהָיוּ מְהַלְכִין בַּדֶּרֶךְ, פָּגְעוּ לָהֶן גּוֹיִם וְאָמְרוּ: תְּנוּ לָנוּ אֶחָד
מִכֶּם וְנַהֲרוֹג אוֹתוֹ, וְאִם לַאו, הֲרֵי אָנוּ הוֹרְגִים אֶת כּוּלְכֶם - אֲפִילוּ כּוּלָן
נֶהֱרָגִים לֹא יִמְסְרוּ נֶפֶשׁ אַחַת מִיִּשְׂרָאֵל.

יִחֲדוּ לָהֶן אֶחָד: כְּגוֹן שֶׁבַע בֶּן בִּכְרִי, יִמְסְרוּ אוֹתוֹ וְאַל יֵיהָרְגוּ.

אָמַר רַבִּי שִׁמְעוֹן בֶּן לָקִישׁ: וְהוּא שֶׁיְּהֵא חַיָּיב מִיתָה כְּשֶׁבַע בֶּן בִּכְרִי.

וְרַבִּי יוֹחָנָן אָמַר: אַף עַל פִּי שֶׁאֵינוֹ חַיָּיב מִיתָה כְּשֶׁבַע בֶּן בִּכְרִי.

If a traveling group is confronted by Gentiles who say, "Give us one of your number so that we can kill him; if not, we will kill all of you"—even if all of them are truly going to be killed, they should not hand over a single soul.

If, however, they specified a particular person, as in the story of Sheva ben Bichri, then they should hand that person over, so that they are not all killed.

Rabbi Shimon ben Lakish said: This permission only applies if the specified person had incurred the death penalty like Sheva ben Bichri.

Rabbi Yochanan said: This permission applies even if the specified individual hadn't incurred the death penalty.

JERUSALEM TALMUD

A commentary to the Mishnah, compiled during the 4th and 5th centuries. The Jerusalem Talmud predates its Babylonian counterpart by 100 years and is written in both Hebrew and Aramaic. While the Babylonian Talmud is the most authoritative source for Jewish law, the Jerusalem Talmud remains an invaluable source for the spiritual, intellectual, ethical, historical, and legal traditions of Judaism.

RABBI SHIMON BEN LAKISH (REISH LAKISH) CA. 200–? CE

Second-generation Talmudic sage (*amora*). Rabbi Shimon was raised in the Land of Israel when it was under Roman rule. In his youth, he was a gladiator and led a gang of bandits. A chance encounter with Rabbi Yochanan led Rabbi Shimon to embrace Torah study. He married Rabbi Yochanan's sister and became his study partner. Many of his debates with Rabbi Yochanan on various points of Jewish law are quoted in the Talmud.

RABBI YOCHANAN CA. 180–280 CE

Second-generation Talmudic sage (*amora*). Rabbi Yochanan was born in the Galilee region of Israel when it was under Roman rule. As a young boy, he studied under Rabbi Yehudah Hanasi, the redactor of the Mishnah. Rabbi Yochanan later moved to Tiberias, where he established an academy, and was eventually recognized as the leading scholar in the Land of Israel. Over the course of his long life, he laid the foundations for the Jerusalem Talmud.

QUESTIONS FOR DISCUSSION

1 What is the rational basis for the positions of Rabbi Shimon ben Lakish and Rabbi Yochanan?

2 How would Rabbi Shimon ben Lakish and Rabbi Yochanan rule in Case Study C?

	RABBI SHIMON BEN LAKISH	RABBI YOCHANAN
Case Study C		

TEXT 7

MICHAEL SANDEL, *JUSTICE: A READER* (OXFORD: OXFORD UNIVERSITY PRESS, 2007), P. 9

One way of thinking about the right thing to do, perhaps the most natural and familiar way, is to ask what will produce the greatest happiness for the greatest number of people. This way of thinking about morality finds its clearest statement in the philosophy of Jeremy Bentham (1748–1832). In his *Introduction to the Principles of Morals and Legislation* (1789), Bentham argues that the principle of utility should be the basis of morality and law. By utility, he means whatever promotes pleasure or prevents pain.

MICHAEL SANDEL
1953–

Political philosopher. Dr. Sandel is the Anne T. and Robert M. Bass professor of government at Harvard University, where he has taught political philosophy since 1980. His legendary undergraduate course, "Justice," has enrolled more than 15,000 students, and is the first Harvard course to be made freely available online and on public television. The *Guardian* called him "one of the most popular teachers in the world."

JEREMY BENTHAM
1748–1832

English philosopher and founder of modern Utilitarianism. Bentham devoted himself to the scientific analysis of morals and law. His *Introduction to the Principles of Morals and Legislation* argues that the greatest happiness of the greatest number should govern our judgment of every institution and action. Many of the reforms in the 19th-century England owe much to Bentham's activism.

TEXT 8

RABBI ELIEZER WALDENBURG, *RESPONSA TSITS ELIEZER* 15:70

כְּגוֹן עַל כְּלִי רֶכֶב, כְּשֶׁנּוֹסְעִים בְּדוֹמֶה לְמָשָׁל, וְנִקְלָעִים פִּתְאוֹמִית לִפְנֵי
אֲנָשִׁים רַבִּים שֶׁחוֹצְצִים אָז הַכְּבִישׁ, וְיֵשׁ לַעֲשׂוֹת עֲצִירָה פִּתְאוֹמִית עַל
יְדֵי נְסִיגָה אֲחוֹרַנִית כְּדֵי שֶׁרַבִּים מֵהָעוֹבְרִים לֹא יֵהָרְגוּ, אֲבָל בָּאֲחוֹרָה
נִמְצָא שָׁם יָחִיד עוֹמֵד בְּאוֹפֶן שֶׁבָּרוּר שֶׁיֵּהָרֵג עַל יְדֵי כֵן, וְכֵן בְּכָל הַדּוֹמֶה
לָזֶה. וְהַשְּׁאֵלָה נִשְׁאֶלֶת בְּכָאֲמוּר בְּמַה יֵּשׁ לוֹ לִבְחוֹר יוֹתֵר לִנְהוֹג בְּמַצָּב
כָּזֶה, אִם לִישָּׁאֵר בְּמַצָּב שֶׁל שֵׁב וְאַל תַּעֲשֶׂה וְעַל יְדֵי כֵן יֵהָרְגוּ אֲחָדִים
שֶׁלְּפָנָיו, אוֹ לָסֶגֶת אֲחוֹרָה בְּקוּם וַעֲשֵׂה, וְעַל יְדֵי זֶה יֵהָרֵג הַיָּחִיד.

וְכָאָמוּר לְדַעְתֵּנוּ יֵשׁ לִהְיוֹת בְּזֶה בְּשֵׁב וְאַל תַּעֲשֶׂה . . . וְלֹא לַעֲשׂוֹת שׁוּם
פְּעוּלָה הַמִּתְבַּטֵּאת בְּמַעֲשֶׂה שֶׁל קוּם וַעֲשֵׂה, וְלֹא מְשַׁנֶּה הַדָּבָר מַה שֶׁהוּא
כַּוָּנָתוֹ בָּזֶה לְשֵׁם פְּעוּלַת הַצָּלָה, בִּהְיוֹת וּלְמַעֲשֶׂה הוּא יַהֲרוֹג עַל יְדֵי כֵן
בְּוַדָּאוּת אֶת הַיָּחִיד.

**RABBI ELIEZER YEHUDAH WALDENBERG
1915–2006**

Noted halachic authority. Rabbi Waldenberg served as a judge on the Supreme Rabbinical Court in Jerusalem and was known as an eminent authority on Jewish medical ethics and Jewish law. He published his halachic responsa, *Tsits Eliezer,* which is viewed as one of the great achievements of halachic scholarship of the 20th century. He served as rabbi for the Shaare Zedek Medical Center in Jerusalem.

A driver suddenly encounters many people who are crossing the street. The only way to save these people would be to shift into reverse, but behind the vehicle there is one person who would definitely be killed by this. What should the driver do? Should the driver remain passive, killing the people in front of the car, or should the driver change course and kill the single person behind the car?

According to our analysis, the driver should remain passive. . . . The driver should not perform any act of commission. It makes no difference that the driver's intention in reversing is not to kill the one person but to save the larger number of people, because ultimately, the driver's act will in actual fact cause a death.

Figure 5.2

The Driver's Dilemma

	CASE	DIRECTIVE	RESULT
Case Study A	Driver notices pedestrian ahead. There is a brick wall on each side of the road.	Do not turn	Driver is saved
Case Study B	Driver notices construction barrier ahead. There is one pedestrian on each side.	Do not turn	Pedestrians are saved
Case Study C	Driver notices ten pedestrians ahead. There is one pedestrian on each side of the road.	Do not turn	Pedestrians on the side of the road are saved

TEXT 9

MISHNAH, SANHEDRIN 4:5

הֱווּ יוֹדְעִין שֶׁלֹּא כְּדִינֵי מָמוֹנוֹת דִּינֵי נְפָשׁוֹת. דִּינֵי מָמוֹנוֹת אָדָם נוֹתֵן מָמוֹן
וּמִתְכַּפֵּר לוֹ. דִּינֵי נְפָשׁוֹת, דָּמוֹ וְדַם זַרְעִיּוֹתָיו תְּלוּיִין בּוֹ עַד סוֹף הָעוֹלָם.
שֶׁכֵּן מָצִינוּ בְּקַיִן שֶׁהָרַג אֶת אָחִיו, שֶׁנֶּאֱמַר (בְּרֵאשִׁית ד, י) "דְּמֵי אָחִיךָ
צֹעֲקִים", אֵינוֹ אוֹמֵר "דַּם אָחִיךָ" אֶלָּא "דְּמֵי אָחִיךָ" - דָּמוֹ וְדַם זַרְעִיּוֹתָיו.

Know that capital cases are not like monetary cases. In civil suits, you can make monetary restitution [if you testify falsely] and thereby gain atonement; but [for testifying falsely] in capital cases, you are held responsible for the accused's life and the lives of the accused's unborn descendants until the end of time.

Thus, we find in the case of Cain who killed his brother Abel that it is written, "The bloods of thy brother cry unto Me" (GENESIS 4:10). It does not say "the blood of thy brother," but "bloods"—referring to Abel's blood and the blood of his unborn descendants.

MISHNAH

The first authoritative work of Jewish law that was codified in writing. The Mishnah contains the oral traditions that were passed down from teacher to student; it supplements, clarifies, and systematizes the commandments of the Torah. Due to the continual persecution of the Jewish people, it became increasingly difficult to guarantee that these traditions would not be forgotten. Rabbi Yehudah Hanasi therefore redacted the Mishnah at the end of the 2nd century. It serves as the foundation for the Talmud.

TEXT 10

RABBI JONATHAN SACKS, "THE PRACTICAL IMPLICATIONS OF INFINITY," *TO TOUCH THE DIVINE* (BROOKLYN, N.Y.: MERKOS L'INYONEI CHINUCH, 1989), PP. 83–84

Finitude is quantifiable, infinity is not.

If human life is very precious, and yet still finite in its value, then there is a difference between one man dying and many. And this difference makes it sometimes—*in extremis*—justifiable to sacrifice the one for the sake of the many. . . .

[But] each individual life is literally infinite. . . . And infinity cannot be quantified. Infinity times one and infinity times one hundred are the same. So devastating is the loss of a single life that the enormity is infinite. And as between the death of one and the death of many there can be no calculations. This total refusal to enter into any quantification where "one Jewish soul" is concerned is the strict consequence of taking infinity with absolute seriousness.

RABBI JONATHAN SACKS, PHD
1948–

Former chief rabbi of the United Kingdom. Rabbi Sacks attended Cambridge University and received his doctorate from King's College, London. A prolific and influential author, his books include *Will We Have Jewish Grandchildren?* and *The Dignity of Difference*. He received the Jerusalem Prize in 1995 for his contributions to enhancing Jewish life in the Diaspora, was knighted and made a life peer in 2005, and became Baron Sacks of Aldridge in 2009.

KEY POINTS

1 Your life takes precedence over the life of another. Hence, if you have a single bottle of water, enough to save only one person, and you and a friend are dying of thirst, you are permitted to keep the water for yourself.

2 One may not actively kill another person in order to save his or her own life, even if the potential victim is elderly and with little quality of life. To say that one's life is more valuable than another's, and to use this reasoning to kill another, is arrogant and immoral.

3 If an enemy threatens to kill an entire group, but would be mollified if a random innocent person were surrendered, the group may not surrender one person to save the rest. This teaches us to what extent we must avoid being an accomplice to murder. It also reminds us about the infinite worth of each individual life.

4 If a driver is about to crash into a barrier, which would result in the driver's death, it is forbidden for the driver to swerve and kill a pedestrian in order to save him- or herself.

5 If a driver is about to hit a pedestrian, and the only way to avoid this is to turn toward a barrier that would kill the driver, the driver should not take this turn.

6 If a driver is about to hit a group of pedestrians, and there is an option to swerve and kill one pedestrian instead, the driver should not take this turn.

7 Our tentative halachic conclusion is that when faced with these types of dilemmas, the algorithm of an autonomous vehicle should take the path of least intervention and shut down.

8 It would be permissible to purchase a car that is programmed to save the greatest number of people, even if this is not the optimal way of programming the car. This is because the likelihood of such a scenario occurring is extremely remote.

Continue your learning experience

ONLINE

Visit www.myJLI.com/dilemma5 for insightful and inspiring videos, articles, and readings on this topic.

Additional Readings

ROBOT ETHICS AND SELF-DRIVING CARS
HOW ETHICAL DETERMINATIONS IN SOFTWARE WILL REQUIRE A NEW LEGAL FRAMEWORK

NICK BELAY

I. Introduction

Automated decision making in vehicles has played an increasing role in transportation as technology has yielded improvements to machine learning, sensing, and processing.[1] Today, cars perform complex tasks related to braking, steering, and object detection, often without the awareness of the driver.[2] Multiple major automotive companies already plan on releasing technologies that allow for hands-free driving assistance in the next couple of model years.[3] Indeed, Google—one of the leading companies in self-driving cars—has publicly stated its intention to bring entirely autonomous cars to consumer markets within the next five years.[4]

Once considered science fiction, self-driving cars are becoming more of a reality every day.[5] However, along with the numerous benefits to convenience and safety,[6] these new technologies pose major ethical dilemmas.[7] Perhaps most notably, machines will have to make decisions regarding whom to save or protect in the event of a collision or unforeseen obstacle.[8] Inseparable from these ethical considerations is the issue of legal liability,[9] for whoever dictates the car's behavior in these situations will also most likely be subject to the liability surrounding the outcome.[10] This article aims to survey the various approaches to the legal and ethical aspects of self-driving cars and offer the best strategy going forward to meet these considerations without deterring innovation in the market.

NICK BELAY

J.D. Candidate at the University of Alabama School of Law. His previous experience includes working for the US Environmental Protection Agency. He now resides in Tuscaloosa, Alabama.

II. The Trolley Problem Comparison

Consider the following classic thought experiment in ethics: A runaway trolley is barreling down the tracks towards five unsuspecting railroad workers and will kill them if nothing is done.[11] Watching from a distance, you see a lever positioned next to you.[12] If you pull this lever, the trolley will switch to a separate set of tracks.[13] You notice, however, that the alternative tracks have a single railroad worker on them.[14] Your options are to either: 1) do nothing and allow the trolley to kill the five workers; or 2) pull the lever to divert the trolley and kill the one worker.[15] The experiment illustrates the difficult distinction between affirmative action that *causes* one death vs. "letting circumstance lie" and *allowing* five.[16]

A number of answers and justifications exist to this dilemma, known as "The Trolley Problem,"[17] dependent on one's personal moral values. According to a psychology study conducted at Michigan State University, roughly 90% of individuals would choose to kill the one worker instead of the five.[18] However, altering the scenario slightly (i.e., instead of switching the track, you would have to push a bystander in front of the train to save the five people) yields a far less confident response, despite the end result being the same.[19] This variability makes it difficult to determine a consistent ethically "correct" course of action. Certainly from a utilitarian perspective, saving five people outweighs the cost of losing one.[20] However, what if, for example, the one is a child and the others are adults?[21] Five adults might provide a higher net utility than one child, but western society often places a high moral value on saving the latter.[22] Moreover, at what point does general welfare impede on notions of personal liberty? The deaths of the five men can be characterized as a product of external factors (the trolley);[23] pulling the lever, however, would directly cause a person to die where he otherwise would not have.[24]

These are the sorts of considerations that both companies developing self-driving cars and their stakeholders will have to solve in order to curb liability and remain ethically sound. In fact, manufacturers of self-driving cars may even face a more difficult situation than that of the Trolley Problem due to the decision being premeditated.[25] In the case of a human, tort law provides a malleable scale of accountability for negligence cases (the Reasonable Person Standard)[26] to determine whether an individual fell short of his duty to others.[27] This test takes into account limitations in a human's ability to make the best decision given the specific circumstances (e.g., stress, time to react, etc.).[28] In the case of self-driving cars, however, the machine makes decisions based on the algorithms coded into its software.[29] Which is to say, the car will react in accordance to how the manufacturer predetermined it should react in those circumstances.[30]

Imagine a scenario where a child runs in front of a car approaching a tunnel.[31] The options are to either hit and kill the child or swerve into the wall and kill the driver.[32] Or perhaps there is a scenario where a dog runs in front of the car.[33] To what degree should the car attempt to swerve (and potentially endanger the driver or others) in order to avoid the dog? Does it make a difference if it is a squirrel?[34] Or perhaps there is a scenario where a human driver would ethically be justified in breaking the law, like a husband rushing his wife who is in labor to the hospital.[35] Should the car take such situations into account when determining its behavior? It may be tempting to conclude that self-driving cars will encounter these situations so infrequently that they hardly pose an issue.[36] However, by nature of operating in imperfect systems filled with human drivers, pedestrians, and animals that behave unpredictably, autonomous vehicles encountering these ethical calculations is all but guaranteed.[37] Thus, as long as there exists even the slightest possibility that a self-driving car will have to make an ethical decision, programmers will have to account for the various choices and moral reasoning in the car's software.[38]

On a systemic level, this raises the question of who exactly should have the power to determine who lives and who dies or else who will suffer injury to self or property. Should it lie in the legislature in the form of laws and policy that detail whom exactly to save? Should it be left up to the manufacturer of the machine in question? Should it minimize damage from an insurer's point of view? Or, ultimately, perhaps it should rest with the individual. While laws regarding automated cars are currently scarce,[39] an application of legal ethics from established areas of law, like tort law, provides a framework to guide early law and policy as we move into the inevitable future of AI/Human interaction.

III. Examining the Assignment of Responsibility (Legal and Ethical) for the Decisions Made by Machines
A. The Manufacturer

Perhaps the most obvious choice to determine the behavior of self-driving cars in ethical situations is the manufacturer. This designation would be consistent under traditional product liability notions where the manufacturer is "ultimately responsible for the final product."[40] That is, if there is a design defect within the control of the manufacturer that leads to some sort of harm, and the manufacturer knew or should have known of the defect, then they are going to be liable for the harm.[41] This raises the issue, however, as to whether an ethical determination that very well could have been made by a human driver in the same situation can be considered a "defect" so as to impose product liability. While tort law varies by state,[42] a majority of courts follow a similar two-part test for design defects as laid out by the California Supreme Court:[43]

> First, a product may be found defective in design if the plaintiff establishes that the product failed to perform as safely as an ordinary consumer would expect when used in an intended or reasonably foreseeable manner. Second, a product may alternatively be found defective in design if the plaintiff demonstrates that the product's design proximately caused his injury and the defendant fails

to establish, in light of the relevant factors, that, on balance the benefits of the challenged design outweigh the risk of danger inherent in such design.[44]

Under this reasoning, a plaintiff would have a difficult time proving the second test given the benefits detailed previously in this article;[45] however, a plaintiff could have a case for the first test depending on the circumstances. For example, if the manufacturer programmed the car to minimize overall damage, which resulted in the car injuring the driver instead of multiple pedestrians, this result might be contrary to an ordinary consumer's expectation that a product would protect the owner first and foremost. In fact, according to a survey conducted by the Open Roboethics Initiative,[46] roughly 64% of people polled would prefer the car to protect their lives and those of their passengers before a pedestrian's.[47]

From an ethical standpoint, a manufacturer would likely have to apply a one-size-fits-all set of behaviors that may be inconsistent with those of the user.[48] For example, the manufacturer might program the car to always try to protect the driver seat,[49] but one can imagine a scenario where the driver would rather protect their significant other or child in the passenger seat. Or alternatively, the car might be programmed to save a pedestrian over a passenger when a human might value the opposite.[50] Such a system would subject the user to the values of the manufacturer, creating a situation where "cars [would] not respect drivers' autonomous preferences in . . . deeply personal moral situations."[51]

Ultimately, however, the reasoning against making the manufacturer responsible might be much more grounded: if the manufacturer were responsible for all the ethical decisions of a self-driving car, "the liability burden on the manufacturer may be prohibitive of further development."[52] This would potentially deter manufacturers from developing the autonomous vehicle altogether—a socially undesirable result.[53]

B. The Individual

If not the manufacturer, perhaps the next most intuitive party to hold responsibility over the vehicle's actions is the individual owner/user.[54] This designation would be consistent with the already well-established concept of liability resting with the driver.[55] However, as the "driver" in self-driving cars will have theoretically no role in the decision making process,[56] assigning liability will surpass the traditional negligence standard associated with vehicles in favor of strict liability.[57] Such a system would remove significant ambiguity from the legal side, but is it too much to ask a driver to potentially face full liability for the moral decisions of the car?

Holding the driver responsible creates two major issues that could cripple the self-driving car from ever taking hold. First, a strict liability standard would create a strong disincentive against individuals adopting the new technology. How many people would consistently agree to be at the mercy of liability they do not control, especially when said liability could potentially deal with significant damages to life or property? Strict liability operates best as a deterrent against a specific behavior,[58] whereas negligence encourages a greater level of care when conducting that behavior.[59] Assuming that self-driving cars are a societally desirable change, as this article does, strict liability would not make sense as the controlling standard. Moreover, strict liability for the driver would (at least in part) remove incentives for the manufacturer to program smart decisions, as the manufacturer would share none of the risk associated with those decisions.[60]

One counterargument might be that driving is already essentially a strict liability activity.[61] Statistically, the average driver is likely to have a collision roughly once every 17.9 years.[62] Thus, just by engaging in the activity a driver is agreeing to be liable at some point. Under this rationale, the assignment of liability would not be based on the end result but rather the risk created merely by entering a car (driverless or otherwise).[63] Under such a model, owners of self-driving cars would share the responsibility of the risks the car creates.[64] This result could be achieved through some sort of tax or mandatory insurance.[65] The problem with this position, however, is that it ignores the idea of being morally "blameworthy" currently attributed to driving liability.[66] Even if a traditional driver's fault in an accident is inevitable,[67] the reprehensible conduct that led to that specific accident still would exist.[68]

The other issue is that the driver would be liable for the decisions of the manufacturer but shares no role in determining the ethical values of those decisions.[69] One possible solution would be to allow the driver to determine the ethical priorities of the car through a system of adjustable ethics.[70] Thus, the users of self-driving cars would be able to customize their car to reflect their own personal moral values.[71] In a poll by the Open Roboethics Initiative, 44% of respondents said the passengers in the vehicle should control how it responds in ethical situations.[72] Moreover, adjustable ethics might carry the added bonus of making consumers feel more comfortable holding end liability. Still, such a system would not be without drawbacks: it would create a level of unpredictability among self-driving cars, as each would behave uniquely depending on the specific ethics of the user. This might mirror more traditional driving today, but would potentially lessen the safety and efficiency benefits that come with self-driving cars being predictable to both other cars and the environment.[73]

The simplest solution to both the ethical and legal side of individual responsibility might be to require that a driver always be behind the wheel and ready to take over in emergency situations.[74] Under this "duty to intervene" model, the liability would be based on the driver's failure to pay attention and take over when necessary.[75] This model would mirror the traditional decision making process made currently by drivers, thus both making liability clear and removing the need for machines to make ethical determinations in place of a human driver.[76] In fact, such a requirement is already consistent with current legislation regarding self-driving cars requiring an operator present in the driver's seat.[77]

However, this model poses multiple practical issues. First, requiring an operator would eliminate much of the consumer appeal of a self-driving car.[78] Not only would this make impossible the comfortable notion of reading or browsing the internet while your car drives you to a destination,[79] but it would also prevent self-driving cars from performing one of their largest selling points: being controlled remotely.[80] For example, a consumer would not be able to use the car for tasks like sending it to pick up a child from school[81] or bringing someone home from a bar.[82] Second, a duty to intervene assumes the capability of humans to properly recognize dangers and react in time—something that may not be possible given the split-second in which a collision can present itself.[83] Further, even if a person could react in time, there would be no guarantee that the reaction would be desirable.[84] After all, approximately 90% of all accidents are caused by human error.[85] Moreover, users may overreact to avoid liability and create risk where there otherwise would have been none;[86] for example, if an operator mistakenly believes the car to be nearing a collision and swerves into traffic in response. For these reasons, requiring a duty to intervene may serve as a functional legal tool while the technology behind self-driving cars is still being explored but does not offer a long-term solution.

C. The Insurer

If the aim is to maximize total welfare for society, then attributing responsibility to the insurer of a self-driving car seems to effectively produce that prima facie result. One of the fundamental tenets of an insurance provider is to pool risk and minimize loss.[87] This goal falls in line with traditional utilitarian theory,[88] which finds that actions that increase total utility are morally justified.[89] Thus, a self-driving car under an insurer's influence will always choose the "lesser of two evils" from an economic standpoint. Moreover, strong statistical evidence and a repeat presence place insurance providers in an advantageous position to justify a car's behavior from a liability standpoint.[90]

Two main issues, however, surround the insurer as the responsible party—one moral and one practical. The moral issue remains the same as previously discussed: why should the owner of a vehicle be subject to the ethical values of some other entity when there exists no morally "right" answer?[91] Or from a pedestrian's perspective, why should a working class individual be targeted over a corporate executive in the event the car has to hit one? Certainly, the latter provides greater overall economic utility, but does this not infringe upon the rights of the individual?[92]

One does not have to entirely rely on the moralistic argument, for there is a practical reason a utilitarian perspective does not work for self-driving cars. Namely, it would create improper incentives.[93] An automated car that aims to minimize overall damage will target people and objects that are less likely to suffer costly injuries. Thus, the self-driving car would choose to swerve into a car with high safety ratings rather than one with low safety ratings. Or the car would choose to hit the cyclist wearing a helmet over one without. In effect, this would create an environment where people were placed at greater risk of personal or economic harm because they took more responsible safety measures—the opposite of a societally desired effect.

D. The Legislature

Ultimately, the legislature may be in the best position to meet the legal and ethical demands of self-driving cars. Indeed, self-driving cars are not entirely unique in posing new issues on these fronts. The shift from horse and buggy to cars, for example, posed its own set of legal and ethical challenges.[94] Without transitionary laws, liability would have been too great for automobiles to take hold,[95] thus highlighting an additional consideration when assigning responsibility: the existence of a *transitional* period.[96] Many of the ethical and legal issues surrounding self-driving cars will become significantly less pressing as more and more people adopt self-driving cars.[97] According to the Eno Center for Transportation,[98] as many as 4.2 million accidents could be avoided if 90% of vehicles in the U.S. were self-driving.[99] Moreover, roughly $450 billion could be saved in related costs.[100] While unpredictable behavior from pedestrians and animals would still exist, accidents among passenger vehicles (estimated at 65% of all automobile related deaths)[101] pose the largest issue to safety going forward.[102] Therefore, the focus in the present should be on minimizing liability for manufactures and consumers to incentivize early adopters and allow the market to grow to the amount ideal for safety and utility.

IV. Framing a Legislative Solution

The key to accomplishing these goals will be consistency in behavior, so the legislature needs to determine a consistent code by which all self-driving cars abide. The idea being that uniformity will relieve the manufacturer and consumer from large lawsuits contingent on how their one car in particular behaved.[103] In line with this reasoning, the legislature should determine that all self-driving cars must act in the *interest of their passengers* over anything else. The idea of self-preservation is both ethically neutral and societally accepted.[104] Moreover, it is consistent with current tort law that does not favor an affirmative duty to risk one's own well-being for others.[105] Further, the legislatures should consider the application of a "reasonableness standard" to machines making decisions. While certainly people's expectation of machines is to act perfectly according to programming, it is unrealistic given the current limitations in computer science and sensory hardware to expect a self-driving car to always execute the best decision in a complex environment.[106] The application of a reasonableness standard will allow for situational flexibility as a way of limiting liability as the technology improves.

Overall, an ideal painless solution to the ethical and legal issues posed by self-driving cars may not exist. If we are to see this future become a reality, however, consistent behavior and limited liability is a necessity as we transition away from human-controlled vehicles.

The Journal of the Legal Profession, 40 (Fall 2015), pp. 119–130
Reprinted with permission of the publisher

Endnotes
[1] *See* Noah J. Goodall, "Machine Ethics and Automated Vehicles," *Road Vehicle Automation*, (Gereon Meyer & Sven Beiker, eds., Springer International Publishing, 2014), p. 93.
[2] *See* Russ Heaps, "8 Great New Advances in Auto Technology," *Bankrate* (May 27, 2009), http://www.bankrate.com/finance/money-guides/8-great-new-advances-in-auto-technology-1.aspx.
[3] *See, e.g.*, C.C. Weiss, "Cadillac to Introduce Automated Driving and Vehicle-to-Vehicle Tech in 2016," *Gizmag* (Sept. 12, 2014), http://www.gizmag.com/cadillac-super-cruise-v2v-2016/33769/.
[4] Donna Tam, "Google's Sergey Brin: You'll Ride in Robot Cars within 5 Years," *CNET* (Sept. 25, 2012, 2:01 PM), http://www.cnet.com/news/googles-sergey-brin-youll-ride-in-robot-cars-within-5-years/.
[5] *See* "Self-Driving Cars Coming to a Street near You," *The Economist* (Sept. 18, 2014), http://www.economist.com/news/business-and-finance/21618531-making-autonomous-vehicles-reality-coming-street-near-you.
[6] *See* Don Howard, "Robots on the Road: The Moral Imperative of the Driverless Car," *Sci. Matters* (Nov. 13, 2014), http://

donhoward-blog.nd.edu/2013/11/07/robots-on-the-road-the-moral-imperative-of-the-driverless-car/#.VGVY6FfF8QS; *See also* Christopher Mims, "The Potential Benefits of Driverless Cars Are Stunning," *Quartz* (Oct. 22, 2013), http://qz.com/138367/the-potential-benefits-of-driverless-cars-are-stunning/.

[7] *See* Adam Gopnik, "A Point of View: The Ethics of the Driverless Car," *BBC News Magazine*, http://www.bbc.com/news/magazine-25861214 (last updated Jan. 24, 2014).

[8] *Id.*, *supra* note 7.

[9] *See* Alexis C. Madrigal, "If a Self-Driving Car Gets in an Accident, Who—or What—Is Liable?," *The Atlantic* (Aug. 13, 2014), http://www.theatlantic.com/technology/archive/2014/08/if-a-self-driving-car-gets-in-an-accident-who-is-legally-liable/375569/ [hereinafter "If a Self-Driving Car Gets in an Accident"].

[10] *Id.*, *supra* note 9.

[11] Judith J. Thomson, "The Trolley Problem," 94 *Yale Law Journal*, 1395–96 (1985).

[12] *Id.*, *supra* note 11.

[13] *Id.*

[14] *Id.*

[15] *Id.*

[16] *Id.* at 1396–97.

[17] *Id.*, *supra* note 11, at 1395.

[18] David C. Navarrete et al., "Virtual Morality: Emotion and Action in a Simulated Three-Dimensional 'Trolley Problem,'" 12 *Emotion* 364, 367 (2012).

[19] *See* Thomson, *supra* note 11, at 1409–10.

[20] *Id.* at 1408.

[21] *Id.* at 1405.

[22] *See generally* Viviana A. Zelizer, *Pricing the Priceless Child: The Changing Social Value of Children* 22–58 (Princeton U. Press, 1994).

[23] *See* Thomson, *supra* note 110, at 1397.

[24] *Id.* at 1395–96.

[25] *See* Patrick Lin, "The Ethics of Autonomous Cars," *The Atlantic* (Oct. 8, 2013), http://www.theatlantic.com/technology/archive/2013/10/the-ethics-of-autonomous-cars/280360/?single_page=true.

[26] *Restatement (Second) of Torts*, § 283 (1965).

[27] *See Restatement (Third) of Torts*, § 7 (2010).

[28] *See Restatement (Second) of Torts*, § 283 (1965).

[29] Alexis C. Madrigal, "The Trick That Makes Google's Self-Driving Cars Work," *The Atlantic* (May 15, 2014), http://www.theatlantic.com/technology/archive/2014/05/all-the-world-atrack-the-trick-that-makes-googles-self-driving-cars-work/370871/ [hereinafter "The Trick"].

[30] *See* "The Trick," *supra* note 29.

[31] *See* Jason Millar, "Should Your Robot Driver Kill You to Save a Child's Life?," *The Conversation* (Aug. 1, 2014), http://theconversation.com/should-your-robot-driver-kill-you-to-save-a-childs-life-29926.

[32] *Id.*, *supra* note 31.

[33] *See* Gopnik, *supra* note 7.

[34] *See id.*

[35] Dave Dickinson, "5 Issues Concerning Driverless Cars," *Listosaur* (Nov. 27, 2014), http://listosaur.com/science-a-technology/5-issues-concerning-driverless-cars/.

[36] *See* Goodall, *supra* note 1, at 94–98.

[37] *See id.*

[38] *See id.*

[39] *See id.* at 97.

[40] Gary E. Marchant and Rachel A. Lindor, "The Coming Collision between Autonomous Vehicles and the Liability System," 52 *Santa Clara Law Review* 1321, 1329 (2012).

[41] *See id.*, *supra* note 40, at 1329.

[42] *See* Thomson Reuters, *50 State Statutory Surveys: Civil Laws: Torts*, 0020 Surveys 29 (Westlaw) (2015).

[43] *See id.*, *supra* note 42.

[44] Barker v. Lull Engineering Co., 573 P.2d 443, 455-56 (1978).

[45] *See* "Self-Driving Cars Coming to a Street near You," *supra* note 5.

[46] Open Roboethics Initiative, http://robohub.org/author/ori/ (last visited Nov. 13, 2014).

[47] Open Roboethics Initiative, "If Death by Autonomous Car Is Unavoidable, Who Should Die? Reader Poll Results," *Robohub* (June 23, 2014), http://robohub.org/if-a-death-by-an-autonomous-car-is-unavoidable-who-should-die-results-from-our-reader-poll/.

[48] *See* Millar, *supra* note 31.

[49] *See* Kyle Stock, "The Problem with Self-Driving Cars: They Don't Cry," *Bloomberg Business Week* (April 03, 2014), http://www.businessweek.com/articles/2014-04-03/the-problem-with-self-driving-cars-they-dont-cry.

[50] *See id.*, *supra* note 49.

[51] Millar, *supra* note 31.

[52] Marchant and Lindor, *supra* note 40, at 1334.

[53] *See id.*

[54] Alexander Hevelke and Julian Nida-Rümelin, "Responsibility for Crashes of Autonomous Vehicles: An Ethical Analysis," *Science and Engineering Ethics* 620, 623–627 (June 11, 2014), *available at* http://link.springer.com/article/10.1007%2Fs11948-014-9565-5.

[55] Tim Worstall, "When Should Your Driverless Car from Google Be Allowed to Kill You?," *Forbes* (June 18, 2014), http://www.forbes.com/sites/timworstall/2014/06/18/when-should-your-driverless-car-from-google-be-allowed-to-kill-you/.

[56] *See* Samuel Gibbs, "Google's Self-Driving Car: How Does It Work and When Can We Drive One?," *The Guardian* (May 29, 2014), http://www.theguardian.com/technology/2014/may/28/google-self-driving-car-how-does-it-work.

[57] *See generally* Hans-Bernd Schäfer and Andreas Schönenberger, *Strict Liability Versus Negligence* (Munich Pers. RePEc Archive, Working Paper No. 5, 2008), *available at* http://mpra.ub.uni-muenchen.de/40195/1/MPRA_paper_40195.pdf.

[58] *See id.*, *supra* note 57, at 6–8.

[59] *See id.* at 6.

[60] *See* Lin, *supra* note 25.

[61] *See* Worstall, *supra* note 55.

[62] Des Toups, "How Many Times Will You Crash Your Car?," *Forbes* (July 27, 2011), http://www.forbes.com/sites/moneybuilder/2011/07/27/how-many-times-will-you-crash-your-car/.

[63] Hevelke and Nida-Rümelin, *supra* note 54, at 626–627.

[64] *Id.* at 626.

[65] *Id.* at 626–627.

[66] *Id.* at 627.

[67] *See* Toups, *supra* note 62.

[68] Hevelke and Nida-Rümelin, *supra* note 54, at 627.

[69] *See id.* at 626–627.

[70] David Tuffley, "Self-Driving Cars Need 'Adjustable Ethics' Set by Owners," *The Conversation* (Aug. 24, 2014), http://theconversation.com/self-driving-cars-need-adjustable-ethics-set-by-owners-30656.

[71] *Id.*, *supra* note 70.

[72] Open Roboethics Initiative, *supra* note 46.

73 *See* Howard, *supra* note 6.

74 *See* Hevelke and Nida-Rümelin, *supra* note 54, at 623–624.

75 *Id.*

76 *See id.*

77 *Cal. Veh. Code* § 38750(b)(2) (West 2015).

78 Hevelke and Nida-Rümelin, *supra* note 54, at 624.

79 *See* Sherry Stokes, *Consumers Expect to Use Mobile Devices, Read and Eat in Self-Driving Cars of Tomorrow*, Carnegie Mellon University (Jan. 22, 2015), http://engineering.cmu.edu/media/press/2015/01_22_autonomous_vehicle_survey.html.

80 *See* Kevin Maney, "Google Has Shown That Self-Driving Cars Are Inevitable—and the Possibilities Are Endless," *The Independent* (June 18, 2014), http://www.independent.co.uk/lifestyle/motoring/features/google-has-shown-that-self-driving-cars-are-inevitable — and-the-possibilities-are-endless-9547231.html.

81 Hevelke & Nida-Rümelin, supra note 54, at 624.

82 *Id.*

83 *Id.*

84 *See* Bryant W. Smith, "Human Error as a Cause of Vehicle Crashes," *The Center for Internet and Society* (Dec. 18, 2013), http://cyber-law.stanford.edu/blog/2013/12/human-error-cause-vehicle-crashes.

85 *Id., supra* note 84, at 624.

86 *See* Hevelke and Nida-Rümelin

87 Brian Boone, "How Auto Insurance Companies Work," *Howstuffworks* (May 30, 2012), http://money.howstuffworks.com/personal-finance/auto-insurance/auto-insurance-company2.htm.

88 "Utilitarianism." *BusinessDictionary.com.*, WebFinance, Inc., http://www.businessdictionary.com/definition/utilitarianism.html (last visited Nov. 13, 2014) [defined as "(a)n ethical philosophy in which the happiness of the greatest number of people in the society is considered the greatest good. According to this philosophy, an action is morally right if its consequences lead to happiness (absence of pain), and wrong if it ends in unhappiness (pain)"].

89 *See generally* John C. Harsanyi, "Morality and the Theory of Rational Behavior," in *Utilitarianism and Beyond* 39, 62 (Amartya Sen and Bernard Williams, Cambridge U. Press, 1982).

90 "Self-Driving Cars and Insurance," *Insurance Information Institute* (Feb. 2015), http://www.iii.org/issue-update/self-driving-cars-and-insurance.

91 *See* Tuffley, *supra* note 70.

92 *See id.*

93 *See id.*

94 *See generally* Eric Morris, *From Horse to Horsepower: The External Costs of Transportation in the 19th Century City* (2006) (M.A. Thesis, UCLA), *available at* http://www.uctc.net/access/30/Access%2030%20-%2002%20-%20Horse%20Power.pdf.

95 Morris, *supra* note 94.

96 *See id.*

97 Phil LeBeau, "Take the Wheel Please, I'm Done Driving," *CNBC* (Aug. 18, 2014), http://www.cnbc.com/id/101913796#.

98 *Eno Center for Transportation*, https://www.enotrans.org/ (last visited Nov. 13, 2014).

99 "Preparing a Nation for Autonomous Vehicles," *Eno Center for Transportation* 8 (Oct. 2013), https://www.enotrans.org/wp-content/uploads/wpsc/downloadables/AV-paper.pdf.

100 "Preparing a Nation for Autonomous Vehicles," *supra* note 99, at 17.

101 NHTSA, *2012 Motor Vehicle Crashes: Overview*, U.S. Department of Transportation (2012), http://wwwnrd.nhtsa.dot.gov/Pubs/811856.pdf.

102 NHTSA, *supra* note 101, at 8.

103 *See* Hevelke and Nida-Rümelin, *supra* note 54, at 629.

104 *See* Erich Fromm, *Man for Himself: An Inquiry into the Psychology of Ethics* 19 (Open Road Media, 2013).

105 *Restatement (Third) of Torts*, § 7 (2010).

106 *See* Lin, *supra* note 24; *See also* Stock, *supra* note 49.

SACRIFICING THE FEW TO SAVE THE MANY

RABBI J. DAVID BLEICH

...for one life is not set aside for another
OHOLOT 7:6

The date 9/11 is indelibly imprinted upon the national consciousness of America. The horrific loss of life in the terrorist attacks upon the Twin Towers of the World Trade Center was an unforgettable tragedy; the attack upon the Pentagon, the nerve-center of military security, exposed the vulnerability of the nation's defense apparatus. But it was the fourth, thwarted, attack that is remembered for the heroism of the victims.

A domestic passenger flight flying from Newark International Airport to San Francisco, United Airlines Flight 93, was hijacked by terrorists some forty-five minutes into the flight. The hijackers breached the cockpit, overpowered the pilots and, taking control of the aircraft, directed it towards Washington, D.C. The hijackers' intended target is thought to have been the White House or possibly the Capitol.

The terrorists' master plan apparently called for carrying out that attack simultaneously with the attacks upon the World Trade Center and the Pentagon. However, due to airport congestion, the airplane was delayed on the ground more than half an hour. During the course of the hijacking, flight attendants and passengers, using GTE air phones and cell phones succeeded in making numerous calls to family and friends as a result of which they learned of the other terrorist attacks.

The passengers, apparently on the basis of a vote, determined to seize the controls of the plane from the hijackers. Of the ensuing events little is known with

certainty. Early reports conjectured that the passengers were successful in overtaking the plane and that they knowingly caused the plane to crash in order to prevent greater loss of life. Strikingly, the mother of one of the passengers, herself a United Airlines flight attendant, left a message on her son's cell phone urging an attempt to take over the aircraft. Much later, a report issued by a government investigating commission gave no indication that the passengers broke through the cockpit door but made it clear that the passengers' actions thwarted the plans of the terrorists. Recordings of the cockpit conversations reveal that the terrorists feared that they would imminently lose control and debated whether to crash the plane immediately or whether to delay such action. The passengers' death certificates state the cause as homicide and those of the hijackers list suicide as a cause of death. It is unclear whether the hijackers ultimately did crash the plane deliberately or whether they simply lost control. Had the passengers been successful in gaining control of the plane, the ending might well have been much happier. Among the passengers was an aviation executive who had extensive experience in a cockpit as a private pilot. Another passenger was experienced as an air traffic controller with the Air National Guard. Given those facts, there is scant reason to question the halakhic propriety of the course of action taken by the passengers.

Far more complex is the issue of purposely shooting down the plane and thereby causing the death of the innocent passengers.[1] Air Force and Air National Guard fighter jets were unable to intercept the planes headed to the World Trade Center and the Pentagon but indications are that they would have reached the fourth plane in time to prevent it from reaching Washington. The option of shooting down the commercial jet was certainly given serious consideration and a decision to do so may actually have been reached.

The propriety of purposely causing the immediate death of the passengers aboard the plane in order to prevent further loss of life hinges upon the

RABBI J. DAVID BLEICH

Expert on Jewish law, ethics, and bioethics. Rabbi Bleich serves as professor of Talmud at the Rabbi Isaac Elchanan Theological Seminary, an affiliate of Yeshiva University, as well as head of its postgraduate institute for the study of Talmudic jurisprudence and family law. A noted author, he is most famous for his 6-volume Contemporary Halakhic Problems.

applicability of a provision of Halakha recorded by Rambam, *Hilkhot Yesodei ha-Torah* 5:5:

> ...*if the heathen said to them, "Give us one of your company and we shall kill him; if not we will kill all of you," let them all be killed but let them not deliver to them [the heathens] a single Jewish soul. But if they specified [the victim] to them and said, "Give us so and so or we shall kill all of you," if he had incurred the death penalty as Sheba the son of Bichri, they may deliver him to them...but if he has not incurred the death penalty let them all be killed but let them not deliver a single Jewish soul.*

Rambam's ruling is based upon the explication of the narrative of II Samuel 20:4-22 found in the Palestinian Talmud. *Terumot* 8:12. .Joab, commander of King David's troops, had pursued Sheba the son of Bichri and besieged the town of Abel in which Sheba sought refuge. Thereupon Joab demanded that Sheba be delivered to the king's forces; otherwise, Joab threatened to destroy the entire city. On the basis of the verse, "Sheba the son of Bichri has lifted up his hand against the king, against David" (II SAMUEL 20:21), Resh Lakish infers that acquiescence with a demand of such nature can be sanctioned only in instances in which the victim's life is lawfully forfeit, as was the case with regard to Sheba the son of Bichri who is described as being guilty of *lèse majesté*. However, in instances in which the designated victim is guiltless, all must suffer death rather than become accomplices to murder. R. Yohanan maintains that the question of guilt is irrelevant; rather, the crucial factor is the singling out of a specific individual by the oppressor. Members of a group have no right to select one of their number and deliver him to death in order to save their own lives. Since the life of each individual is of inestimable value there is no basis for preferring one life over another. However, once a specific person has been marked for death in any event, either alone if surrendered by his companions or together with the entire group if they refuse to comply, those who deliver him are not to be regarded as accessories. Rambam´s ruling is in accordance with the opinion of Resh Lakish. Both opinions are cited by Rema, *Shulhan Arukh, Yoreh De'ah* 157:1.[2]

Sheba ben Bichri was doomed to die in any event. Since Sheba would perish together with the other inhabitants of the besieged city, refusal to deliver him to the hands of the enemy would have served to spare his life for only a brief period. It is evident that the discussion in the Palestinian Talmud is predicated upon the premise that it is forbidden to cause the loss of even *hayyei sha'ah*, i.e., a brief or limited period of longevity anticipation, of a particular individual in order to preserve the normal longevity anticipation of a multitude of individuals.

Hazon Ish, Gilyonot le-Hiddushei Rabbenu Hayyim ha-Levi, Hilkhot Yesodei ha-Torah 5:1, s.v. *u-mi-kol makom*, demonstrates the same principle on the basis of his analysis of the well-known controversy between R. Akiva and Ben Petura recorded by the Gemara, *Bava Mezi'a* 62a. The case involves two people who are stranded in a desert with but a single container of water. There is sufficient water to sustain one person until he reaches safety; however, if the water is shared, neither will survive. Ben Petura declares that they should share the water and "let not one witness the death of his fellow." R. Akiva rules that the owner of the water should drink it himself in order to save his own life. In support of that ruling R. Akiva cites the verse, "that your brother may live with you" (LEVITICUS 25:36). That biblical command requires that a person enable his brother to live with him but not that he prefer his brother over himself. If so, the life of another person should not be preferred over one's own life with the result, as announced by R. Akiva. That "your life takes precedence."

Hazon Ish, as were others before him, was troubled by the fact that Ben Petura's conflicting ruling is apparently refuted by R. Akiva's quite cogent inference drawn from the verse, "that your brother may live with you"—but not at the expense of your life.[3] Accordingly, *Hazon Ish* asserts that Ben Petura is actually in agreement with the basic principle enunciated by R. Akiva with the result that, in a situation in which only one person can receive any longevity benefit, one's own life takes precedence over that of another. Thus, for example, if two individuals have been poisoned and one of the two is in possession of a sufficient quantity of an antidote to save one person but, if divided, the quantity available will prolong the life of neither, Ben Petura would agree that the owner of the antidote must administer it to himself. Ben Petura would also concede that, if the antidote belongs to a third party, the halakhic rules of triage would apply. Ben Petura, asserts *Hazon Ish*, disagrees only in the case of the container of water because, if the water is shared, the life of each of the stranded persons will be prolonged at least minimally, whereas administering less than the requisite dose of the antidote would be entirely without purpose. Ben Petura, in disagreeing with R. Akiva, does so because he recognizes a duty of rescue with regard to even *hayyei sha'ah*. Since sharing the water serves to prolong the life of both at least minimally, such sharing is an act of loving one's fellow as oneself, i.e., both lives are rendered equal. Put in somewhat different terms, since every moment of life is of infinite value and all infinities are equal, the fact that if one person drinks the entire quantity of water he will survive and enjoy a normal life-span is of no consequence. R. Akiva disagrees in maintaining that loving one's fellow as oneself, but not more than oneself, requires preservation of one's own normal longevity anticipation even if such rescue precludes prolongation of the *hayyei sha'ah* of another.

Consequently, argues *Hazon Ish*, even according to R. Akiva, it is only self-preservation that can excuse ignoring the *hayyei sha'ah* of another. It would then follow that, if the container of water belongs to a third party who is not in danger of perishing as a result of dehydration, that person, even according to R. Akiva, must divide the water equally between the two persons at risk. The principle that emerges is that a person dare not ignore the *hayyei sha'ah* of one putative victim even to carry out the complete rescue of another victim or even of many such victims.[4] *A fortiori*, an overt act having the effect of extinguishing even an ephemeral period of life-anticipation of even a single individual cannot be countenanced in order to save the lives of many.

The only situation in which the life of another individual may be sacrificed in order to rescue a putative victim is the case of *rodef*, or pursuer. In such cases, as codified by Rambam, *Hilkhot Rozeah* 1:9, intervention in order to preserve the life of the victim is mandatory. In the case under discussion, the airplane pilot certainly must be categorized as a *rodef* even though he acts under duress. However, the passengers inside the airplane are in no way complicit in the potential death of the innocent people in the building targeted for destruction. Although the life of the *rodef* is forfeit, provided that taking the life of the *rodef* is necessary in order to rescue the victim, it is not permissible to cause collateral damage in the nature of the death of an innocent third party in eliminating the threat posed by the *rodef*. The pilot, who is intent upon using the airplane to bring death upon innocent victims, may be prevented from doing so even if it is necessary to kill him in order to accomplish that end[5] but it is not permissible to cause the death of innocent passengers who are no more than passive bystanders even for the purpose of preserving the lives of a greater number of people.[6]

Some time ago, Phillippa Foot presented a moral dilemma in formulating the "Trolley Problem."[7] The situation involved the driver of a trolley rounding a bend. Five track workmen are seen to be engaged in repairing the track. The track is surrounded on two sides by a steep mountain and the trolley is travelling much faster than the workmen could possibly run. The driver steps on the brake in order to avoid striking the five men. Tragically, the brakes fail. The driver sees a spur of track in front of him leading off to one side. The driver can quite easily steer the trolley so that it will travel down the spur and thus save the lives of the five men on the track straight ahead. Unfortunately, there is a single workman who is repairing that spur. The workman cannot possibly get off the track before the trolley hits him. If the driver does nothing, five men will perish. If he turns the trolley onto the spur only one person will die but that person is at this moment in no danger whatsoever. Is it morally permissible to turn the trolley so that it claims the life of a single person in order to rescue five individuals?[8]

A situation quite similar to that of the runaway trolley in described by *Hazon Ish, Sanhedrin*, no. 25, *s.v. ve-zeh le-ayyein, Hazon Ish* describes a situation in which a bystander witnesses the release of an arrow aimed at a large group of people. The bystander has the ability to rescue the intended victims by deferring the arrow; however, if he does so, the arrow will claim a single victim who heretofore was endangered in no way whatsoever. *Hazon Ish* expresses doubt with regard to the permissibility of such intervention. If the hypothetical is changed from an arrow to a hand grenade, the moral dilemma acquires contemporary relevance.

Hazon Ish's perplexity seems to be based upon the possibility of considering the situation to be analogous to triage. A person who comes upon multiple innocent victims must perforce choose which of the many victims he will attend. Triage for the purpose of rescue is quite different from selection for death. A person does not have license to designate another individual for death even if his motive is the rescue of a far larger number of lives. However, if the same person can save one, but not all, of the victims, he is required to intervene. In doing so, he is in no way complicit in the death of others. His selection is for rescue rather than for death: acts of rescue are profoundly different from acts of homicide. A person capable of doing do may, and indeed must, save as many lives as possible even if such rescue entails abandoning one or more victims to their fate.

To be sure, in the case of the runaway trolley, the flying arrow, or the hand grenade, the original act to which the ultimate death of the victims is to be attributed was already completed before the moral agent confronts a choice between intervening for the purpose of deflecting a lethal weapon and passive non-intervention. The motive for intervention is certainly the rescue of those who will be saved, not the death of the person who will actually die in their stead. It is, however, difficult to understand how intervention in the form of deflecting a lethal weapon can be regarded as a simple act of rescue governed by principles of triage. In the given hypothetical, it is the act of deflection that endangers a previously unendangered person. The intervener has not simply rescued a larger group of victims; he has in an active, overt manner caused the death of an innocent person. *Hazon Ish* himself emphasizes that even R. Yohanan, who maintains that in the event that the victim has already been designated for execution he may be delivered to the enemy, would agree that one may not actually kill

the designated victim in order to spare other victims. *Hazon Ish* argues that R. Yohanan permits only indirectly hastening the death of a designated victim by delivering him to the enemy but does not sanction a direct act of homicide.[9] It seems to this writer that deflection of a lethal weapon constitutes a direct rather than an indirect act. That objection has been raised by R. Benjamin Rabinowitz—*Te'umim, No'am*, VII (5724), 375.[10] R. Eli'ezer Waldenberg, *Ziz Eli'ezer*, XV, no. 70, addresses *Hazon Ish's* hypothetical and concludes that passive non-intervention is the only acceptable mode of conduct.

Putting that point aside, any argument in support of deflecting the arrow must be based on the premise that a distinction can be drawn between intervention for purposes of neutralizing a direct danger and overt delivery to death in order to ward off future deaths.

There are authorities who, in certain limited cases, permit sacrificing one life to save another when failure to intervene would result in the death of both persons. The question of killing a neonate whose forehead has emerged from the birth canal in order to save the life of the mother when, otherwise, the lives of both would be forfeit is raised by R. Akiva Eger, *Tosafot R. Akiva Eger, Oholot* 7:6, no. 16, but left unresolved. R. Akiva Eger does however cite *Teshuvot Panim Me'irot*, III, no.8, who rules that such a course of action is permissible. R. Israel Lipschutz, *Tiferet Yisra'el, Oholot* 7:6, *Bo'az*, sec. 10, similarly comments that, "perhaps it is permissible to destroy the infant in such circumstances in order to rescue the mother."[11]

R. Saul Mordecai Arieli, *Or Yisra'el*, vol. 8, no.3 (Adar Sheni 5763), compares the case of the airplane seized by terrorists planning to crash it into the Pentagon to the situation of the mother in childbirth in arguing that it is permissible to cause the death of innocent passengers by shooting down the plane since the latter are doomed in any event. Nevertheless, it is virtually self-evident that such a comparison is inapt. If correct, that reasoning should apply as well to the situation described in the Palestinian Talmud in which one person has already been designated for death and failure to deliver him to the enemy will result in the death of all. R. Yohanan and Resh Lakish disagree with regard to whether it is permissible to become even indirectly complicit in the death of the doomed victim by delivering him for execution, but all agree that he may not actively be put to death in order to spare the lives of others.[12] The case of the woman in childbirth is quite different because both mother and child are reciprocal pursuers, i.e., each is in the process of causing the death of the other. Non-intervention is mandated as explained by the Babylonian Talmud, *Sanhedrin* 72b, because "heaven is pursuing her" or, in the words of the Palestinian Talmud, because "you do not know who is pursuing whom." The rationale for non-intervention is either that a natural physiological process is an "act of God," and hence the person who is the instrument of danger cannot be categorized as a pursuer, or that intervention in cases of pursuit is warranted only in order to preserve the life of the victim but in a case of mutual pursuit each party is both victim and aggressor and, consequently, the rule is non-intervention.

The authorities who permit intervention in childbirth do so only because they regard the exception to the law of the pursuer formulated by the Gemara to be limited to activities of mutual aggression in which, barring intervention, one will prevail while the other will perish but the bystander is in no position to determine which of the two will live and which will die. In such situations the understanding that the bystander may not choose between the two is on the basis of the law of pursuit. However, they contend, if in the absence of intervention, both will die, each of the two must be regarded with certainty as being a *rodef*. Accordingly, those authorities regard intervention in order to rescue one of the parties to be permissible since, fundamentally, intervention is for the purpose of eliminating a *rodef* whose life is forfeit. Consequently, they regard intervention as a permissible act of rescue rather than as an act of selection for death. However, it is quite evident that this line of reasoning is not applicable in the case of innocent airplane passengers who are not at all engaged in pursuit. There are no grounds actively to cause the death of passengers in order to save others despite the fact that they, too, are doomed.

Me'iri, *Sanhedrin* 72b, expresses the novel view that, in the case of a woman in "hard travail," although

a third party is barred from destroying the infant in order to save the mother because of inapplicability of the law of pursuit, nevertheless the mother herself may exercise the right of self-defense to save her own life. A similar view is held by R. Joseph Saul Nathanson, *Teshuvot Sho´el u-Meshiv*, I, no. 22.[13]

Nor is the situation comparable to that described by the Gemara, *Bava Kamma* 26b, in which a child is thrown from a roof but, before landing and perishing from the fall, he is stabbed to death by another person. The majority view is that neither party incurs capital punishment. As explained by the medieval commentaries, the first performed a lethal act but did not actually kill. The second administered a *coup de grace*, but only after a lethal act had already been initiated and thus his act is comparable to extinguishing the life of a *treifah*. Causing the death of a *treifah* is an act of non-capital homicide because the cause of death has already been set in motion and capital punishment is administered only if the perpetrator has extinguished *kol nefesh*, i.e., "an entire life." The airplane passengers cannot be considered as being in that category because no lethal act that would result in the loss of their lives has actually been initiated.[14] Moreover, in terms of normative Halakhah, a *treifah* may not be killed to preserve the life of another individual.[15]

Rescue of human life is a divine mandate, but that imperative does not constitute license to commit an overt act of homicide. At times, passive non-intervention is the only morally acceptable option.

Contemporary Halakhic Problems, Volume VI (Jersey City: Ktav Publishing, 2012), ch. 2, pp. 39–50
Reprinted with permission of the author

Endnotes

1 Voluntary self-sacrifice in order to rescue the community of Israel is sanctioned by *Yeshu'ot Ya'akov*, *Yoreh De'ah* 157:1, on the basis of a report of such an act recorded in *Bava Batra* 10b and the approbation lavished upon those individuals. Cf., however, R. Abraham I. Kook, *Mishpat Kohen*, no. 143, who states that the incident described in *Bava Batra* demonstrates only that persons who would themselves perish together with the community may act in that manner. Nevertheless, *Mishpat Kohen*, nos. 143–144, presents another argument in sanctioning martyrdom for the purpose of rescuing the community of Israel. See also R. Meir Don Plocki, *Hemdat Yisra'el*, *Parashat Pinhas*, sec. 1. Cf., however, R. Meir Simcha ha-Kohen of Dvinsk,

Or Sameach, Hilkhot Rozeah 7:8 and *idem, Meshekh Hakhmah, Parashat Shemot,* s.v. *lekh shuv mizraymah.* Nevertheless, voluntary self-sacrifice is not sanctioned simply to rescue a larger number of people. Cf., *Ve-Ha'arev Na,* 106–107.

2 In the case of the hijacked airplane the passengers may be regarded as specified because, in the absence of intervention, they would all die. If intervention were sanctioned, sacrificing their lives would save others but there was no possibility of sacrificing others in order to save them. Nevertheless, even if victims are specified, R. Yohanan does not sanction actively hastening death in order to save others.

3 Cf., Ramban, *Commentary on the Bible,* Leviticus 19:18, who observes that, according to R. Akiva, "and you shall love your neighbor as yourself" should be understood in a similar manner.

4 Cf., however, *Hazon Ish's* apparently contradictory comments, *Hoshen Mishpat Nezikin, Likkutim,* no. 20, *Bava Mezi'a* 62a.

5 The plane itself also has the status of a *rodef* despite the absence of any element of moral culpability because it is the weight and velocity of the plane that will cause the victims to perish. However, it is unlikely that the incremental weight of the passengers presents a danger that would otherwise not exist; hence, none of the passengers can be considered a *rodef.* See R. Shlomoh Zefrani, *Shimru Mishpat* (January 5, 5764), no. 128.

6 A case of such nature arose during World War II. A German "spy ring" consisting of double agents supplied the German government with information concerning the areas in which V1 and V2 rockets were falling. It was proposed that the double agent transmitting information to the German military report that most aimed a number of miles to the south. The purpose was to assure that future rockets would fall in Kent, Surrey or Sussex where there would be far fewer casualties than in London. The proposal was reportedly placed before the Cabinet by Herbert Morrison, the Home Secretary, but with the negative comment that the report would soon be known by the British populace to be untrue and "doubts would be cast upon the accuracy of Government statements generally." Churchill was abroad at the time, but the Cabinet rejected the proposal on the grounds that the British government was not justified in choosing to sacrifice unendangered citizens in order to save others. See Sefton Delmer, *The Counterfeit Spy* (London, 1971), p. 209. Despite the Cabinet veto, the deception team continued with their efforts to trick the Germans into correcting the aim and range of the German rockets. Morrison, with furious indignation, once again brought the matter before the Cabinet. He is reported to have exclaimed, "Who are we to act as God? Who are we to decide that one man shall die because he lives on the South Coast while another survives because he lives in London?" Morrison's view ultimately prevailed. See *ibid.,* p. 214.

7 The problem was first advanced by Philippa Foot, "The Problem of Abortion and the Doctrine of the Double Effect," *Oxford Review,* no. 5 (Oxford, 1967), pp.5–15, reprinted in Philippa Foot, *Virtues and Vices and Other Essays in Moral Philosophy,* 2nd ed. (Oxford, 2002), pp. 19–32.

8 Philippa Foot's example is somewhat complicated by the fact that, if the five were already on the track before the locomotive was set in motion, it is the driver who set in motion the chain of events that will lead to loss of life. Can he "remedy" an act that would cost five lives by modifying the act so that it will result in the loss of a different, but single, life? The hypothetical could just as readily involve a situation in which the driver has had a seizure and it is now a passenger who must take over the controls. The difference is that the passenger has heretofore been in no way involved in the performance of an act that will lead to fatality. May he now cause the death of one person in order to save five others? That dilemma is discussed by Professor Foot in "Killing and Letting Die," *Abortion: Moral and Legal Perspectives,* J. Garfield, ed. (Amherst, 1985), pp. 177–85, reprinted in Philippa Foot, *Moral Dilemmas and Other Topics in Moral Philosophy* (Oxford . 2002), pp. 78–87, seemingly without an awareness of the difference between the two hypotheticals. See *Moral Dilemmas,* p. 85. It is not at all clear that a distinction should be made between the two cases. If a distinction is to be made it would be on the basis of the following consideration: Although overtly causing the death of one person to save a group of individuals is forbidden because each life is of infinite value, nevertheless, if the potential intervener himself set the chain of events in motion, even unintentionally, he has a duty to minimize his own transgression. That consideration may be sufficient grounds to deflect the arrow or trolley so that he is responsible for fewer acts of homicide. A discussion of that issue is beyond the scope of this endeavor but should focus upon an analysis of *Shabbat* 4a.

9 Absent designation, even indirectly causing the death of another in order to save one's own life is included in the category of *yeharag ve-al ya-avor.* See R Yeruchem Yehuda Perilman, *Or Gadol* (Vilna, 5684), no. 1, *Hilkhot Yesodei ha-Torah* 5:2, s.v. *veh-ha-nireh* (p. 5a) and s.v. *ve-ha-iker* (p. 10b) and *Hazon Ish, Gilyonot le-Hiddushei Rabbenu Hayyim ha-Levi, Hilkhot Yesodei ha-Torah* 5:1, s.v. *ve-yesh lomar.* Cf., however, *Galya Masekhta* (Vina, 5605), *Yoreh De'ah,* no. 5, s.v. *u-ke-ein he'arah* (p. 92a).

10 Capital culpability is an entirely different matter. The arrow, for example, reaches its goal only because of the combination of the force imparted by the archer and the channeling of that force by the intervener. The situation seems analogous to a case of an arsonist who lights a fire that is carried by the wind and causes death. In that case, it is the act of lighting a fire together with the force of wind that causes death. Capital culpability in such circumstances is dependent upon the Talmudic controversy regarding *isho mishum hizav* or *isho mishum memmono.*

11 For fuller discussion of this question see this writer's Contemporary Halakhic Problems, Vol. 1 (New York, 1977), 355–361.

12 See also *Ve'Ha'arev Na,* I, 106.

13 That view is dismissed by R. Moshe Yonah Zweig, *No'am,* Vll, 55, as "the opinion of an individual" having no standing in the determination of Halakhah.

14 Depiction of such a victim as a *gavra ketila,* or "dead man," is equally specious. That classification is applicable to a transgressor actually under sentence of death pronounced by a *bet din.* Causing a death of such an individual is no more than giving effect to the sentence of the *bet din.*

15 See R. Ezekiel Landau, *Teshuvot Noda bi-Yehuda, Mahadura Tinyana, Hoshen Mishpat,* no. 59 and R. Schneur Zalman of Lublin, *Teshuot Torat Hesed. Even ha-Ezer.* no. 42. Cf., however, *Minhat Hinnukh,* no. 296, R. Judah Rosannes, *Parashat Derakhim, Derush* 17, and R. Jacob Emden, *Migdal Oz, Even Bohen* 1:79, and R. Meir Arak, *Tel Torah, Yerushalem, Terumot* 8.3.

Lesson

6

HASTENING THE INEVITABLE

IS ONE RESPONSIBLE FOR EXPEDITING INESCAPABLE HARM?

The popular adage claims that "nothing can be said to be certain except death and taxes." In reality, however, many of life's outcomes can be said to be certain and inevitable. So how are we to react when someone intervenes and hastens a harm or loss that would have occurred moments later? In this lesson we examine whether such perpetrators, whose actions appear to be of no consequence, should be absolved or held accountable.

CASE STUDY **A**

SOURCE: *DILLON V. TWIN STATE GAS & ELECTRIC CO.,* 85 N.H. 449, 163 A. 111

A fourteen-year-old boy by the last name of Dillon often played with his friends on a public bridge in Berlin, New Hampshire. The boys had been accustomed for a number of years to climb the sloping girders to reach the horizontal girders, on which they would sit and walk.

One afternoon, while Dillon was sitting on a horizontal girder, he leaned over and lost his balance. He instinctively threw out his arm to take hold of electrical wires to save himself from falling. These wires provided the electricity for the bridge's lamps, and they were owned and maintained by Twin State Gas & Electric Company. The wires were charged with a high voltage current when Dillon took hold of them. He was electrocuted and died instantly.

Dillon's father sued Twin State Gas & Electric Company for its negligence in not insulating their wires. Twin State conceded that the wires were not insulated properly, but they argued that without the wires, the boy would have fallen anyway to his death onto the roadway or into the river below.

POLL 1

Should Twin State be liable for Dillon's death?

1 Yes

2 No

3 Not sure

CASE STUDY B

SOURCE: *RULINGS OF THE JERUSALEM RABBINICAL COURT* 6:111

Reuben arrived early at his store one morning and saw two burglars loading his merchandise into a vehicle. In an attempt to prevent them from fleeing, he shattered the windshield of the car and contorted its steering wheel. Seeing that their getaway vehicle was disabled, the thieves fled empty-handed. When the police arrived, it became apparent that the vehicle did not belong to the thieves. It was stolen.

The owner of the vehicle demanded that Reuben pay for the damaged windshield and steering wheel. Reuben argued that without him damaging the vehicle, the thieves would have stolen it, and thus, his action, in effect, caused no loss to the owner.

POLL 2

Should Reuben be liable to pay for the damage he caused to the vehicle?

1 Yes

2 No

3 Not sure

CASE STUDY C

SOURCE: RABBI YITSCHAK BEN SHESHET, *RESPONSA* 506

Reuben and Simeon jointly owned a house. Reuben owned the ground level, which he used for storage, and Simeon owned the upper two floors.

One day, Simeon decided to demolish a portion of his third-floor wall that required repair. In so doing, a large portion of the wall accidently fell inward. The impact broke the second floor ceiling, which in turn destroyed the ceiling of the lowest level, where Reuben stored wine. Three of Reuben's wine barrels that were stored there were destroyed.

Reuben sued Simeon, claiming he was negligent for not hiring a professional contractor to perform the repairs.

He demanded compensation for the lost wine and for the cost of repairing his ceiling.

Simeon argued that he was not responsible for any of the damages, because Reuben's ceiling was going to collapse on its own imminently. In fact, he claimed that an assessment would show that the falling debris on its own should not have been enough to break Reuben's ceiling, proving that Reuben's ceiling was about to cave in on its own. In effect, he argued, he had caused no harm.

POLL 3

If Simeon's claim can be substantiated, should he be responsible to compensate Reuben for his ceiling and wine?

1 Yes

2 No

3 Not sure

CHAVRUTA A

TEXT 1

TALMUD, BAVA KAMA 17B

אָמַר רַבָּה: זָרַק כְּלִי מֵרֹאשׁ הַגַּג, וּבָא אַחֵר וּשְׁבָרוֹ בְּמַקֵּל - פָּטוּר. דְּאַמְרִינָן לֵיהּ: מָנָא תְּבִירָא תָּבַר.

Rabah said: If someone throws another's vessel from a rooftop, and a second person comes along and shatters it with a stick [before it hits the ground], the second person is exempt. For we say, "The second one broke a broken vessel."

BABYLONIAN TALMUD

A literary work of monumental proportions that draws upon the legal, spiritual, intellectual, ethical, and historical traditions of Judaism. The 37 tractates of the Babylonian Talmud contain the teachings of the Jewish sages from the period after the destruction of the 2nd Temple through the 5th century CE. It has served as the primary vehicle for the transmission of the Oral Law and the education of Jews over the centuries; it is the entry point for all subsequent legal, ethical, and theological Jewish scholarship.

RABAH BAR NACHMANI (RABAH)
CA. 270–330

Third-generation Talmudic sage (*amora*). Rabah headed the Talmudic academy of Pumbedita, Babylonia. His prodigious ability to debate, resolve, and apply earned him the nickname "uprooter of mountains." He was known for beginning his Torah lectures with a witticism to put his students in a good mood.

TEXT **2**

TOSAFOT, AD LOC.

אִם זָרַק אֶבֶן אוֹ חֵץ עַל הַכְּלִי, וּבָא אַחֵר וְקָדַם וּשְׁבָרוֹ, דִּפְשִׁיטָא דְּחַיָּיב, וְלֹא שַׁיָּיךְ כַּאן מָנָא תְּבִירָא תָּבַר . . . וּסְבָרָא פְּשׁוּטָה הִיא לְחַלֵּק בֵּין זוֹרֵק אֶבֶן לְזוֹרֵק כְּלִי עַצְמוֹ.

If a person throws a rock or arrow toward a vessel, and another person comes along and shatters the vessel before the projectile strikes it, certainly, the one who shattered the vessel [and not the one who threw the rock] is liable. In this instance, we do not apply the rationale of "the second one broke a broken vessel." Simple logic calls for us to distinguish between throwing a rock [toward a vessel] and throwing the vessel itself.

TOSAFOT

A collection of French and German Talmudic commentaries written during the 12th and 13th centuries. Among the most famous authors of *Tosafot* are Rabbi Ya'akov Tam, Rabbi Shimshon ben Avraham of Sens, and Rabbi Yitschak ("the Ri"). Printed in almost all editions of the Talmud, these commentaries are fundamental to basic Talmudic study.

?

QUESTIONS FOR DISCUSSION

1 How do you understand the rationale of Rabah's ruling?

2 Why does this rationale not apply in the case described in Text 2? What is the "simple logic" that differentiates between the two cases?

TEXT **3**

RABBI CHAIM BENVENISTE, *KENESET HAGEDOLAH, CHOSHEN MISHPAT, BEIT YOSEF* 386:33

בְּזוֹרֵק כְּלִי עַצְמוֹ בְּמָקוֹם שֶׁאֵין כָּאן כָּרִים וּכְסָתוֹת, אַף עַל גַּב דְּבָעִידָנָא דְּשַׁדְיֵיהּ אַפְסְקֵי גִּירֵיהּ דִּידֵיהּ, הֲוֵי פְּסִיק רֵישֵׁיהּ וְלֹא יָמוּת, דְּאִי אֶפְשָׁר דְּכָל שֶׁנִּזְדַּק בְּכֹחַ וְנָפַל עַל הָאָרֶץ שֶׁלֹּא יִשָּׁבֵר בְּוַדַּאי, בִּכְלִי חֶרֶשׂ אוֹ שֶׁל עֵץ דְּוַדַּאי הֵם נִשְׁבָּרִים עַסְקִינָן.

אֲבָל בְּזוֹרֵק חֵץ אוֹ אֶבֶן, לֹא הֲוֵי פְּסִיק רֵישֵׁיהּ וְלֹא יָמוּת, שֶׁאֶפְשָׁר שֶׁאֲפִילוּ יַגִּיעַ הָאֶבֶן אוֹ הַחֵץ בַּכְּלִי לֹא יִשָּׁבֵר, דְּאֶפְשָׁר דְּלֹא הָיָה כֹּחַ בַּזּוֹרֵק שֶׁעַל יְדֵי זְרִיקַת הָאֶבֶן אוֹ הַחֵץ יִשָּׁבֵר הַכְּלִי. וְאֶפְשָׁר גַּם כֵּן . . . דְּשֶׁמָּא הַחֵץ אוֹ הָאֶבֶן לֹא הָיָה מַגִּיעוֹ וְהָיָה מִסְתַּלֵּק לַצְּדָדִים וְלֹא הָיָה נוֹגֵעַ בַּכְּלִי. וְלָכֵן זֶה שֶׁקָּדַם וּשְׁבָרוֹ לֵיכָּא לְמֵימַר מָנָא תְּבִירָא תָּבִיר לִיחַיֵּיב הַזּוֹרֵק וְלֹא הַמְשַׁבֵּר.

RABBI CHAIM BENVENISTE
1603–1673

Leading 17th-century Torah scholar in Constantinople. Rabbi Chaim was born in Constantinople to a family descended from Spanish exiles. He became famous in his youth for authoring *Dina Dechayei*, a commentary on *Sefer Mitzvot Gadol (Semag)*. He later wrote *Keneset Hagedolah*, a collection of halachic decisions and commentary, written as notations to the *Beit Yosef* and the *Shulchan Aruch*.

When one throws a vessel from a rooftop and there are no cushions on the ground, the vessel is certain to break, albeit after a small delay. It is impossible for pottery or a wooden vessel not to shatter when it is thrown to the ground with force.

However, when throwing an arrow or rock [at a vessel], the intended vessel is not certain to shatter. Perhaps the thrower did not put enough strength into the throw to shatter it. It is also possible . . . that the arrow or rock will miss the intended target altogether. Therefore, the person who shatters the vessel cannot be excused from liability by saying, "I broke a broken vessel."

TEXT 4

RABBI YISRAEL GUSTMAN, *KUNTRESEI SHIURIM,* BAVA KAMA 10:9

אִם הַזְּמַן שֶׁל בֵּינְתַּיִם אֵינוֹ רָאוּי לְהִשְׁתַּמְשׁוּת, אָז שַׁיָּיךְ לוֹמַר דַּהֲרֵי הוּא כְּשָׁבוּר עַכְשָׁיו עַל זְמַן הַשְּׁבִירָה. מַה שֶּׁאֵין כֵּן בְּרָאוּי לְהִשְׁתַּמְשׁוּת עַד זְמַן הַשְּׁבִירָה, שׁוּב לֹא שַׁיָּיךְ כְּלָל לוֹמַר דַּהֲוֵי מָנָא תְּבִירָא, דְּכֵיוָן דְּיֵשׁ לוֹ הִשְׁתַּמְשׁוּת . . . שׁוּב עֲדַיִין שֵׁם כְּלִי עָלָיו, וְלֹא שַׁיָּיךְ לוֹמַר . . . יְהֵא כְּמָנָא תְּבִירָא.

**RAV YISRAEL ZE'EV GUSTMAN
1908–1991**

Rabbi Gustman was born near Bialystok. In 1931, Rabbi Chaim Ozer Grodzinski appointed him to the rabbinical court in Vilna. During World War II, he escaped the Vilna Ghetto with his wife and daughter and took refuge for many months on the farm of a kind Gentile. After the war, he taught for a few years in the Central Lubavitch Yeshiva in New York. He made *aliyah* in 1971.

If between the first person's act and the breaking of the object, the object does not provide utility, then we already regard it as broken from the time of the initial act. When, however, it still provides utility before it is actually broken, we cannot say that it is already broken from the time the first person acted. If it still has utility . . . it is still legally regarded as a vessel, and it is impossible to call it . . . broken.

POLL 4

In Case Study B, is Reuben liable to pay for the damage he caused to the vehicle?

1 Yes

2 No

3 Not sure

POLL 5

In Case Study C, if Simeon's claim can be substantiated, is he responsible to compensate Reuben for his ceiling and wine?

1 Yes

2 No

3 Not sure

TEXT 5a

RABBI YITSCHAK BEN SHESHET, *RESPONSA* 506

שֶׁכֵּיוָן שֶׁהָיְתָה נִרְקֶבֶת וְנִתְלַעַת, עַד שֶׁלֹּא הָיָה אֶפְשָׁר לְשִׁמְעוֹן לְהִשְׁתַּמֵּשׁ בָּהּ אִם לֹא בְּסַכָּנָה, כְּבָר נִתְחַיֵּיב רְאוּבֵן לְסָתְרָהּ עַל מְנַת לִבְנוֹתָהּ. וְאִם כֵּן, מָנָא תְּבִירָא תָּבַר, וְאֵין כָּאן הֶזֵּק.

וּמַה שֶּׁאָמַר: שֶׁהָיְתָה רְאוּיָה לַעֲמוֹד זְמַן מְרוּבֶּה, אוֹ קְצַת זְמַן, אוּלַי סָמַךְ עַל מַה שֶׁהִזְכִּירוּ שְׁנֵי הָעֵדִים הָאוּמָּנִין בְּעֵדוּתָם בְּאָמְרָם: שֶׁהָיְתָה נִרְקֶבֶת וְנִתְלַעַת, עַד שֶׁלְּכָל הַיּוֹתֵר שֶׁהָיְתָה יְכוֹלָה לְהִתְקַיֵּים לֹא הָיְתָה מִתְקַיֶּימֶת מִשָּׁנָה אַחַת וְאֵילָךְ.

וְלֹא דְקַדֵּק בְּעֵדוּתָם. כִּי הֵם לֹא הֵעִידוּ שֶׁיָּכוֹלָה לְהִתְקַיֵּים בְּבָרִי שָׁנָה וְלֹא חֲצִי שָׁנָה. אֶלָּא שֶׁבָּרִי לָהֶם שֶׁלֹּא תִּתְקַיֵּים יוֹתֵר מִשָּׁנָה לְכָל הַיּוֹתֵר, וּפָחוֹת מִכֵּן הוּא סָפֵק וְסַכָּנָה. כִּי הַדָּבָר יָדוּעַ: שֶׁכָּל תִּקְרָה שֶׁנּוֹפֶלֶת מֵחֲמַת רִקָּבוֹן וְהַתְלָעָה, קוֹדֶם נְפִילָתָה יוֹתֵר מִשָּׁנָה וּשְׁנָתַיִם הִיא בְּחֶזְקַת סַכָּנָה.

וְאִם כֵּן, אֵין כָּאן יוֹם אֶחָד וְלֹא שָׁעָה אַחַת שֶׁלֹּא תִּהְיֶה בְּסַכָּנָה. וּמִקּוֹדֶם נְפִילָתָה הָיָה מְחוּיָּיב רְאוּבֵן לְסָתְרָהּ. וְאִם כֵּן אֵין כָּאן הֶזֵּק כְּלָל, דְּמָנָא תְּבִירָא תָּבַר.

RABBI YITZCHAK PERFET (RIVASH, RABBI YITZCHAK BEN SHESHET) 1326–1408

Halachist. Rivash studied under Rabbeinu Nisim of Gerona (Ran) in Barcelona, and served as rabbi there and in other important Jewish communities in Spain. Because of the eruption of anti-Jewish riots in 1391, he fled to North Africa and settled in Algiers. He was the first to address the halachic status of Marranos. Rivash's Halachic responsa are his most important work; the contain sources no longer extant and served, in part, as a basis for the Code of Jewish Law.

Because Reuben's ceiling was decaying and rotting, to the extent that Simeon could not walk on the floor above it safely, Reuben was already required to demolish it and rebuild it. Thus, Simeon damaged a broken ceiling.

Reuben claims that the ceiling could have lasted a long while, or at least a little bit. Presumably, Reuben is basing this claim on the testimony from the experts who said that the ceiling could have lasted for a year at most.

However, Reuben is twisting their words. They did not say it would for sure last a year or even half a year; they only said it will certainly not last more than a year, and that it was at immediate risk of collapse. For it is well-known that a rotting and decaying ceiling can collapse at any moment for at least two years prior to its actual collapse.

Accordingly, there was no moment free of danger, and therefore, Reuben was responsible to demolish his ceiling before the accident occurred. Simeon, then, caused no damage inasmuch as "he broke a broken vessel."

TEXT 5b

RABBI YITSCHAK BEN SHESHET, IBID. 👥

וְהָיָה הָאֱמֶת שֶׁהָיְתָה הַתִּקְרָה יְכוֹלָה לְהִתְקַיֵּים בְּוַדַּאי שָׁנָה אוֹ שְׁנָתַיִם, וְהָיָה שִׁמְעוֹן יָכוֹל לְהִשְׁתַּמֵּשׁ עָלֶיהָ בְּלִי סַכָּנָה תּוֹךְ הַזְּמַן הַהוּא . . . הָיָה לוֹ לְחַיֵּיב רְאוּבֵן לִבְנוֹת הַתִּקְרָה בְּנְיָן חָזָק. וְשִׁמְעוֹן יְסַיֵּיעַ לוֹ בְּבִנְיָן כְּדֵי שׁוּמַת נֶזֶק תִּקְרָה הָרִאשׁוֹנָה לְשָׁנָה אוֹ לִשְׁנָתַיִם.

What if it were true that the ceiling was not at all in danger of collapsing for a year or two, which would have meant that Simeon could walk upon it and use it safely during that time frame? . . . If this were the case, Reuben, who is responsible for the ceiling, should construct a new and sturdy one, but Simeon must reimburse Reuben for the one or two years' time that he deprived Reuben of his previous ceiling.

Figure 6.1

Preemptive Cause — Halachic Rulings

		VARIABLES	RULINGS
Case Study B		Vehicle had theft insurance	Reuben is liable
		Vehicle did not have theft insurance	Reuben is liable
Case Study C	Reuben's ceiling	Was in danger of immediate collapse	Simeon is not liable
		Was not going to collapse for another year	Simeon is liable to pay the value of one year
	Reuben's wine	N/A	Simeon is liable

POLL 6

Should the alcohol vandal (Lesson One, Case Study C) be exonerated, considering that he broke a barrel that would have soon been confiscated?

1 Yes

2 No

3 Not sure

TEXT **6**

RABBI CHAIM SEGALOWITZ, *RESPONSA MEKOR CHAYIM* 33

לְכְאוֹרָה נִרְאֶה שֶׁהוּא פָּטוּר מִלְשַׁלֵּם מֵהַהִיא (דְּבָבָא קַמָּא יז, ב) "דְּאָמַר רַבָּה: זָרַק כְּלִי מֵראשׁ הַגַּג וּבָא אַחֵר וּשְׁבָרוֹ בְּמַקֵּל פָּטוּר, דְּאָמְרִינָן לֵיהּ, מָנָא תְּבִירָא תָּבַר". וְכֵן פָּסְקוּ כָּל הַפּוֹסְקִים.

וְאִם כֵּן הָכָא נַמִי, לְבַד שֶׁיָּצָא לוֹ טוֹבָה מִזֶּה שֶׁשָּׁבַר, הֲרֵי אִם לֹא הָיָה שֹׁבֵר, הָיָה לֹקֵחַ הַמְּמוּנֶּה אֶת הַיַּיִן שָׂרָף, וְאִם כֵּן מָנָא תְּבִירָא תָּבַר.

אַךְ מִדְּבְרֵי הַתּוֹסָפוֹת שָׁם (דִּיבּוּר הַמַּתְחִיל: זָרַק) נִרְאֶה דְּחַיָּיב. דְּכָתְבוּ שָׁם, וְזֶה לְשׁוֹנָם: "נִרְאֶה דְּאִם זָרַק אֶבֶן אוֹ חֵץ עַל הַכְּלִי, וּבָא אַחֵר וְקָדַם וּשְׁבָרוֹ, דִּפְשִׁיטָא דְּחַיָּיב, וְלֹא שַׁיָּיךְ כָּאן מָנָא תְּבִירָא תָּבַר כוּ', וּסְבָרָא פְּשׁוּטָה הִיא לְחַלֵּק בֵּין זוֹרֵק אֶבֶן לְזוֹרֵק כְּלִי עַצְמוֹ", עַד כָּאן לְשׁוֹנָם.

וְאִם כֵּן, הָכָא נַמִי פְּשִׁיטָא דְּדָמֵי לְזוֹרֵק חֵץ וְהַמְשַׁבֵּר חַיָּיב.

At first glance, I would have said that the vandal is exempt per Rabah's teaching (T a l m u d ,   B a v a   K a m a 1 7 b) . For Rabah taught, "If someone throws another's vessel from a rooftop, and a second person comes along and shatters it with a stick [before it hits the ground], the second person is exempt. For we say, 'The second one broke a broken vessel.'" All halachic authorities have accepted this ruling.

Now, in this case, in addition to causing a great benefit to the liquor owner [by enabling him to avoid a harsh penalty], the vandal broke a broken vessel, for the wine would have been confiscated had he not broken it.

However, from the ruling of *Tosafot* it seems that the vandal is unable to employ this defense. For *Tosafot* writes, "If a person throws a rock or arrow toward a vessel, and another person comes along and shatters the vessel before the projectile strikes it, certainly, the one who shattered the vessel [and not the one who threw the rock] is liable. In this instance, we do not apply the rationale of 'the second one broke a broken vessel.' Simple logic calls for us to distinguish between throwing a rock [toward a vessel] and throwing the vessel itself."

Our case of the alcohol vandal seems to be analogous with *Tosafot's* variation of the case.

RABBI CHAIM SEGALOWITZ
1844–1925

Rabbi Chaim Segalowitz served as rabbi in Salcininkai, near Vilna, from 1870–1884, and later moved to Vilna, where he served until his passing in 1925. In 1894 he published his work *Mekor Chayim*, which includes halachic responsa as well as Talmudic commentaries and his homilies.

QUESTION FOR DISCUSSION

How might the aforementioned passages apply to Case Study A?

TEXT 7a

TALMUD, BAVA KAMA 10B

אָמַר רַבָּה: זָרַק תִּינוֹק מֵרֹאשׁ הַגַּג וּבָא אַחֵר וְקִבְּלוֹ בְּסַיָּיף - פְּלוּגְתָּא דְּרַבִּי יְהוּדָה בֶּן בְּתֵירָא וְרַבָּנָן.

Rabah said: If a person throws an infant from a rooftop, and another person comes along and kills the infant with a sword before it hits the ground—this issue is debated by Rabbi Yehudah ben Beteira and the sages.

TEXT 7b

TALMUD, IBID.

דְּתַנְיָא: הִכּוּהוּ עֲשָׂרָה בְּנֵי אָדָם בְּעֲשָׂרָה מַקְלוֹת, בֵּין בְּבַת אַחַת בֵּין בָּזֶה אַחַר זֶה - כּוּלָן פְּטוּרִין.

It was taught: If ten people strike a victim with ten clubs, whether they do it simultaneously or consecutively, they are all exempt.

TEXT 7c

TALMUD, IBID.

רַבִּי יְהוּדָה בֶּן בְּתֵירָא אוֹמֵר: בָּזֶה אַחַר זֶה - הָאַחֲרוֹן חַיָּיב, מִפְּנֵי שֶׁקֵּירַב מִיתָתוֹ.

Rabbi Yehudah ben Beteira said: When done consecutively, the last person is liable for expediting the victim's death.

RABBI YEHUDAH BEN BETEIRA

There seems to have been two sages by this name, and it is not always possible to differentiate them. The first Rabbi Yehudah ben Beteira lived during Temple times in Nisibis, Mesopotamia. It is likely that he had a grandson by the same name, who was a contemporary of Rabbi Yehudah Hanasi, redactor of the Mishnah.

TEXT 8a

MAIMONIDES, *MISHNEH TORAH,* LAWS OF MURDER AND PRESERVATION OF LIFE 2:6–7

אֶחָד הַהוֹרֵג אֶת הַגָּדוֹל אוֹ אֶת הַקָּטָן בֶּן יוֹמוֹ, בֵּין זָכָר בֵּין נְקֵבָה, הֲרֵי זֶה נֶהֱרַג עָלָיו אִם הָרַג בְּזָדוֹן, אוֹ גוֹלֶה אִם הָרַג בִּשְׁגָגָה . . .
וְאִם הָיָה גוֹסֵס בִּידֵי אָדָם, כְּגוֹן שֶׁהִכּוּהוּ עַד שֶׁנָּטָה לָמוּת וַהֲרֵי הוּא גוֹסֵס, הַהוֹרֵג אוֹתוֹ אֵין בֵּית דִּין מְמִיתִין אוֹתוֹ.

Whether a person kills an adult or a one-day-old infant, a male or female, the killer should be executed if he killed intentionally, and exiled if he killed unintentionally. . . .

If, however, one kills a person who is about to die because of wounds inflicted by other perpetrators—for example, if the victim is on the verge of death because of repeated blows—the killer should not be executed by the court.

RABBI MOSHE BEN MAIMON (MAIMONIDES, RAMBAM) 1135–1204

Halachist, philosopher, author, and physician. Maimonides was born in Cordoba, Spain. After the conquest of Cordoba by the Almohads, he fled Spain and eventually settled in Cairo, Egypt. There, he became the leader of the Jewish community and served as court physician to the vizier of Egypt. He is most noted for authoring the *Mishneh Torah,* an encyclopedic arrangement of Jewish law, and for his philosophical work, *Guide for the Perplexed.* His rulings on Jewish law are integral to the formation of halachic consensus.

TEXT **8b**

RABBI CHAIM BENVENISTE, *DINA DECHAYEI*, MITZVAH 163

מַשְׁמַע דְּאֵין בֵּית דִּין מְמִיתִין אוֹתוֹ, אֲבָל חַיָּיב בְּדִינֵי שָׁמַיִם. וּמִסְתַּבֵּר הָכִי, שֶׁהֲרֵי לְעִנְיָן שַׁבָּת אָמְרוּ (יוֹמָא פה, א) שֶׁאִם נָפְלָה עָלָיו מַפּוֹלֶת מְפַקְּחִין אֶת הַגַּל אִם מְצָאוּהוּ חַי, אַף עַל פִּי שֶׁיּוֹדְעִים שֶׁלֹּא יִחְיֶה כִּי אִם שָׁעָה אַחַת, דִּלְחַיֵּי שָׁעָה חַיְישִׁינָן.

The implication is that the court cannot execute this person, but he is liable under the laws of Heaven. This makes sense. For if a building collapses on Shabbat, the law is (TALMUD, YOMA 85A) that we must excavate through the rubble to rescue those buried beneath it. Even if we discover someone who is about to die, we must continue to work to extract this person to gain a short extension of life, because even mere moments of life are meaningful.

TEXT 8c

RABBI MEIR SIMCHAH OF DVINSK, *OR SAME'ACH,* LAWS OF MURDER AND PRESERVATION OF LIFE 2:4

וְדַע, דִּבְגוֹסֵס בִּידֵי אָדָם נֶחְלְקוּ אִם חַיָּיב הָרוֹצֵחַ. וְרַבֵּינוּ פָּסַק בְּהֲלָכָה
ז' דְּפָטוּר. מִכָּל מָקוֹם, גַּם בָּזֶה מִדִּין מֶלֶךְ יִשְׂרָאֵל חַיָּיב, וְיָכוֹל הַמֶּלֶךְ
לְהָרְגוֹ . . . וְזֶה הִרְגִּישׁ רַבֵּינוּ בִּלְשׁוֹן קָדְשׁוֹ: "וְאִם הָיָה גוֹסֵס בִּידֵי אָדָם
כו', הַהוֹרְגוֹ אֵין בֵּית דִּין מְמִיתִין אוֹתוֹ" - דְּקָדֵק בֵּית דִּין, הָא מִדִּין מַלְכוּת
חַיָּיב מִיתָה.

There is a Talmudic debate as to whether one is liable for killing a person who was already attacked by others and on the verge of death. Now, while Maimonides rules that the final attacker is exempt, he can still be executed by the rules of justice administered by the monarch. . . . Notice how this can be seen in Maimonides' words. He writes, "If one kills a person who is about to die because of wounds inflicted by other perpetrators, the killer should not be executed by the court." He was careful to say "the court," implying that the king is lawfully allowed to execute this person.

RABBI MEIR SIMCHAH HAKOHEN OF DVINSK 1843–1926

Served as rabbi of Dvinsk for nearly 40 years. He is renowned for two works: *Or Same'ach,* a commentary on Maimonides' *Mishneh Torah,* and *Meshech Chochmah,* a profound commentary on the Bible. In the latter work, Rabbi Meir Simchah demonstrates the unity between the Written and Oral Laws and presents original interpretations of biblical and Talmudic passages. In 1906, he was offered the position of rabbi of Jerusalem but bowed to the entreaties of the city folk to remain in Dvinsk.

TEXT 9

RABBI ISSER ZALMAN MELTZER, *EVEN HA'AZEL, HILCHOT NIZKEI MAMON* 2:14

דְּדִין רוֹצֵחַ לֹא תָּלֵי בְּדִין חֲשִׁיבוּת חַי, אֶלָּא בְּפוֹעַל אִם הוּא חַי.

The laws of murder have nothing to do with utility; all that matters is the taking of a life.

RABBI ISSER ZALMAN MELTZER 1870–1953

Rabbi Meltzer was born in Mir, Belarus. He studied in the yeshiva of Volozhin under Rabbi Chaim of Volozhin and Rabbi Chaim Soloveitchik. In 1903, he was appointed rabbi of Slutsk. He wrote a commentary to Maimonides' *Mishneh Torah* entitled *Even Ha'azel.*

Learning Exercise 1

Choose one teaching, law, or quote from this course for each of the criteria below.

CRITERIA	TEACHING, LAW, OR QUOTE
Wisest concept	
Most controversial concept	
Concept that resonated most	
Concept that did not resonate	
Concept I will likely share with others	
Most surprising concept	

KEY POINTS

1 If someone throws an object from a rooftop and a second person shatters it before it hits the ground, the second person is not liable to pay damages. But if someone throws a rock at an object, and a second person shatters the object before the rock reaches it, the second person is held liable.

2 For the second person to be exempt, it must be a case in which the owner's loss was definitely inevitable and where the owner had already lost all utility from the given object.

3 When someone hastens an inevitable death, it is an act of forbidden murder that carries Heavenly liability, though whether a court of law can execute this wrongdoer is a matter of dispute.

4 The value of life on its truest level lies in the very fact that a divine soul is present in a human body, regardless of the degree of visible function it exhibits. This explains why each moment of life is valuable.

5 Under biblical law, one who is responsible for negligently causing a death is exiled. When the laws of exile do not apply, there are specific and rigorous paths of repentance that are suggested by rabbinic authorities.

Continue your
learning experience

ONLINE

Visit www.myJLI.com/dilemma6
for insightful and inspiring videos,
articles, and readings on this topic.

Additional Readings

CAUSATION IN TORT LAW

RICHARD W. WRIGHT

Editor's note: The following is an excerpt from Part II of Professor's Wright "Causation in Tort Law." Please consult the original for the rest of the article and its footnotes.

A. The But-For Test and Its Limits: Duplicative and Preemptive Causation

The most widely used test of actual causation in tort adjudication is the but-for test, which states that an act (omission, condition, etc.) was a cause of an injury if and only if, but for the act, the injury would not have occurred. That is, the act must have been a necessary condition for the occurrence of the injury. The test reflects a deeply rooted belief that a condition cannot be a cause of some event unless it is, in some sense, necessary for the occurrence of the event. This view is shared by lawyers, philosophers, scientists, and the general public.

In the vast majority of cases, the but-for test works quite well as a test of actual causation. But in certain types of cases, it results in a finding of no causation even though it is clear that the act in question contributed to the injury. These are cases of overdetermined causation: cases in which a factor other than the specified act would have been sufficient to produce the injury in the absence of the specified act, but its effects either (1) were preempted by the more immediately operative effects of the specified act or (2) combined with or duplicated those of the specified act to jointly produce the injury.

I will refer to the first type of situation as a case of preemptive causation. For example, D shoots and kills P just as P was about to drink a cup of tea that was poisoned by C. D's shot was a preemptive cause of P's death; C's poisoning of the tea was not a cause because its potential effects were preempted. I will refer to the second type of situation as a case of duplicative causation. For example, C and D independently start separate fires, each of which would have been sufficient to destroy P's house. The fires converge and together burn down the house. Each fire was a duplicative cause of the destruction of the house. Yet, application of the but-for test would result in a finding that D's shot was not a cause of P's death in the first example and that neither C's nor D's fire was a cause of the destruction of P's house in the second example.

A different sort of objection to the but-for test focuses on the hypothetical or counterfactual nature of the inquiry that the test calls for. A number of writers have asserted that the hypothetical nature of the but-for inquiry necessarily involves or at least invites introduction of policy considerations into a supposedly factual inquiry.

While it might be thought that these difficulties could be avoided by substituting a sufficient condition test for the but-for necessary-condition test, this substitution would eliminate almost every potential cause, since few if any acts are sufficient by themselves to produce any particular consequence. Thus, in the scientific and philosophic literature on causation, it is usually stressed that the cause of an event must include all the conditions which together are sufficient to produce the consequence. Consequently, both lawyers and philosophers often conclude that this scientific or philosophic concept of causation is of little relevance or use in the law.

On the other hand, the sufficient-condition test could be interpreted to mean any condition that is sufficient in combination with other conditions to produce the consequence, even though it is not sufficient

RICHARD W. WRIGHT

Associate Professor of law, Chicago-Kent College of Law, Illinois Institute of Technology. B.S. 1968, California Institute of Technology; J.D. 1973, Loyola University, Los Angeles; LL.M. 1976, Harvard University.

by itself. Under this interpretation, however, anything could be treated as a cause simply by adding it to an already sufficient set of conditions.

Judges and legal writers have responded to the actual and perceived deficiencies in the but-for test in several different ways. A few writers have tried to improve the but-for test by modifying the manner in which it is applied. Most judges and writers, however, have adopted the substantial-factor formula, either as a supplement to or as a substitute for the but-for test depending on their degree of dissatisfaction with the but-for test. Others have relied on an undefined and irreducible notion of directly observable causal contribution.

Each of these approaches will be discussed in subsequent sections of this Part. It will be demonstrated that, under each approach, the analysis ultimately must fall back on the but-for test in order to be useful and coherent. The necessary-condition element, in some form, indeed seems to be fundamental to the concept of causation. But it obviously is too restrictive when applied in the usual way to the overdetermined-causation cases. Some writers treat the overdetermined-causation cases as genuine instances of causation that must be admitted as unexplained exceptions to the but-for test. A larger and growing number of writers treat the overdetermined-causation cases as policy-based exceptions to the actual-causation requirement, which is equated with the but-for test.

B. Efforts to Modify the But-For Test

As mentioned above, the but-for test works well as a test of actual causation in the vast majority of cases, but produces obviously incorrect results in the overdetermined-causation cases. A few writers have tried to extend the but-for test's range of application by modifying the way in which it is applied. Rollin Perkins, Arno Becht, and Frank Miller apply the test to a detailed description of the injury or the manner of its occurrence. Glanville Williams excludes consideration of hypothetical facts. And the editors of the fifth edition of Prosser's hornbook on tort law apply the test to multiple potential causes in the aggregate. None of these approaches works. Several of them assume the very answer the test is supposed to provide.

1. Detailing the Manner of Occurrence

Perkins tries to resolve the causal issue in the overdetermined-causation cases by detailing the manner in which the injury occurred: "Whenever that would not have happened when and as it did happen, had it not been for this, this is an actual cause of that." For example, if a victim is killed instantaneously by a bullet wound while already dying from a knife wound, he would not have died, as he in fact did, at the earlier moment and by a bullet wound if not for the firing of the bullet. Without the bullet wound, he would have died later, from the effects of the knife wound. This, however, did not in fact happen. Thus, the bullet wound, but not the knife wound, is a but-for cause of the death "when and as" it happened.

This form of reasoning is nothing more than proof by tautology. For example, consider Perkins' treatment of the case in which the victim is struck simultaneously by two bullets, each of which would have been instantly fatal by itself: "[He] would not have died when and as he did die (by two bullets) had only one been fired. 'One might have caused the result, but in fact both did so.'" The factors believed to be causally relevant (the two bullets) are incorporated into the description of the manner of occurrence of the injury (death by two bullets), and they are then demonstrated to be causally relevant because we cannot construct that precise description without them.

Such an approach could just as easily have included the victim's knife wound, his silk shirt, or the air temperature in the description of the manner of occurrence of the injury. If so included, each of these conditions would also be proven under Perkins' test to be but-for causes of the harm. We do not include them because we do not believe they were causally relevant. But that is precisely the issue the test is supposed to determine. The test "proves" only what has already been decided. It does not tell us how that decision was made or help us to make it in hard cases.

2. Detailing the Injury

Becht and Miller accept Perkins' reasoning, but they focus more on the details of the harm itself—the final result—than on the manner of its occurrence. For example, in the case of the two fires, one set by the defendant and each sufficient to destroy the plaintiff's house, Becht and Miller assert that, using the but-for test applied "in minute detail, it would probably appear that the defendant's fire was a cause, for the positions of the smoke, ashes, and some parts of the ruins might well have been caused by [i.e., not have existed but for] the defendant's fire."

Again, this assertion begs the question. Under this approach, the defendant's fire was a but-for cause only of the precise "positions of the smoke, ashes, and some parts of the ruins," not of the destruction of the house, for which these precise details are irrelevant. The detailed description will be useful only if the plaintiff wishes to recover for damages that would not have occurred but for the precise position of the smoke and debris—a most unlikely lawsuit.

If being a but-for cause of even the most trivial detail of a harm were sufficient to make the defendant a cause of all the harm, the detailed but-for approach would prove too much. Becht and Miller discuss an example in which an inattentive driver hits a pedestrian who suddenly ran into the path of the driver's car. If the driver had been attentive, he could have swerved a little, but not enough to avoid impact with serious injury. Nevertheless, a detailed application of the but-for test shows that the driver's inattentiveness "was a cause of the injuries actually suffered," since "the injuries would have been at least slightly different and would have been inflicted by different parts of the car if the driver had swerved." Becht and Miller admit that both laypersons and lawyers, using the common knowledge of causation upon which Becht and Miller rely so strongly, would conclude that the driver's inattentiveness was not a cause in such a case. They suggest that laypersons and lawyers make this mistake by failing to pay careful attention to the precise details. But laypersons and lawyers, even after considering the precise details, would still assert correctly that the inattentiveness was not a cause of the serious injury, although it may have been a (but-for) cause of some details associated with the injury. These details have causal significance only if they contributed to the seriousness of the injury.

Becht and Miller realize that they, rather than the laypersons and lawyers, must give way on this issue. They compromise their usual causal principles by "equating the injuries." They reluctantly disregard minor differences and conclude that the inattentiveness was not a cause. Although they do not acknowledge it, they thereby destroy the alleged usefulness of the minute-detail approach. After utilizing the minute-detail approach to support a finding of causation, they then are forced to ignore the details and reject causation by equating the injuries. The concept of "equating the injuries" introduces an inconsistency into their theory that undermines their use of the minute-detail approach to support a finding of causation in the merged-fires case.

3. Excluding Hypothetical Facts
Glanville Williams also refers to Perkins' approach of detailing the manner in which the harm occurred, but he proposes a different approach for the preemptive-causation cases. In such cases, facts that did not actually occur must not be "invented" and considered, no matter how likely they were to occur. Thus, the hypothesized but almost certain fact that P would have been shot by C if he hadn't already been shot by D cannot be considered. However, on the very next page, Williams is obliged to depart from this rule to reach the correct causal conclusion in a case of negligent omission. Moreover, such a rule is of no help at all in cases where the preempted condition actually has occurred—for example, when P actually was shot by C after he already had been shot and killed by D. In this type of preemptive-causation case, and in the duplicative-causation cases, Williams abandons the but-for test for actual causation and treats the causal issue as a policy issue.

4. Aggregating Multiple Potential Causes
The editors of the fifth edition of Prosser's hornbook on tort law attempt to resolve the causal issue in the overdetermined-causation cases by applying the but-for test to the aggregate of potential causes:

When the conduct of two or more actors is so related to an event that their combined conduct, viewed as a whole, is a but-for cause of the event, and application of the but-for rule to them individually would absolve all of them, the conduct of each is a cause in fact of the event.

This version of the but-for test, like Perkins's version, works only if the person applying the test already has correctly determined which factors are sufficiently "related" to the event to be treated as its causes. On its own, the test cannot distinguish duplicative causes from preempted conditions. Moreover, it would treat totally unrelated conditions as causes.

For example, consider the case in which C poisons P's tea and D shoots P before P drinks the tea. Assume also that B was climbing Mt. Everest. Clearly, D's shooting P was a preemptive cause of P's death, and neither C's poisoning the tea nor B's climbing Mt. Everest was a cause. The proposed test, however, would treat all three activities as causes. In the aggregate they were a but-for cause of P's death, while individually none of them was a but-for cause.

C. The Substantial-Factor Formula

Those theorists and judges who are unwilling to engage in contortions such as the ones illustrated above to rescue the but-for from its inadequacies usually have turned to the substantial-factor formula, either as a supplement to the but-for test (to apply to the overdetermined-causation cases) or as a complete substitute for it.

The substantial-factor formula was created originally not as a test of actual causation but as a guide for resolving proximate-cause issues. The originator of the formula, Jeremiah Smith, was content with the but-for test as a test of cause-in-fact, with the usual exception for the overdetermined-causation cases. He wanted to devise a practical alternative to the probability or foreseeability tests for determining the proximate-cause limitations on liability, because he believed that those tests were unsound and inconsistent with the results in many cases. He proposed the following formula: "Defendant's tort must have been a substantial factor in producing the damage complained of." The accompanying explanation and alternative formulations clearly stated that the defendant's tort could not be a substantial factor unless it satisfied the but-for test (with an exception for simultaneous independent sufficient causes); in addition, it would have to be an appreciable and continuously effective or efficient factor in producing the harm, up to the time of occurrence of the harm.

Thus, the substantial-factor formula was meant to be used as the test of legal (proximate) cause, but also incorporated the but-for test (and its exception) for cause-in-fact. Smith's approach was adopted

essentially intact in the original Restatement of Torts. It has persisted in the Restatement (Second) of Torts' treatment of legal causation and cause-in-fact, despite an attempt by Prosser and others to confine the substantial-factor formula to the question of causation-in-fact.

Leon Green first suggested that the substantial-factor formula be applied to the actual-causation issue. He completely rejected the but-for test, since it "take[s] the eye off the ball" by asking what would have happened rather than focusing on what did happen and thereby denies causation in many cases where causal contribution to the injury is obvious. In his view, the substantial-factor formula was the best available alternative. He argued that it should be used without elaboration to pose the issue of causal contribution to the jury in every case, not just in the overdetermined-causation cases. Green's view was accepted by Prosser, who passed it on to several generations of law students and lawyers through the various editions of his hornbook, even after Green himself became disenchanted with the formula.

The problem with the substantial-factor formula as a test of actual causation (apart from its complete lack of guidance on what constitutes a "factor") is that the alleged cause must be a substantial factor. Thus, paradoxically, at the same time that Green was arguing strenuously and cogently that the issue of causation should be completely divorced from the policy issues camouflaged in proximate-cause analysis, he adopted a formula for actual causation that required the judge or jury to determine not only whether the actor's tortious conduct had contributed to the injury (been a factor), but whether it had contributed enough to make the actor responsible—whether, "in the light of all the other factors, the defendant's conduct played an appreciable part in the result." Green seemed to believe that the resulting inquiry retained its character as a factual, causal inquiry because it allegedly relied on quantitative rather than qualitative measures of relative contribution.

Even if quantitative measures of relative contribution are used, however, the question of limiting liability due to the extent of contribution, rather than due to the absence of any contribution, is clearly a proximate-cause issue of policy or principle, rather than an issue of actual causation (contribution to the injury). Moreover, the substantial-factor formula inherently invites consideration of qualitative measures as well as quantitative ones.

Green himself, immediately after emphasizing the quantitative nature of the inquiry, used qualitative considerations when discussing a series of cases involving multiple causes. For example, he asserted that it is "perhaps clear" that the hole poked by D's tug in P's barge, three feet above the water line, was not an appreciable factor in the sinking of the barge when compared with the continued loading of the barge which brought the hole below the waterline, since those who were loading the barge were fully conscious of what had occurred but made no effort to repair the hole. Similarly, he suggested that there would be little possibility of a finding that D's driving over a small flat box, which unbeknown to him contained a highly explosive substance, was a substantial factor in producing the resulting explosion. And, when discussing the cases in which P is negligently or intentionally pushed by X into a hole negligently maintained by D, Green stated that "what would be considered appreciable in one case might not in another. So, as compared with X's negligence, [D's] conduct might be considered appreciable, while as compared with X's intended violence, [D's] conduct might not be so considered."

In each of these cases, the defendant's tortious act was a necessary condition for the occurrence of the injury. When an act (omission, condition) was a necessary condition for the occurrence of an injury, it is unnatural to deny that the act was, as a matter of fact, not only a factor in producing the injury, but also a substantial or appreciable factor. To state otherwise is to make a non-causal, nonfactual policy judgment about responsibility for the injury.

Prosser and, eventually, Green seem to have recognized the emptiness of the undefined substantial-factor formula and the danger of its being used to introduce proximate-cause issues into the actual-causation inquiry. Prosser, in the various editions of his hornbook, concluded his brief discussion of the formula by equating it with the but-for test, with an exception for the overdetermined-causation cases, and in his articles he relied primarily on the but-for test.

In his later writings, Green abandoned his earlier substantive interpretation of the substantial-factor formula. He treated it as a meaningless label for the judge to attach to her determination on the actual-causation issue or to use as a hortatory device "to caution a jury to weigh the evidence carefully." He also criticized the view that the causal inquiry involves not only the question of contribution to the injury, but also the question of how significant the contribution was, without noting that he previously had been the major proponent of this view. However, he continued to reject the but-for test and to insist that the issue of causal contribution be submitted to the jury without any elaboration or guidance.

D. Undefined, Directly Observable Causal Contribution

Lacking any satisfactory test, Green and a few other writers have treated causation as an undefinable and irreducible factual relation between events that can be directly perceived or inferred without explicitly or implicitly resorting to any generalization, definition, or test. Most of these writers do not attempt to explain how this concept would be applied in the various types of causation cases. However, there is one notable exception: Becht and Miller's book, The Test of Factual Causation.

Becht and Miller's book is a comprehensive attempt to demonstrate how the concept of undefined, directly observable causal contribution is applied in tort analysis. They argue that we determine whether a causal relation exists between an act and an injury by breaking down the sequence of events to the appropriate level of detail to see if we can "perceive" a causal connection. If we can, the act is deemed to be a cause of the injury even if the injury can also be traced back to another act or event through a different causal sequence as in the merged-fires case. However, when Becht and Miller attempt to show how this approach would work in the myriad variety of actual-causation cases, they are forced to rely on the but-for test in an increasingly wide range of cases.

Initially, they are forced to use the but-for test to handle causal inquiries involving omissions. By definition an omission is a nonevent—something which did not happen—which only rarely will trigger an actual causal sequence that can be directly perceived or traced. Instead, an omission is almost always a "negative" cause of an injury: it represents a missed opportunity to prevent the injury. That is, an omission is a cause of an injury only if the omitted act would have been part of a hypothetical causal sequence that would have prevented, terminated, or deflected the different causal sequence that actually occurred and produced the injury. Thus, in order to determine whether an omission was a cause of an injury, it is necessary to conduct a hypothetical inquiry. The omitted act must be hypothetically supplied, and a hypothetical causal sequence (which Becht and Miller call a "parallel series") must be constructed and traced to determine whether it would have prevented the occurrence of the injury.

The hypothetical inquiry (but-for test) also must be used whenever an actual ("positive") causal sequence becomes a negative cause by blocking or terminating some preventive effort for example, by blocking a fire engine or cutting off its supply of water. This inquiry also must be employed to determine whether the excess (negligent) portion of a certain speed or weight, or the difference between being in a safe position or an unsafe (negligent) position, contributed to the injury. Indeed, as Becht and Miller reluctantly admit, the hypothetical inquiry must be used whenever the negligent aspect of an act does not encompass the act as a whole. For example, in the excess-speed case, the act is driving at a certain speed. We observe the car at that speed hit the child. The negligent aspect of the speeding is the excess speed, which Becht and Miller note "is not an extent but a concept. Like an omission, it did not happen, and it cannot be a simple [perceived] cause of events in the world."

Becht and Miller recognize the possible criticism that they are implicitly using the hypothetical inquiry with all negligent acts, rather than just with negligent acts that have a non-negligent aspect, "but are unconscious of [doing so] when the [hypothetical inquiry] shows clearly that the negligent act was a cause of the harm." They admit that they cannot disprove this contention, but they continue to claim that they are using direct perception of causation in such cases. However, they have some difficulty with a case in which the defendant negligently welds the roof of a car, leaving a sharp edge, and the driver's head is crushed against the roof at the weld point when the roof is smashed in during an accident. They steadfastly assert that the case is one in which direct perception or inference, unaided by any hypothetical inquiry, shows a lack of causation by the sharp weld, just as direct perception or inference shows that the color of the roof was not a cause of the injury.

The direct-perception argument relies on the notion that there are observable and describable causal qualities or forces in objects or events. Becht and Miller eventually concede that this notion is naive as compared with the Human account, which is based on causal generalizations. Even if the direct-perception notion were creditable, it is difficult to imagine how the lack of causation by the sharp weld could be perceived in the circumstances given. It is also difficult to understand what is meant by "direct inference." An inference is based on some concept of how things generally happen—that is, on causal generalizations. Causal generalizations incorporate the belief that the cause is in some sense necessary for the occurrence of the consequence. The but-for test is simply the means by which we determine whether this element of necessity exists in the particular case.

Becht and Miller argue that, even if it is true that they are explicitly or implicitly using the but-for test in every case, they are using a less restrictive version. Unlike the usual version, they compare what happened with what would have happened in as minute detail as possible. Moreover, in those cases in which there was more than one positive causal sequence that led to the injury, they only require that the defendant's act or omission have been necessary for the continuation of the positive causal sequence with which it was associated, rather than requiring that it have been necessary for the injury itself.

The first distinction—their use of minute detail—is nullified by their tactic of "equating the injuries" to avoid finding but-for causation whenever there is a slight difference between the actual process or result and the hypothesized process and result.

The second distinction, however, is a real one. It enables them to find that causation exists in many of the overdetermined-causation cases. For example, in the merged-fires case the defendant's tortious conduct will be treated as a cause of the destruction of the house if it was a but-for cause of one of the fires, even though the house would have been burnt down by the other fire anyway. The defendant's tortious conduct was a but-for cause of one of the duplicative causal sequences, and that is sufficient to establish the causal connection to the destruction of the house.

Becht and Miller's causal-contribution analysis ends up being very similar to the "necessary element of a sufficient set" test. However, it is not exactly equivalent. Indeed, it produces anomalous results precisely to the extent that it varies from the latter test. Becht and Miller's approach requires that the tortious act or omission have been a necessary condition for one of the positive (actual) causal sequences that contributed to the injury. They are therefore forced to deny that causation exists when the overdetermined-causation problem results from duplicative or preempted conditions that affect the same positive causal sequence, rather than from the existence of multiple positive causal sequences.

For example, they discuss the case in which C negligently fails to discover and repair defective brakes in a car before renting the car to D, who, unaware of the defective condition of the brakes, negligently fails to try to use them to avoid hitting P. P is hit, but he would not have been hit if the brakes had been working properly and D had used them. C's omission (the failure to inspect and repair the brakes) was not a necessary condition for the occurrence of the positive causal sequence that produced the injury, since D made no attempt to use the brakes. Similarly, given C's omission, D's omission (the failure to try to use the brakes) was not a necessary condition either. Becht and Miller unhappily but firmly conclude that neither omission was a cause of the injury, but would hold both C and D liable to avoid a "morally indefensible" and "inexcusable" result.

The same problem occurs with acts. Assume that a cable has a maximum safe load capacity of one ton when it is in good condition. C negligently weakens the cable (for example, by cutting a few of its strands) so that it will now break if a one-ton load is applied. D negligently overloads the cable with a two-ton load, which would cause it to break even if it were in good condition. The cable breaks at the weakened point, and the load falls on and injures P. Since the negligent

acts of C and D are both part of the same positive causal sequence that produced the injury, but neither was a necessary condition for the occurrence of the sequence, neither is a cause of the injury under Becht and Miller's approach.

Becht and Miller's book contains illuminating discussions on many points—for example, the distinction between acts and omissions and the need to focus on the tortious aspect of the actor's conduct. Perhaps its most valuable contribution, however, is an unintended one: the demonstration of the unavoidability of the but-for (necessary condition) test in causal analysis. This unavoidability is most clear when the causal inquiry focuses on omissions or the tortious aspect of acts, but it is implicit in all causal inquiries.

E. The NESS (Necessary Element of a Sufficient Set) Test

In this section, I turn at last to a test for causal contribution that is applicable to the entire spectrum of causation cases. This test incorporates the indispensable notion of necessity, but subordinates it to the notion of sufficiency. I call this test the NESS (Necessary Element of a Sufficient Set) test.

The NESS test was first suggested by H.L.A. Hart and Tony Honore. However, their brief exposition of this test was overshadowed and distorted by their primary emphasis on proximate-cause issues. The test has received very little notice and even less acceptance in the subsequent legal literature. One of the principal purposes of this Article is to draw renewed attention to the NESS test, by demonstrating its fundamental identity with the basic concept of causation and its utility in resolving the cases that have proved troublesome for several generations of tort scholars.

1. The Philosophic Basis of the NESS Test

The NESS test captures the essential meaning of the concept of causation. This meaning was first articulated by the philosopher David Hume. Hume rejected the earlier notion that we acquire causal knowledge through direct sensory perception of causal qualities or forces inherent in objects or events. Instead, he insisted that we only observe certain successions of events, more or less frequently repeated. From these observations, we inductively derive the belief that certain antecedent events are not only always conjoined with, but also are sufficient for the occurrence of, certain subsequent events. That is, we form a belief in more or less well-grounded causal laws or generalizations. Causal knowledge or belief also can be based on reasoning by analogy from such observations or can be acquired through education, which passes on the causal knowledge of others. Any singular causal statement about a particular occurrence is not a reporting of direct sensory perception of causal forces, but rather an assertion of the belief that the occurrence instantiates one or more causal laws or generalizations.

A fully specified causal law or generalization would state an invariable connection between the cause and the consequence: given the actual existence of the fully specified set of antecedent conditions, the consequence must follow. In other words, the fully specified set of antecedent conditions is sufficient for the occurrence of the consequence. In the typical singular causal statement, the causal assertion includes, explicitly or implicitly, only a few of the antecedent conditions but nevertheless asserts that they were part of an incompletely specified (and incompletely understood or known) set of actual conditions that was sufficient for the occurrence of the consequence.

Hume was primarily interested in elaborating and defending this "regularity" account of causation and causal knowledge, which insists that the meaning of causation is to be found in causal laws or generalizations rather than in some notion of causal qualities or forces. However, while pursuing this primary objective, he occasionally noted that one must be careful when constructing a causal law or generalization to distinguish the causally relevant antecedent conditions from the causally irrelevant antecedent conditions. This differentiation is necessary to insure that the set of jointly sufficient antecedent conditions includes only those that are indeed invariably connected with the consequence. Thus, the antecedent conditions must be restricted to those that are necessary for the sufficiency of the set.

Hume also maintained that a certain consequence is always produced by the same cause—that is, that there is a unique sufficient set of antecedent conditions that always must be present to produce a particular consequence. Hume's successor, John Stuart Mill, disagreed. He asserted that there may be a plurality

of potential causes for any consequence. For example, death may be caused by poison on one occasion, by a bullet wound on another, by fire on yet another, and so forth. Hume's defenders have argued that such seemingly different causes may upon further investigation turn out to be overly broad specifications of a single common cause, or that the seemingly identical consequence may turn out to be distinct consequences. However, they also admit that ordinary experience provides strong support for the plurality-of-potential-causes theory. Indeed, the plurality theory has become part of the dominant "regularity" account of the meaning of causation.

As Hart and Honore noted in 1959, the "necessary element of a sufficient set" (NESS) test of causal contribution follows directly from this dominant "regularity" account of the meaning of causation. The essence of the concept of causation under this philosophic account is that a particular condition was a cause of (condition contributing to) a specific consequence if and only if it was a necessary element of a set of antecedent actual conditions that was sufficient for the occurrence of the consequence. (Note that the phrase "a set" permits a plurality of sufficient sets.) This is the more precise, extended statement of the NESS test.

Surprisingly, however, this notion of a contributing condition appears only infrequently in the philosophic literature on causation. The literature continues to be characterized by arguments based on necessary conditions, sufficient conditions, or necessary and sufficient conditions. After Hart and Honore's book was published, several non-legal philosophers articulated NESS-like notions of causal contribution. In each instance, however, they burdened the NESS test with the additional requirement that the sufficient set be necessary for the occurrence of the consequence in the particular circumstances. This requirement converts the NESS test to a necessary and sufficient condition test, which cannot accommodate the duplicative-causation cases (for example, the merged-fires cases).

Hart and Honore do not make this mistake, because they recognize that there may be a plurality of causes in a particular instance. However, their version of the NESS test is also deficient in several respects.

First, they apparently require that a duplicative or preemptive cause be independently "sufficient" for the occurrence of the injury. That is, it must be sufficient in conjunction with the "background" conditions, but excluding the duplicated or preempted conditions. Second, they submerge the critical distinction between duplicative and preemptive causation by constructing an overlapping typology of overdetermined-causation cases. Finally, they confuse the factual issue of causal contribution with the issues of policy or principle involved in determining ultimate liability in certain types of cases.

2. The Duplicative-Causation Cases

As elaborated, Hart and Honore's NESS test is only slightly less restrictive than the Restatement's substantial-factor exception to the butfor test, which only applies when each of two actively operating factors was sufficient by itself for the occurrence of the injury. Hart and Honore do not require that each of the factors have been actively operating, but they seem to require that each have been sufficient by itself for the occurrence of the injury. For example, in the merged-fires cases, they assume that each fire would have been sufficient by itself for the destruction of the plaintiff's house. The NESS test then confirms causal contribution by each fire. Each fire was necessary for the sufficiency of a set of actual antecedent conditions that did not include the other fire.

The requirement that each factor have been sufficient by itself (when combined with the background conditions) is too restrictive and is not a part of the basic concept of causation that is reflected in the NESS test. Moreover, the independent-sufficiency requirement is not followed by the courts. For example, in two duplicative-causation cases involving merged fires and noisy motorcycles, respectively, the courts did not require the plaintiff to prove the independent sufficiency of each contributing factor, but rather required him to prove only that each factor contributed to the injury. Similarly, in the pollution cases, the courts have allowed the plaintiff to recover from each defendant who contributed to the pollution that caused the injury, even though none of the defendants' individual contributions was either necessary or sufficient by itself for the occurrence of the injury.

Malone argues that the courts' departure from the but-for test in the overdetermined-causation cases is further evidence of the policy-dependent nature of the causal inquiry. He contends that the courts are willing to replace the but-for test with the substantial-factor formula in cases like the merged-fires cases because of the important policies that underlie "the well-established rules that prohibit the setting into motion of a destructive force."

But, contrary to Malone's assertion, the policies or principles at work in these cases are not those underlying the particular rule that was violated. They are the ones underlying the actual causation requirement itself. As Malone himself notes, the courts feel impelled to depart from the but-for test in these overdetermined-causation cases because, although the but-for test is not satisfied, it is clear that the defendant's tortious conduct contributed to the injury: "Our senses have told us that he did participate… In the language of the layman, the defendant's fire 'had something to do with' the burning of the plaintiff's property." Just as Newtonian mechanics serves as an adequate substitute for the more accurate and comprehensive theories of relative and quantum mechanics in ordinary physical situations, the but-for test serves as an adequate substitute for the NESS test in ordinary causal situations. In each context, however, the substitute must give way to the more accurate and comprehensive concept when the situation is more subtle and complex.

In the pollution cases, the NESS test confirms that each defendant's pollution contributed to the injury, even though it was neither necessary nor independently sufficient for the injury. For example, assume that five units of pollution were necessary and sufficient for the injury and that each of seven defendants discharged one unit of pollution. Each defendant can truthfully say that its one unit was neither necessary nor independently sufficient for the injury. But each defendant's one unit was necessary for the sufficiency of a set of actual antecedent conditions that included only four of the other units, and the sufficiency of this particular set of actual antecedent conditions was not affected by the existence of two additional duplicative units.

A similar causal situation exists even if one defendant discharges five units of pollution and a second defendant discharges two units. The two units still mix with the five units to produce the injurious seven units. More rigorously, the two units were necessary for the sufficiency of a set of actual antecedent conditions that included only three of the first defendant's five units, a set whose sufficiency was not affected by the existence of two additional duplicative units also provided by the first defendant.

The analysis of the merged-fires cases is analogous. Thus, if any two of three fires were sufficient for the injury, but none by itself was sufficient, each was a cause of the injury since each was necessary for the sufficiency of a set of actual antecedent conditions that included only one of the other fires. The same causal situation exists even if there were only two fires, one of which was independently sufficient and the other of which was not. The first fire was clearly a cause, since it was independently sufficient. But the second fire also was a cause. It was necessary for the sufficiency of a set of actual antecedent conditions which included another fire (the first) that was "at least large enough to be sufficient for the injury if it merged with a fire the size of the second fire." The sufficiency of this set is not affected by the fact that the first fire was so large that it would have been sufficient by itself.

The wording of the quoted condition, "at least large enough," is not a verbal gimmick. The condition is an actual one that existed on the particular occasion. It describes a certain factual situation, as much as the condition in the pollution case that referred to only three of the first defendant's five units of pollution. In the former case, the size of the first fire is broken down into portions; in the latter case, the amount of the first defendant's pollution is broken down into portions.

The NESS test would attribute causal status to a very small fire that merged with an overwhelming large fire. The very small fire was a duplicative cause of any resulting injury. Whether the person who tortuously caused the very small fire should be held liable for any or all of the resulting injury is an issue of policy or principle that comes under the heading of damages.

The same analysis applies to the weakened-cable hypothetical. In that example, a cable with a maximum safe load capacity of one ton was weakened by C, who negligently cut a few of its strands so that it would break if subjected to a one-ton load. D then negligently put a two-ton load on the cable, which would have caused it to break even if the cable were in good condition, and the cable broke at the weakened point. C's weakening of the cable was necessary for the sufficiency of a set of actual antecedent conditions which included a load of at least one ton, and the sufficiency of this set was not affected by the fact that the load was more than one ton. Indeed, the causal contribution of C's weakening of the cable is evidenced by the fact that the cable broke at the weakened point. Similarly, D's overloading of the cable was necessary for the sufficiency of a set of actual antecedent conditions that included a cable with a load capacity of at most one ton, and the sufficiency of this set was not affected by the fact that the cable had a capacity of less than one ton as a result of the weakening. C's weakening of the cable and D's overloading of it are duplicative causes of the cable's breaking and the resulting injury to the plaintiff.

3. The Preemptive-Causation Cases

So far, the discussion has concentrated on the duplicative-causation cases. I turn now to the preemptive-caution cases. Hart and Honore mention situations in which the defendant asserts that someone else would have shot the plaintiff or stolen his property if the defendant had not done so. The defendant's argument would succeed under a literal application of the Restatement, which adheres to the but-for test unless the alternative factor was "actively operating." But, under the NESS test, the defendant's tortious act clearly was a cause of the injury, since it was a necessary element of the set of actual antecedent conditions that was sufficient for the injury. Under this test, moreover, only the defendant's actions would be deemed a cause. The potential actions of others that did not in fact occur could not be a part of any set of actual antecedent conditions that was sufficient for the injury.

Preemptive causation also is present in many cases where the alternative factor actually did occur. For example, in my initial illustration where D shot and killed P just as P was about to drink a cup of tea that had been poisoned by C, D's shot was necessary for the sufficiency of a set of actual antecedent conditions that did not include the poisoned tea. Conversely, C's poisoning of the tea was not a necessary element of any sufficient set of actual antecedent conditions. A set that included the poisoned tea but not the shooting would be sufficient only if P actually drank the tea, but this was not an actual condition. The shooting preempted the potential causal effect of the poisoned tea.

Moreover, even if P actually had drunk the poisoned tea, C's poisoning of the tea still would not be a cause of P's death if the poison did not work instantaneously but the shot did. The poisoned tea would be a cause of P's death only if P drank the tea and was alive when the poison took effect. That is, a set of actual antecedent conditions sufficient to cause P's death must include poisoning of the tea, P's drinking of the poisoned tea, and P's being alive when the poison takes effect. Although the first two conditions actually existed, the third did not. D's shooting P prevented it from occurring. Thus, there is no sufficient set of actual antecedent conditions that includes C's poisoning of the tea as a necessary element. Consequently, C's poisoning of the tea fails the NESS test. It did not contribute to P's death.

As the last example illustrates, a necessary condition for the sufficiency of any set of actual antecedent conditions is that the injury not have occurred already as a result of other actual conditions outside the set. The determination of whether this condition existed, as with all the other conditions, is an empirical judgment. For example, in the weakened-cable hypothetical, C's weakening of the cable was considered to be a duplicative cause when the cable broke at the weakened point. If the cable had broken instead at some other point, our empirical evaluation would be that the potential causal effect of C's weakening of the cable was preempted by the existence of this other weaker point in the cable. This other weaker point prevented the cable from staying together long enough for C's weakened point to have any effect. In those circumstances, C's weakening of the cable would not be a necessary element of any sufficient set of actual antecedent conditions.

The key to the overdetermined-causation cases, therefore, is the distinction between duplicative and preemptive causation. In each case, an empirical judgment must be made: was the tortious aspect of the defendant's conduct a necessary element in a set of actual antecedent conditions that was sufficient for the occurrence of the injury, or was it not a necessary member of any actually sufficient set because its potential effects were preempted by other actual conditions outside the set?

In the merged-fires cases or the noisy-motorcycles case, we believe that each factor duplicates or reinforces the effects of the other factor, rather than preempting those effects—that is, that there is more than one sufficient cause. In the shooting case, however, we believe that there was only one sufficient cause (the shooting), which preempted the effects of the other potential cause (the poisoning) and thereby prevented it from being a necessary member of an actually sufficient set. We would believe otherwise if medical experts testified that the effects of the poison combined with the effects of the shooting to cause the victim's death, although either alone would have been sufficient. The critical issue is whether one factor completely preempted the potential effects of the other factor, so that there was only one sufficient (preemptive) cause in the actual circumstances, or whether each factor was a necessary part of a different (but overlapping) actually sufficient set, in which case there was more than one sufficient (duplicative) cause.

Hart and Honore submerge this critical issue in their discussion of the overdetermined-causation cases. They construct a typology that first divides the cases into those involving "additional causes" and those involving "alternative causes." The alternative-cause category is meant to include those cases in which there was a potential alternative cause which never occurred. Examples include the cases where the defendant assets that someone else would have shot or robbed the plaintiff if he had not. However, Hart and Honore also include a bridge-delay case in which there was an actual second bridge that would have delayed the plaintiff's boat even if the first bridge had not. It is misleading to speak of these cases as alternative-cause cases. As Hart and Honore clearly indicate, the alternative cause was not a cause. It was a preempted potential cause, best referred to as a "preempted condition." The category is a subset of the preemptive-causation cases.

Their additional-cause category is subdivided into three subcategories. The "combinatory" or "reinforcing" cause subcategory, however, is the only one that actually involves additional (duplicative) causes. The other two subcategories are subsets of the preemptive-causation cases, where again it is misleading to refer to the preempted condition as an additional cause. The "neutralizing" cause subcategory covers situations in which the effective cause prevents an alternative active causal process from being completed. For example, a fire approaching a house is quenched by a flood which destroys the house, or a poison victim is killed by a bullet before the poison kills him. The "overtaking" cause subcategory originally was limited to situations in which a subsequent actual injury would have caused the same damage as the initial injury: for example, two successive injuries, each of which would have been sufficient to disable the victim totally. However, the subcategory has been expanded in the second edition to encompass situations in which the effective cause frustrates an active causal process, so that the subcategory now overlaps the "neutralizing" cause subcategory.

Perhaps as a result of their confusing typology, Hart and Honore lose sight of the basic concept of causation embodied in the NESS test. In the double-bridge and successive-injury cases, for example, the defendant's tortious conduct was a (preemptive) cause of the boat's delay in the double-bridge case and a (preemptive) cause of the victim's loss of a limb and resulting total disability in the successive-injury case. But Hart and Honore claim that the tortious conduct was not a cause of the victim's economic loss in either case, since the victim would have suffered the economic loss anyway as a result of the second bridge or the second injury, respectively.

This causal argument, however, is based on the but-for test rather than the NESS test. In each case, the defendant's tortious conduct was a necessary element of a set of actual antecedent conditions that did not include the subsequent condition (the second bridge or the second injury) and was sufficient for the occurrence of the economic loss. The existence of the subsequent condition did not prevent this set from being sufficient to produce the economic loss. On the other hand, neither the second bridge nor the second injury

was a necessary element of any set of actual antecedent conditions that was sufficient for the occurrence of the loss. The second bridge will cause a delay only if the boat reaches it, but the boat did not reach it. The second injury will cause total disability and resulting economic loss only if the victim is not already totally disabled, but this also was not one of the actual conditions. In each instance, the defendant's tortious act is a preemptive cause of the injury and the resulting economic loss, and the subsequent preempted condition is not a cause of the economic loss.

4. Distinguishing the Damages Issue: The Successive-Injury and Overwhelming-Force Cases

The successive-injury cases have engendered much debate and confusion, particularly in the Commonwealth countries, where the legal community seems unable to free itself from the but-for concept of causation. The causal situation is clear in these cases. The first injury caused the economic loss; the second did not. The issue is not causal. It is a proximate-cause issue of policy or principle that is most appropriately placed under the heading of damages, and it also arises in the duplicative-causation cases. The issue is whether a defendant who has tortuously caused injury to the plaintiff nevertheless should be absolved from liability if the injury would have occurred anyway as a result of independent duplicative or preempted conditions.

Courts generally absolve the defendant from liability if he proves that the injury would have occurred anyway as a result of independent non-tortious conditions. In such a case, the plaintiff's corrective-justice claim—that he would not have been injured if not for the tortious conduct of others—fails. On the other hand, if the duplicative or preempted conditions also resulted from tortious conduct, the plaintiff's corrective-justice claim is intact. Nevertheless, it may seem unfair to hold a defendant liable for the entire injury if his contribution to the injury was relatively minor compared to the other contributing conditions. But this proximate-cause problem has been greatly lessened by the recent widespread liberalization of the rules governing contribution among defendants. Therefore, once the plaintiff has established that the tortious aspect of a certain defendant's conduct contributed to the injury, many courts shift the burden to the defendant to establish that (1) the injury would have occurred anyway as a result of independent non-tortious conditions, (2) he contributed to only a part of the injury, or (3) he is entitled to contribution from the other defendants based on relative tortious contribution.

The causal issue is almost always confused with the policy-laden damages issue in the overwhelming-force cases involving passive conditions. When an overwhelming force combines with an active condition, the courts are less likely to confuse the two issues. Thus, in the merged-fires cases, the courts generally recognize that the defendant's smaller fire that combined with a much large fire nevertheless contributed to the injury. If the defendant avoids liability, it is not due to a lack of causal contribution but rather due to non-causal limitations. For example, the defendant usually can avoid liability if he proves that the other fire was independently sufficient and of non-tortious origin, or perhaps even if it was also of tortious origin if it was so overwhelming as to make the defendant's contribution relatively insignificant. On the other hand, the defendant is unlikely to escape liability even though his contribution was a very small part of the total cause if it was necessary for the consequence or, although unnecessary, was combined with a large number of similarly small contributions, as in the pollution cases.

When the overwhelming force combines with a passive condition, however, most courts and commentators tend to fall back on the but-for test and erroneously deny causal contribution. For example, the courts deny that the defendant's negligent failure to construct an adequate dam or to keep runoff pipes free of debris was a cause of flooding that would have occurred given a normal storm, if the actual storm was an extraordinary one that would have caused flooding even if the defendant had not been negligent. Similarly, they have stated that the defendant's negligent failure to remove a rotten pole is not a cause of injury when the pole is knocked down by a car that hits it with such force that it would have been knocked down even if it were not rotten.

These are overdetermined-causation cases that are entirely analogous to the merged-fires cases and the weakened-cable case. Thus, if the rotten pole broke at its weak point, the weak condition clearly contributed to the injury. It was a necessary element of a sufficient set of actual antecedent conditions that included an impact with at least enough force to knock down a rotten pole. The sufficiency of the set was not affected by the fact that the impact had a greater force, unless the impact knocked the pole over in its entirety rather than breaking it at its weak point. Similarly, the failure to remove debris from a dam's runoff pipes or to build it high enough to prevent flooding during a normal storm is a duplicative cause of flooding that occurs during an extraordinary storm. The unremoved debris or inadequate height is a necessary element in a sufficient set of actual antecedent conditions that includes an at least normal storm, and the sufficiency of this set is not affected by the fact that the storm was larger than normal.

A few courts have recognized that the defendant's tortious conduct contributed to the injury in these passive-condition cases. Indeed, some courts have held the defendant liable even when the injury would have occurred anyway as a result of independently sufficient non-tortious conditions. However, if the non-causal policy limitations adopted in the merged-fires and successive-injury cases are followed, the defendant should be able to avoid liability in such circumstances. These policy limitations, rather than the false denial of causation, explain the ultimate result in those cases in which liability is denied because the injury would have occurred anyway due to the extraordinary force of a storm.

Conversely, given the usual policy limitations, the defendant should not escape liability when the duplicative or preempted condition was also of tortious origin—for example, when the defendant's rotten pole is knocked down by a negligent driver and an innocent third party is injured. This case is the same as a merged-fires case in which the defendant's insufficient fire joins with an independently sufficient fire, also of tortious origin. In each case, both conditions are tortious duplicative causes of the injury, and liability should be imposed jointly on both toreadors with a right of contribution.

5. Theft, Nonuse, or Misuse of Defective or Missing Safety Devices

Some of the most difficult overdetermined-causation cases are the preemptive-causation cases involving theft, nonuse, or misuse of defective or missing safety devices. A familiar example is the case in which C negligently failed to discover and repair defective brakes in a car that he rented to D, and D negligently failed to try to use the brakes to avoid running into P. It is assumed that the injury to P would have been avoided if and only if C had repaired the brakes and D had tried to use them. As we saw above, Green asserts that C's conduct as a whole and D's conduct as a whole were each causes of the injury, but that only C should be held liable. Becht, Miller, Prosser, and Fleming assert that neither C's negligence nor D's negligence was a cause of the injury, but that both C and D should be held liable.

Under the NESS test, it is clear that D's negligence was a preemptive cause of P's injury, and that C's negligence did not contribute to the injury. D's failure to try to use the brakes was necessary for the sufficiency of a set of actual antecedent conditions that did not include C's failure to repair the brakes, and the sufficiency of this set was not affected by C's failure to repair the brakes. A failure to try to use brakes will have a negative causal effect whether or not the brakes are defective. On the other hand, C's failure to repair the brakes was not a necessary element of any set of antecedent actual conditions that was sufficient for the occurrence of the injury. Defective brakes will have an actual causal effect only if someone tries to use them, but that was not an actual condition here. The potential negative causal effect of C's failure to repair the brakes was preempted by D's failure to try to use them.

The same analysis applies in every case involving nonuse or misuse of a missing or defective safety device, unless the actor did not try to use the device because he knew it was missing or defective. For example, failure to provide a fire escape was not a cause of P's injury if P could not have gotten to the fire escape anyway or would not have tried to get to it even if it existed. Similarly, failure to provide safety equipment to a worker is not a cause of his injury if he would not have used it anyway, and failure to pack a parachute properly is not a cause of death if the deceased never pulled the ripcord to release the parachute.

A somewhat different situation is presented by McLaughlin's hypothetical in which D empties P's water keg and refills it with salt before P is dropped into the middle of a desert. C subsequently steals the keg, thinking that it contains water, and P dies of thirst. This case is different from the previous cases because it is assumed that P would have used the water ("safety device") if it had been available. D's emptying the keg made the water unavailable and was a preemptive cause of P's death. C's theft of the keg was not a cause of P's death. Its potential effect (making the water unavailable) depended on the keg's having water in it when it was stolen, but that was not an actual condition.

Hart and Honore modify the facts by having D poison the water in the keg rather than replacing it with salt. They conclude that neither C nor D was a cause of P's death, but only because they equate causing death with shortening life and note that P would have died sooner by poisoning if C had not stolen the keg. As Becht and Miller point out, and as a NESS analysis demonstrates, the lack of water (fluid) caused the death, and it is irrelevant that P would have died sooner if he had drunk the poisoned water. He in fact did not drink the poisoned water, because C stole it. C's theft caused P's death and preempted the potential causal effect of D's poisoning the water.

It should be clear by now that the NESS test not only resolves but also clarifies and illuminates the causal issues in the problematic causation cases that have plagued tort scholars for generations. It does so because it is not just a test for causation, but is itself the meaning of causation. When there is no overdetermined-causation problem—that is, when there is only one actual or hypothetical sufficient set of conditions for a particular event—the NESS test collapses into the simple, traditional but-for test. But the concept of causation is much subtler and complex than the but-for test. Thus, whenever the but-for test is not satisfied, the factfinder must utilize this more complex notion of causation, with its often subtle distinction between actual sufficiency and mere apparent (preempted) sufficiency, before the causal inquiry can be concluded.

Excerpted from "Causation in Tort Law," *California Law Review* 73:6 (December 1985), pp. 1775–1803
Reprinted with permission of the publisher

MAIMONIDES: LAWS OF THE NEGLIGENT KILLER

**Laws of Murder and Preservation
of Life, Chapter 5**

1. Whenever a person kills unintentionally, he should be exiled from the city in which he killed, to a city of refuge. It is a positive mitzvah to exile him, as implied by Numbers 35:25: "He shall dwell there until the death of the High Priest."

The court is admonished not to accept a ransom from the killer to enable him to remain in his city, as Ibid., 32 states: "You shall not accept a ransom so that he will not have to flee to his city of refuge." . . .

7. At the outset, both a person who killed unintentionally and one who killed intentionally should flee to a city of refuge. The court in the city in which the killing took place sends for the killer and brings him back to that city, as ibid.:12 states: "And the elders of his city shall send and take him from there."

If the killer is condemned to execution, he should be executed, as ibid. continues: "And they shall give him to the hand of the blood redeemer." If a person is absolved, he should be released, as Numbers 35:25 states: "And the congregation shall save the killer from the hand of the blood redeemer." And if the killer is sentenced to exile, he should be returned to his previous place, as ibid. continues: "And the congregation shall return him to his city of refuge."

8. When he is returned to his city of refuge, he is given two Torah sages to accompany him, lest the blood redeemer attempt to kill him on the way. They should tell him: "Do not deal with him in the manner of those who shed blood. It was unintentional that this happened."

9. When a blood redeemer slays a person who killed unintentionally outside the Sabbath limits of his city of refuge, he is not held liable, as Deuteronomy 19:6 states: "He is not judged as liable to be executed."

10. The above applies whether he kills him on the road before he enters his city of refuge or if he kills him when returning together with the two who are guarding him. If he enters his city of refuge and intentionally departs beyond its Sabbath boundaries, he has granted license for his life to be taken. The blood redeemer is permitted to kill him. And if another person kills him, that other person is not liable, as Numbers 35:27 states: "There is no liability for his blood."

11. If the killer leaves his city of refuge unintentionally, whoever slays him—whether the blood redeemer or another person—should be exiled. If the killer is slain within the Sabbath limits of the city of refuge, the one who slayed him should be executed.

12. The altar in the Temple serves as a haven for killers. This is derived from Exodus 21:14, which states with regard to a person who kills intentionally: "You shall take him from My altar to die." One can derive from this, that one who kills unintentionally should not be killed at the altar.

Thus, if a person kills unintentionally and takes refuge at the altar, and the blood redeemer kills him there, he should be executed as if he killed him in a city of refuge.

13. What serves as a haven is only the top of the altar in the Temple. Moreover, it serves as a haven only for a priest who is in the midst of sacrificial worship. For a person other than a priest, a priest who is not involved in the sacrificial worship, or a priest who was involved in the sacrificial worship but was near the altar or holding on to its horns, the altar does not serve as a haven.

14. If someone takes refuge on the altar, he is not left there. Instead, he is given guards and taken to a city of refuge.

When does the above apply? When one is obligated to be exiled. If, however, a person feared that a king will have him executed as is the king's authority, or that the court will execute him as an immediate directive, and fled to the altar and held on to it, he should be saved.

This applies even if he is a commoner. He should not be taken from the altar to die unless he was sentenced to death because of the testimony of witnesses who delivered a warning, as is always required with regard to those executed by the court.

Laws of Murder and Preservation of Life, Chapter 6

1. There are three categories of unintentional killers.

2. There is a person who kills unintentionally, without at all knowing that this will be the consequence of his actions. Concerning such a person, Exodus 21:13 says: "Who did not lay in ambush." The law applying to such a person is that he should be exiled to a city of refuge, as we have explained in the previous chapter.

3. There is a person who kills unintentionally, whose acts resemble those caused by forces beyond his control—i.e., that the death will be caused by an extraordinary phenomenon that does not commonly occur. Such a person is not liable to be exiled, and if he is slain by the blood redeemer, the blood redeemer should be executed for killing him.

4. There is a person who kills unintentionally, whose acts resemble those willfully perpetrated—e.g., they involve negligence or that care should have been taken with regard to a certain factor and it was not. Such a person is not sentenced to exile, because his sin is very severe and exile cannot bring him atonement, nor do the cities of refuge served as a haven for him. For they serve as a haven only for those obligated to be exiled. Therefore, if the blood redeemer finds this killer anywhere and slays him, he is not liable.

5. What should such a person do? Sit and protect himself from the blood redeemer.

Similarly, if the blood redeemer slays any of the murderers whose acts were observed by only one witness, or who were not given a warning or the like, the blood redeemer is not liable for execution. Killing such individuals should not be considered more severe than killing a person who killed unintentionally.

6. What does the above imply? When a person throws a stone into the public domain and it causes death or he tears down his wall into the public domain, and a stone falls and causes death—whether he tears down the wall during the day or during the night—he is considered to be close to having acted intentionally.

A city of refuge does not serve as a haven for him. For he should have checked the surroundings and then thrown the stone or torn down the wall.

7. The following rules apply if a person tears down a wall into a garbage dump at night. If it is likely that people are there, he is considered to be close to having acted intentionally, and a city of refuge does not serve as a haven for him. If people are never found there, the death is considered close to having been caused by forces beyond his control, and he is not liable for exile.

8. Different rules apply if people would use a garbage dump to relieve themselves at night, but would not use it for this purpose during the daytime. If it happened that a person sat there during the day, and he was killed by a stone that came from a person tearing down his wall, the person who tore down his wall should be exiled.

9. If after the stone began to fall, the person came and sat down, and the stone struck him and caused his death, the person who tore down his wall is not liable to be exiled.

10. Similarly, if a person threw a stone into the public domain, and after the stone left his hand, the victim stuck his head out from a window and was struck by it, the person who threw the stone is not liable for exile. This is derived from Deuteronomy 19:5, which states: "the iron slips from the wood and finds his fellow." This excludes an instance when the victim causes himself to be found by the iron or other object that causes death.

When a person who hates the victim kills unintentionally, the city of refuge does not serve as a haven for him. This is implied by Numbers 35:23, which states that a person who is exiled: "is not the victim's enemy." We operate under the presumption that one who is an enemy is close to having acted willfully.

Who is considered to be an enemy? A person who did not speak to the victim for at least three days because of animosity.

Similarly, all the following individuals are considered close to having acted willfully, and a city of refuge does not serve as a haven for them:

a) a person who entered an intersection holding an open knife in his hand without realizing that the victim was approaching from the other side and unintentionally stabbed him, causing his death;

b) a person who unintentionally pushed a colleague to his death with his body and not with his hands;

c) a person who intended to throw a stone that could kill two cubits, and instead threw it four;

d) a person who thought that it was permitted to kill;

e) a person who intended to kill one person and instead killed another. This applies even if he intended to kill a gentile or an animal and instead killed a Jew.

11. When a person enters a courtyard of a homeowner without permission, and the homeowner kills him unintentionally, the homeowner is not liable to be exiled as can be inferred from Deuteronomy 19:5, which, when describing a person who must be exiled speaks of one: "Who encounters his colleague in the forest." Our Sages commented: A forest is a place that the victim has the right to enter. Similarly, in all such places, and only in such places, is a killer liable to be exiled.

Therefore, if a person enters a carpenter's shop without permission, and a block of wood flies forth and strikes him in the face and kills him, and he dies, the carpenter is not liable to be exiled. If he entered with permission, the carpenter should be exiled.

12. When a person was lifting a barrel with a pulley to bring it up to a roof, and the the rope broke, causing it to fall on a colleague, or a person was climbing up a ladder and fell on a colleague and killed him, the person who caused the death is not liable to be exiled. This is considered to be something beyond his control. For this is not something that is likely to happen, but is rather an extraordinary occurrence.

If, by contrast, a person was lowering a barrel with a rope and it fell on a colleague and killed him, he was descending on a ladder and fell on a colleague, or he was shining with a polisher and it fell on a colleague and killed him, the person responsible should be exiled.

This is derived from Numbers 35:23, which states: "And it fell upon him, and he died," implying that the article must descend in an ordinary manner. An object that descends frequently causes damage. Indeed, it is likely that this will happen, for the nature of a heavy object is to descend downward speedily. Therefore, if the person did not hurry and act appropriately and properly while the object descended, he is responsible and should be exiled. The same applies in other analogous situations.

13. The following rules apply when a butcher was cutting meat and lifted his hands backward while holding a cleaver, and then brought them forward to break a bone, as butchers do. If anyone is killed while he draws the cleaver back—i.e., while he lifts it up in front of him or while he causes it to descend behind him, the butcher is not exiled. If anyone is killed when he brings the cleaver forward—i.e., while he lifts it up behind him or while he causes it to descend in front of him—the butcher should be exiled.

This is the governing principle. Whenever the object that kills is descending, the person responsible should be exiled. If it is not descending, he should not be exiled. Even a descent for the purpose of ascent does not cause the person to be exiled.

14. What is an example of a "descent for the purpose of an ascent"? If a person was ascending on a ladder, and a rung gave way under his feet and fell and caused death, the person climbing is not obligated to be exiled.

Similarly, in the following situations, the death is considered close to having been caused by factors beyond the control of the individuals involved and they are not exiled:

a) a person intended to throw an article in one direction and it went in another direction,

b) a person had a stone in his bosom that he had never been made aware of and when he stood up it fell, or

c) a blind man killed someone unintentionally.

15. If there was a stone in his bosom that he was aware of and he forgot it, and then he stood up, the stone fell and caused death, he is exiled, as implied by Numbers 35:15, which mentions the death taking place

"unintentionally." From the use of that term, we can infer that he knew of the stone's existence beforehand.

If the iron slips from the axe rebounding from the tree he is chopping, he is not exiled, because this does not come from his own force, but from the effect generated by his force. Thus, it is like a factor that is beyond his control.

Similarly, if a person throws a stone into a date palm to knock down dates, and the dates fall on an infant and kill him, the person who throws the stone is not liable to be exiled, because the infant was killed, not by force that he generated, but from the effect generated by his force. Similar principles apply with regard to other blows brought about by analogous situations.

Translated by Rabbi Eliyahu Touger. Published and copyright by Moznaim Publications.
Available at www.chabad.org/682956
Reprinted with permission of the publisher

Acknowledgments

"He has made me dwell in darkness" (LAMENTATIONS 3:6).
This is an allusion to the Babylonian Talmud.

—TALMUD, SANHEDRIN 24A

The methodology of the Babylonian Talmud is hairsplitting analysis via endless queries, debates, and refutations. This style of learning forces the light of knowledge into a labyrinth of darkness, whereby its pristine clarity is significantly dimmed under successive layers of intellectual challenge. But after every possible challenge has been solved or rebuffed, one reaches a far more profound illumination of the concept than was originally available.

—RABBI YOSEF YITSCHAK SCHNEERSOHN, *SEFER HAMA'AMARIM* 5708, P. 123

The Dilemma: Modern Conundrums, Talmudic Debates, Your Solutions features fascinating scenarios plucked straight from the often bizarre and contradictory realties of our modern world. These dilemmas are scrutinized with the illuminating lens of the Talmud, the vast foundational work of Jewish wisdom. The Talmud's methodology, and its dogged pursuit of truth in solving conflicting legal and moral claims, is staggering in skill and profundity. It dares to propel the intellect to a plateau it was unaware that it possessed. This course endeavors to tap into this timeless treasure, which will provide participants with newfound knowledge and skill to issue robust and elegant legal verdicts of their own.

We extend our appreciation to **Rabbis Mordechai Dinerman** and **Naftali Silberberg**, who direct the JLI Curriculum Department and the Flagship editorial team; to **Rabbi Dr. Shmuel Klatzkin**, JLI's senior editor; and to **Rabbi Zalman Abraham**, charged with JLI strategic branding and marketing, who skillfully provides the vision for branding JLI course offerings.

We are grateful to **Rabbis Lazer Gurkow, Sholom Ber Hertzel, Eli Raksin, Shmuel Super,** and **Boruch Werdiger,** who researched extensively the topics for this course, wrote and edited lesson drafts, and made substantial contributions to the course content. **Rabbis Moshe Chanunu** and **Yakov Gershon**, of JLI's **Machon Shmuel: The Sami Rohr Research Institute**, provided research assistance.

We are thankful to **Rivkah Slonim, Rabbi Ari Sollish,** and **Rabbi Avrohom Sternberg**, members of the JLI editorial board, for providing countless useful suggestions that enhanced the course and ensured its suitability for a wide range of students.

We thank **Rivki Mockin,** our exceptional Curriculum Coordinator, for streamlining the course production process and ensuring the smoothness, timeliness, and professionalism of the product; and **Rabbi Levi Kaplan** and **Malka Solomon** for managing many of the components of book production. We are grateful to **Mendel Schtroks** for designing the textbooks with taste, expertise, and patience, and **Mendel Sirota** for directing the book publication. **Lynne Clamage**, **Rabbi Shmuel Super**, **Ya'akovah Weber**, and **Rachel Witty** enhanced the quality and professionalism of the course with their copyediting and proofreading.

We are fortunate to be able to offer this course for CLE credits in many states. We are indebted to **Menachem Sandman, Esq.**, and to **Mindy Wallach** for their research and assistance in bringing this project to fruition.

We thank **Baila Pruss** and **Mushka Pruss** for the design of the course's aesthetically pleasing PowerPoint presentations, and **Moshe Raskin** and **Getzy Raskin** for heading the production team charged with the production of the videos for this course. The video scripts were masterfully written by **Rabbi Yaakov Paley**.

We acknowledge the hard work and efforts of JLI's support staff and administration, whose contributions to this course were critical, but whose names are too many to enumerate here.

We are immensely grateful for the encouragement of JLI's visionary chairman and vice-chairman of Merkos L'Inyonei Chinuch—Lubavitch World Headquarters, **Rabbi Moshe Kotlarsky**. Rabbi Kotlarsky has been highly instrumental in building the infrastructure for the expansion of Chabad's international network, and is the architect of scores of initiatives and services to help Chabad representatives across the globe succeed in their mission. We are blessed to have the unwavering support of JLI's principal benefactor, **Mr. George Rohr**, who is fully invested in our work, continues to be instrumental in JLI's monumental growth and expansion, and is largely responsible for the Jewish renaissance that is being spearheaded by JLI and its affiliates across the globe.

The commitment and sage direction of JLI's dedicated executive board—**Rabbis Chaim Block**, **Hesh Epstein**, **Ronnie Fine**, **Yosef Gansburg**, **Shmuel Kaplan**, **Yisrael Rice**, and **Avrohom Sternberg**—and the countless hours they devote to the development of JLI, are what drive the vision, growth, and tremendous success of the organization.

Finally, JLI represents an incredible partnership of more than fourteen hundred *shluchim* and *shluchot* in over one thousand locations across the globe, who contribute their time and talent to further Jewish adult education. We thank them for generously sharing feedback and making suggestions that steer JLI's development and growth. They are our most valuable critics and our most cherished contributors.

Inspired by the call of the **Lubavitcher Rebbe**, of righteous memory, it is the mandate of the Rohr JLI to encourage all Jews throughout the world to experience and participate in their precious heritage of Torah learning. May this course succeed in fulfilling this sacred charge!

On behalf of the Rohr Jewish Learning Institute,

RABBI EFRAIM MINTZ
Executive Director

RABBI YISRAEL RICE
Chairman, Editorial Board

19 Kislev, 5777

The Rohr Jewish Learning Institute

AN AFFILIATE OF MERKOS L'INYONEI CHINUCH
THE EDUCATIONAL ARM OF THE CHABAD LUBAVITCH MOVEMENT
822 EASTERN PARKWAY, BROOKLYN, NY 11213

JLI INTERNATIONAL

Rabbi Avrohom Sternberg
CHAIRMAN

Rabbi Dubi Rabinowitz
DIRECTOR

Rabbi Berry Piekarski
ADMINISTRATOR

Mendel Schtroks
CONTENT MANAGER

Rabbi Yosef Yitzchok Noyman
ADMINISTRATOR, JLI ISRAEL
IN PARTNERSHIP WITH MIVTZA
TORAH—ISRAEL

Rabbi Israel Ashkenazi
DIRECTOR, JLI ISRAEL

Rabbi Eli Wolf
ADMINISTRATOR, JLI IN THE CIS
IN PARTNERSHIP WITH THE
FEDERATION OF JEWISH
COMMUNITIES OF THE CIS

Rabbi Shevach Zlatopolsky
EDITOR, JLI IN THE CIS

Dr. Arye Olman
TRANSLATOR, RUSSIAN

Rabbi Nochum Schapiro
REGIONAL REPRESENTATIVE,
AUSTRALIA

Rabbi Avraham Golovacheov
REGIONAL REPRESENTATIVE,
GERMANY

Rabbi Shmuel Katzman
REGIONAL REPRESENTATIVE,
NETHERLANDS

NATIONAL JEWISH RETREAT

Rabbi Hesh Epstein
CHAIRMAN

Mrs. Shaina B. Mintz
ADMINISTRATOR

Bruce Backman
Rochelle Katzman
COORDINATORS

Rabbi Shmuly Karp
SHLUCHIM LIAISON

Mrs. Chana Dechter
Mrs. Fraydee Kessler
Aliza Landes
SERVICE AND SUPPORT

JLI LAND & SPIRIT
ISRAEL EXPERIENCE

Rabbi Shmuly Karp
DIRECTOR

Mrs. Shaina B. Mintz
ADMINISTRATOR

Rabbi Yechiel Baitelman
Rabbi Dovid Flinkenstein
Rabbi Chanoch Kaplan
Rabbi Levi Klein
Rabbi Mendy Mangel
Rabbi Sholom Raichik
STEERING COMMITTEE

SHABBAT IN THE HEIGHTS
Shmuly Karp
DIRECTOR

Mrs. Shulamis Nadler
SERVICE AND SUPPORT

Rabbi Chaim Hanoka
Rabbi Zalman Marcus
STEERING COMMITTEE

MYSHIUR
ADVANCED LEARNING INITIATIVE

Rabbi Shmuel Kaplan
CHAIRMAN

Rabbi Levi Kaplan
DIRECTOR

TORAHCAFE.COM
ONLINE LEARNING

Rabbi Levi Kaplan
DIRECTOR

Rabbi Mendy Elishevitz
Rabbi Elchonon Korenblit
WEBSITE DEVELOPMENT

Moshe Levin
CONTENT MANAGER

Avrohom Shimon Ezagui
FILMING

MACHON SHMUEL
THE SAMI ROHR RESEARCH INSTITUTE

Rabbi Avrohom Bergstein
DEAN

Rabbi Moshe Miller
Rabbi Gedalya Oberlander
Rabbi Chaim Rapoport
Rabbi Chaim Schapiro
RABBINIC ADVISORY BOARD

Rabbi Yakov Gershon
RESEARCH FELLOW

FOUNDING DEPARTMENT HEADS

Rabbi Mendel Bell
Rabbi Zalman Charytan
Rabbi Mendel Druk
Rabbi Menachem Gansburg
Rabbi Meir Hecht
Rabbi Yoni Katz
Rabbi Chaim Zalman Levy
Rabbi Benny Rapoport
Dr. Chana Silberstein
Rabbi Elchonon Tenenbaum
Rabbi Mendy Weg

Faculty Directory

ALABAMA

BIRMINGHAM
Rabbi Yossi Friedman 205.970.0100

MOBILE
Rabbi Yosef Goldwasser 718.578.6751

ALASKA

ANCHORAGE
Rabbi Yosef Greenberg 907.279.1200

WASILLA
Rabbi Mendy Greenberg 907.357.8770

ARIZONA

FLAGSTAFF
Rabbi Dovie Shapiro 928.255.5756

FOUNTAIN HILLS
Rabbi Mendy Lipskier 480.776.4763

GILBERT
Rabbi Shimi Ash 480.269.6680

ORO VALLEY
Rabbi Ephraim Zimmerman 520.477.8672

PHOENIX
Rabbi Zalman Levertov
Rabbi Yossi Friedman 602.944.2753

PRESCOTT
Rabbi Elie Filler 928.362.8924

SCOTTSDALE
Rabbi Yossi Levertov 480.998.1410

TUCSON
Rabbi Yehuda Ceitlin 520.881.7956

CALIFORNIA

AGOURA HILLS
Rabbi Moshe Bryski
Rabbi Yisroel Levine 818.991.0991

BAKERSFIELD
Rabbi Shmuli Schlanger 661.331.1695

BEL AIR
Rabbi Chaim Mentz 310.475.5311

BEVERLY HILLS
Rabbi Chaim I. Sperlin 310.734.9079

BURBANK
Rabbi Shmuly Kornfeld 818.954.0070

CARLSBAD
Rabbi Yeruchem Eilfort
Mrs. Nechama Eilfort 760.943.8891

CENTURY CITY
Rabbi Tzemach Cunin 310.860.1260

CHATSWORTH
Rabbi Yossi Spritzer 818.718.0777

CONTRA COSTA
Rabbi Dovber Berkowitz 925.937.4101
Chapter founded by Rabbi Joshua Gordon, OBM

CORONADO
Rabbi Eli Fradkin 619.365.4728

ENCINO
Rabbi Aryeh Herzog 818.784.9986

FOLSOM
Rabbi Yossi Grossbaum 916.608.9811

FREMONT
Rabbi Moshe Fuss 510.300.4090

GLENDALE
Rabbi Simcha Backman 818.240.2750

HUNTINGTON BEACH
Rabbi Aron Berkowitz 714.846.2285

LA JOLLA
Rabbi Baruch Shalom Ezagui 858.455.5433

LAGUNA BEACH
Rabbi Elimelech Gurevitch 949.499.0770

LOMITA
Rabbi Eli Hecht
Rabbi Sholom Pinson 310.326.8234

LONG BEACH
Rabbi Abba Perelmuter 562.621.9828

LOS ANGELES
Rabbi Leibel Korf 323.660.5177

MARINA DEL REY
Rabbi Danny Yiftach-Hashem
Rabbi Dovid Yiftach 310.859.0770

NORTH HOLLYWOOD
Rabbi Nachman Abend 818.989.9539

NORTHRIDGE
Rabbi Eli Rivkin 818.368.3937

OAKLAND
Rabbi Dovid Labkowski 510.545.6770

PACIFIC PALISADES
Rabbi Zushe Cunin 310.454.7783

PALO ALTO
Rabbi Yosef Levin
Rabbi Ber Rosenblatt 650.424.9800

PASADENA
Rabbi Chaim Hanoka 626.564.8820
Rabbi Sholom Stiefel 626-539-4578

RANCHO MIRAGE
Rabbi Shimon H. Posner 760.770.7785

RANCHO PALOS VERDES
Rabbi Yitzchok Magalnic 310.544.5544

RANCHO S. FE
Rabbi Levi Raskin 858.756.7571

REDONDO BEACH
Rabbi Yossi Mintz
Rabbi Zalman Gordon 310.214.4999

S. BARBARA
Rabbi Mendel Loschak 805.683.1544
Chapter founded by Rabbi Yosef Loschak, OBM

S. CLEMENTE
Rabbi Menachem M. Slavin 949.489.0723

S. DIEGO
Rabbi Rafi Andrusier 619.387.8770
Rabbi Motte Fradkin 858.547.0076

S. FRANCISCO
Rabbi Peretz Mochkin 415.571.8770
Rabbi Shlomo Zarchi 415.752.2866

S. LUIS OBISPO
Rabbi Chaim Leib Hilel 805.706.0256

S. MONICA
Rabbi Boruch Rabinowitz 310.394.5699

S. RAFAEL
Rabbi Yisrael Rice 415.492.1666

SOUTH LAKE TAHOE
Rabbi Mordechai Richler 530.314.7677

STUDIO CITY
Rabbi Yossi Baitelman 818.508.6633

TEMECULA
Rabbi Yonasan Abrams 951.234.4196

THOUSAND OAKS
Rabbi Chaim Bryski 805.493.7776

TUSTIN
Rabbi Yehoshua Eliezrie 714.508.2150

VENTURA
Rabbi Yakov Latowicz
Mrs. Sarah Latowicz 805.658.7441

WEST HILLS
Rabbi Avi Rabin 818.337.4544

WEST HOLLYWOOD
Rabbi Mordechai Kirschenbaum 310.275.1215

WEST LOS ANGELES
Rabbi Mordechai Zaetz 424.652.8742

YORBA LINDA
Rabbi Dovid Eliezrie 714.693.0770

COLORADO

ASPEN
Rabbi Mendel Mintz 970.544.3770

DENVER
Rabbi Yossi Serebryanski 303.744.9699

FORT COLLINS
Rabbi Yerachmiel Gorelik 970.407.1613

HIGHLANDS RANCH
Rabbi Avraham Mintz 303.694.9119

VAIL
Rabbi Dovid Mintz 970.476.7887

WESTMINSTER
Rabbi Benjy Brackman 303.429.5177

CONNECTICUT

FAIRFIELD
Rabbi Shlame Landa 203.373.7551

GREENWICH
Rabbi Yossi Deren
Rabbi Menachem Feldman 203.629.9059

MILFORD
Rabbi Schneur Wilhelm 203.878.4569

NEW LONDON
Rabbi Avrohom Sternberg 860.437.8000

STAMFORD
Rabbi Yisrael Deren
Rabbi Levi Mendelow 203.3.CHABAD

WEST HARTFORD
Rabbi Shaya Gopin 860.659.2422

WESTPORT
Rabbi Yehuda L. Kantor
Mrs. Dina Kantor 203.226.8584

DELAWARE

WILMINGTON
Rabbi Chuni Vogel 302.529.9900

FLORIDA

BAL HARBOUR
Rabbi Dov Schochet 305.868.1411

BOCA RATON
Rabbi Zalman Bukiet
Rabbi Arele Gopin 561.487.2934
Rabbi Moishe Denburg 561.526.5760

BOYNTON BEACH
Rabbi Yosef Yitzchok Raichik 561.732.4633

BRADENTON
Rabbi Menachem Bukiet 941.388.9656

BROWARD CO.: SOUTHWEST
Rabbi Mordechai Andrusier 954.074.2200

CAPE CORAL
Rabbi Yossi Labkowski 239.541.1777

CORAL GABLES
Rabbi Avrohom Stolik 305.490.7572

CORAL SPRINGS
Rabbi Yankie Denburg 954.471.8646

DELRAY BEACH
Rabbi Sholom Ber Korf 561.496.6228

EAST BOCA RATON
Rabbi Ruvi New 561.417.7797

FLEMING ISLAND
Rabbi Shmuly Feldman 904.290.1017

FORT LAUDERDALE
Rabbi Yitzchok Naparstek 954.568.1190

FORT MYERS
Rabbi Yitzchok Minkowicz
Mrs. Nechama Minkowicz 239.433.7708

HALLANDALE BEACH
Rabbi Mordy Feiner 954.458.1877

HOLLYWOOD
Rabbi Leizer Barash 954.965.9933
Rabbi Leibel Kudan 954.801.3367

KENDALL
Rabbi Yossi Harlig 305.234.5654

LAKELAND
Rabbi Moshe Lazaros 863.510.5968

LONGWOOD
Rabbi Yanky Majesky 407.636.5994

MAITLAND
Rabbi Sholom Dubov
Rabbi Levik Dubov 470.644.2500

OCALA
Rabbi Yossi Hecht 352.291.2218

ORLANDO
Rabbi Yosef Konikov 407.354.3660

ORMOND BEACH
Rabbi Shmuel Konikov 386.672.9300

PALM BEACH GARDENS
Rabbi Dovid Vigler 561.624.2223

PALM CITY
Rabbi Shlomo Uminer 772.288.0606

PALMETTO BAY
Rabbi Zalman Gansburg 786.282.0413

PLANTATION
Rabbi Pinchas Taylor 954.644.9177

PONTE VEDRA BEACH
Rabbi Nochum Kurinsky 904.543.9301

SARASOTA
Rabbi Chaim Shaul Steinmetz 941.925.0770

SATELLITE BEACH
Rabbi Zvi Konikov 321.777.2770

SOUTH PALM BEACH
Rabbi Leibel Stolik 561.889.3499

SOUTH TAMPA
Rabbi Mendy Dubrowski 813.922.1723

SUNNY ISLES BEACH
Rabbi Alexander Kaller 305.803.5315

VENICE
Rabbi Sholom Ber Schmerling 941.493.2770

WESTON
Rabbi Yisroel Spalter 954.349.6565

WEST PALM BEACH
Rabbi Yoel Gancz 561.659.7770

GEORGIA

ALPHARETTA
Rabbi Hirshy Minkowicz 770.410.9000

ATLANTA
Rabbi Yossi New
Rabbi Isser New
Rabbi Ari Sollish 404.843.2464

GWINNETT
Rabbi Yossi Lerman 678.595.0196

MARIETTA
Rabbi Ephraim Silverman 770.565.4412

HAWAII

PRINCEVILLE
Rabbi Michoel Goldman 808.647.4293

IDAHO

BOISE
Rabbi Mendel Lifshitz 208.853.9200

ILLINOIS

CHAMPAIGN
Rabbi Dovid Tiechtel 217.355.8672

CHICAGO
Rabbi Meir Hecht 312.714.4655
Rabbi Yosef Moscowitz 773.772.3770
Rabbi Levi Notik 773.274.5123

ELGIN
Rabbi Mendel Shemtov 847.440.4486

GLENVIEW
Rabbi Yishaya Benjaminson 847.998.9896

HIGHLAND PARK
Mrs. Michla Schanowitz 847.266.0770

NAPERVILLE
Rabbi Mendy Goldstein 630.778.9770

NORTHBROOK
Rabbi Meir Moscowitz 847.564.8770

OAK PARK
Rabbi Yitzchok Bergstein 708.524.1530

PEORIA
Rabbi Eli Langsam 309.692.2250

ROCKFORD
Rabbi Yecheskel Rothman 815.596.0032

SKOKIE
Rabbi Yochanan Posner 847.677.1770

VERNON HILLS
Rabbi Shimmy Susskind 847.984.2919

WILMETTE
Rabbi Dovid Flinkenstein 847.251.7707

INDIANA

INDIANAPOLIS
Rabbi Dr. Shmuel Klatzkin 317.251.5573

KANSAS

OVERLAND PARK
Rabbi Mendy Wineberg 913.649.4852

KENTUCKY

LOUISVILLE
Rabbi Avrohom Litvin 502.459.1770

LOUISIANA

METAIRIE
Rabbi Yossie Nemes
Rabbi Mendel Ceitlin 504.454.2910

MARYLAND

BALTIMORE
Rabbi Elchonon Lisbon 410.358.4787
Rabbi Velvel Belinsky 410.764.5000
Classes in Russian

BEL AIR
Rabbi Kushi Schusterman 443.353.9718

BETHESDA
Rabbi Sender Geisinsky 301.913.9777

COLUMBIA
Rabbi Hillel Baron
Rabbi Yosef Chaim Sufrin 410.740.2424

FREDERICK
Rabbi Boruch Labkowski 301.996.3659

GAITHERSBURG
Rabbi Sholom Raichik 301.926.3632

OLNEY
Rabbi Bentzy Stolik 301.660.6770

OWINGS MILLS
Rabbi Nochum H. Katsenelenbogen 410.356.5156

POTOMAC
Rabbi Mendel Bluming 301.983.4200
Rabbi Mendel Kaplan 301.983.1485

ROCKVILLE
Rabbi Moishe Kavka 301.836.1242

MASSACHUSETTS

BOSTON
Rabbi Yosef Zaklos 617.297.7282

CAPE COD
Rabbi Yekusiel Alperowitz 508.775.2324

LONGMEADOW
Rabbi Yukov Wolff 413.567.8665

NEWTON
Rabbi Shalom Ber Prus 617.244.1200

SUDBURY
Rabbi Yisroel Freeman 978.443.3691

SWAMPSCOTT
Mrs. Layah Lipsker 781.581.3833

MICHIGAN

ANN ARBOR
Rabbi Aharon Goldstein 734.995.3276

GRAND RAPIDS
Rabbi Mordechai Haller 616.957.0770

WEST BLOOMFIELD
Rabbi Elimelech Silberberg 248.855.6170

MINNESOTA

MINNETONKA
Rabbi Mordechai Grossbaum
Rabbi Shmuel Silberstein 952.929.9922

S. PAUL
Rabbi Shneur Zalman Bendet 651.998.9298

MISSOURI

S. LOUIS
Rabbi Yosef Landa 314.725.0400

NEVADA

SUMMERLIN
Rabbi Yisroel Schanowitz
Rabbi Tzvi Bronchtain 702.855.0770

NEW JERSEY

BASKING RIDGE
Rabbi Mendy Herson
Rabbi Mendel Shemtov 908.604.8844

CHERRY HILL
Rabbi Mendy Mangel 056.074.1500

CLINTON
Rabbi Eli Kornfeld 908.623.7000

FAIR LAWN
Rabbi Avrohom Bergstein 718.839.5296

FORT LEE
Rabbi Meir Konikov 201.886.1238

FRANKLIN LAKES
Rabbi Chanoch Kaplan 201.848.0449

HASKELL
Rabbi Mendy Gurkov 201.696.7609

HILLSBOROUGH
Rabbi Shmaya Krinsky 908.874.0444

HOLMDEL
Rabbi Shmaya Galperin 732.772.1998

MADISON
Rabbi Shalom Lubin 973.377.0707

MANALAPAN
Rabbi Boruch Chazanow
Rabbi Levi Wolosow 732.972.3687

MOUNTAIN LAKES
Rabbi Levi Dubinsky 973.551.1898

MULLICA HILL
Rabbi Avrohom Richler 856.733.0770

OLD TAPPAN
Rabbi Mendy Lewis 201.767.4008

PASSAIC
Rabbi Yitzchak Sebbag
Dr. Michael Akerman 973.246.5251

RANDOLPH
Rabbi Avraham Bekhor
Mrs. Chava Bekhor 973-895-3070

ROCKAWAY
Rabbi Asher Herson
Rabbi Mordechai Baumgarten 973.625.1525

TEANECK
Rabbi Ephraim Simon 201.907.0686

TENAFLY
Rabbi Mordechai Shain 201.871.1152

TOMS RIVER
Rabbi Moshe Gourarie 732.349.4199

WEST ORANGE
Rabbi Mendy Kasowitz 973.486.2362

WOODCLIFF LAKE
Rabbi Dov Drizin 201.476.0157

NEW YORK

BAY SHORE
Rabbi Shimon Stillerman 631.913.8770

BEDFORD
Rabbi Arik Wolf 914.666.6065

BINGHAMTON
Mrs. Rivkah Slonim 607.797.0015

BRIGHTON BEACH
Rabbi Moshe Winner 718.946.9833

BROOKVILLE
Rabbi Mendy Heber 516.626.0600

CEDARHURST
Rabbi Zalman Wolowik 516.295.2478

COMMACK
Rabbi Mendel Teldon 631.543.3343

DIX HILLS
Rabbi Eli Laufer
Rabbi Yaakov Saacks 631.351.8672

DOBBS FERRY
Rabbi Benjy Silverman 914.693.6100

EAST HAMPTON
Rabbi Leibel Baumgarten
Rabbi Mendy Goldberg 631.329.5800

ELLENVILLE
Rabbi Shlomie Deren 845.647.4450

FOREST HILLS
Rabbi Yossi Mendelson 917.861.9726

GREAT NECK
Rabbi Yoseph Geisinsky 516.487.4554

JAMAICA ESTATES
Rabbi Shmuel Kogan 718.480.0100

KINGSTON
Rabbi Yitzchok Hecht 845.334.9044

LARCHMONT
Rabbi Mendel Silberstein 914.834.4321

LONG BEACH
Rabbi Eli Goodman 516.897.2473

NYC KEHILATH JESHURUN
Rabbi Elie Weinstock 212.774.5636

NYC MIDTOWN
Mrs. Raizy Metzger 212.758.3770

NYACK
Rabbi Chaim Zvi Ehrenreich 845.356.6686

OCEANSIDE
Rabbi Levi Gurkow 516.764.7385

OSSINING
Rabbi Dovid Labkowski 914.923.2522

PARK SLOPE
Rabbi Menashe Wolf................347.957.1291

PORT WASHINGTON
Rabbi Shalom Paltiel................516.767.8672

PROSPECT HEIGHTS
Rabbi Mendy Hecht................347.622.3599

RIVERDALE
Rabbi Levi Shemtov................718.549.1100

ROCHESTER
Rabbi Nechemia Vogel................585.271.0330

ROSLYN
Rabbi Yaakov Reiter................516.484.8185

SCARSDALE
Rabbi Avrohom Butman................914.527.2077

SEA GATE
Rabbi Chaim Brikman................718.266.1736

SOUTHAMPTON
Rabbi Chaim Pape................917.627.4865

STATEN ISLAND
Rabbi Mendy Katzman................718.370.8953

STONY BROOK
Rabbi Shalom Ber Cohen................631.585.0521

SUFFERN
Rabbi Shmuel Gancz................845.368.1889

WESTBURY
Rabbi Mendy Brownstein................516.850.4486

NORTH CAROLINA

ASHEVILLE
Rabbi Shaya Susskind................828.505.0746

CARY
Rabbi Yisroel Cotlar................919.651.9710

CHAPEL HILL
Rabbi Zalman Bluming................919.630.5129

CHARLOTTE
Rabbi Yossi Groner
Rabbi Shlomo Cohen................704.366.3984

GREENSBORO
Rabbi Yosef Plotkin................336.617.8120

RALEIGH
Rabbi Pinchas Herman
Rabbi Lev Cotlar................919.637.6950

WILMINGTON
Rabbi Moshe Lieblich................910.763.4770

NORTH DAKOTA

FARGO
Rabbi Yonah Grossman................701.212.4164

OHIO

BEACHWOOD
Rabbi Shmuli Friedman................216.370.2887

BLUE ASH
Rabbi Yisroel Mangel................513.793.5200

COLUMBUS
Rabbi Yitzi Kaltmann................614.294.3296

DAYTON
Rabbi Nochum Mangel
Rabbi Shmuel Klatzkin................937.643.0770

OKLAHOMA

OKLAHOMA CITY
Rabbi Ovadia Goldman................405.524.4800

TULSA
Rabbi Yehuda Weg................918.492.4499

OREGON

BEND
Rabbi Yitzchok Feldman................541.633.7991

PORTLAND
Rabbi Mordechai Wilhelm................503.977.9947

SALEM
Rabbi Avrohom Yitzchok Perlstein................503.383.9569

PENNSYLVANIA

AMBLER
Rabbi Shaya Deitsch................215.591.9310

BALA CYNWYD
Rabbi Shraga Sherman................610.660.9192

CLARKS SUMMIT
Rabbi Benny Rapoport 570.881.1833

LAFAYETTE HILL
Rabbi Yisroel Kotlarsky 484.533.7009

LANCASTER
Rabbi Elazar Green 717.368.6565

NEWTOWN
Rabbi Aryeh Weinstein 215.497.9925

PHILADELPHIA: CENTER CITY
Rabbi Yochonon Goldman 215.238.2100

PITTSBURGH
Rabbi Yisroel Altein .... 412.422.7300 EXT. 269
Rabbi Ely Rosenfeld 412.781.1800

PITTSBURGH: SOUTH HILLS
Rabbi Mendy Rosenblum 412.278.3693

RYDAL
Rabbi Zushe Gurevitz 267.536.5757

WYNNEWOOD
Rabbi Moishe Brennan 610.529.9011

RHODE ISLAND

WARWICK
Rabbi Yossi Laufer 401.884.7888

SOUTH CAROLINA

COLUMBIA
Rabbi Hesh Epstein
Rabbi Levi Marrus 803.782.1831

GREENVILLE
Rabbi Leibel Kesselman 864.256.1770

TENNESSEE

CHATTANOOGA
Rabbi Shaul Perlstein 423.490.1106

MEMPHIS
Rabbi Levi Klein 901.754.0404

TEXAS

ARLINGTON
Rabbi Levi Gurevitch 817.451.1171

AUSTIN
Rabbi Mendy Levertov 512.905.2778

BELLAIRE
Rabbi Yossi Zaklikofsky 713.839.8887

DALLAS
Rabbi Mendel Dubrawsky
Rabbi Moshe Naparstek 972.818.0770
Rabbi Zvi Drizin 214.632.2633

FORT WORTH
Rabbi Dov Mandel 817.263.7701

HOUSTON
Rabbi Dovid Goldstein
Rabbi Zally Lazarus 281.589.7188
Rabbi Moishe Traxler 713.774.0300

HOUSTON: RICE UNIVERSITY AREA
Rabbi Eliezer Lazaroff 713.522.2004

LEAGUE CITY
Rabbi Yitzchok Schmukler 281.724.1554

MISSOURI CITY
Rabbi Mendel Feigenson 832.758.0685

PLANO
Rabbi Mendel Block
Rabbi Yehudah Horowitz 972.596.8270

S. ANTONIO
Rabbi Chaim Block
Rabbi Levi Teldon 210.492.1085

THE WOODLANDS
Rabbi Mendel Blecher 281.719.5213

UTAH

SALT LAKE CITY
Rabbi Benny Zippel 801.467.7777

VERMONT

BURLINGTON
Rabbi Yitzchok Raskin 802.658.5770

VIRGINIA

ALEXANDRIA/ARLINGTON
Rabbi Mordechai Newman..................................703.370.2774

FAIRFAX
Rabbi Leibel Fajnland.......................................703.426.1980

HERNDON
Rabbi Leibel Fajnland.......................................571.594.6490

NORFOLK
Rabbi Aaron Margolin
Rabbi Levi Brashevitzky....................................757.616.0770

TYSONS CORNER
Rabbi Chezzy Deitsch.......................................703.829.5770
Chapter founded by Rabbi Levi Deitsch, OBM

WASHINGTON

BELLINGHAM
Rabbi Yosef Truxton...617.640.8841

MERCER ISLAND
Rabbi Elazar Bogomilsky....................................206.527.1411

SPOKANE COUNTY
Rabbi Yisroel Hahn..509.443.0770

WISCONSIN

KENOSHA
Rabbi Tzali Wilschanski.....................................262.359.0770

MADISON
Rabbi Avremel Matusof......................................608.231.3450

MILWAUKEE
Rabbi Mendel Shmotkin.....................................414.961.6100

WAUKESHA
Rabbi Levi Brook..925.708.4203

DISTRICT OF COLUMBIA

WASHINGTON
Rabbi Levi Shemtov
Rabbi Shua Hecht...202.332.5600

PUERTO RICO

CAROLINA
Rabbi Mendel Zarchi..787.253.0894

ARGENTINA

CAPITAL FEDERAL
Rabbi Mendy Gurevitch...................................54.11.4545.7771

PALERMO NUEVO
Rabbi Mendy Grunblatt...................................54.11.4772.1024

AUSTRALIA

AUSTRALIAN CAPITAL TERRITORY

CANBERRA
Rabbi Shmuel Feldman....................................614.3167.7805

NEW SOUTH WALES

DOUBLE BAY
Rabbi Yanky Berger
Rabbi Yisroel Dolnikov....................................612.9327.1644

DOVER HEIGHTS
Rabbi Motti Feldman......................................612.9387.3822

NORTH SHORE
Rabbi Nochum Schapiro
Mrs. Fruma Schapiro......................................612.9488.9548

SOUTH HEAD
Rabbi Benzion Milecki....................................612.9337.6775

QUEENSLAND

BRISBANE
Rabbi Levi Jaffe...617.3843.6770

VICTORIA

BENTLEIGH EAST
Rabbi Mendel Raskin......................................613.9570.6707

CAULFIELD NORTH
Rabbi Menachem Stern....................................614.4850.4301

ELSTERNWICK
Rabbi Chaim Cowen.......................................614.3330.8584
Rabbi Motty Liberow......................................613.9533.0090

MELBOURNE
Rabbi Sholem Gorelik.....................................614.5244.8770

MOORABBIN
Rabbi Elisha Greenbaum...................................614.0349.0434

S. KILDA EAST
Rabbi Moshe Kahn 613.9522.8217

WESTERN AUSTRALIA

PERTH
Rabbi Shalom White........................618.9275.2106

BRAZIL

RIO DE JANEIRO
Rabbi Yehoshua Binyomin Goldman
Rabbi Avrohom Tsvi Beuthner........................55.21.2294.3138

S. PAULO
Rabbi Avraham Steinmetz........................55.11.3081.3081
Rabbi Yerachmiel Belinow........................55.11.3663.2838

CANADA

ALBERTA

CALGARY
Rabbi Mordechai Groner 403.238.4880

EDMONTON
Rabbi Ari Drelich
Rabbi Mendy Blachman........................780.851.1515

BRITISH COLUMBIA

OKANAGAN
Rabbi Shmuly Hecht 250.575.5384

RICHMOND
Rabbi Yechiel Baitelman........................604.277.6427

VANCOUVER
Rabbi Dovid Rosenfeld........................604.266.1313

VICTORIA
Rabbi Meir Kaplan 250.595.7656

MANITOBA

WINNIPEG
Rabbi Shmuel Altein........................204.339.8737

ONTARIO

LAWRENCE/EGLINTON
Rabbi Menachem Gansburg........................416.546.8770

LONDON
Rabbi Mordechai Silberberg........................519.434.3623

MISSISSAUGA
Rabbi Yitzchok Slavin........................905.820.4432

NIAGARA FALLS
Rabbi Zalman Zaltzman 905.356.7200

OTTAWA
Rabbi Menachem M. Blum........................613.843.7770

RICHMOND HILL
Rabbi Mendel Bernstein 905.770.7700

GREATER TORONTO REGIONAL OFFICE & THORNHILL
Rabbi Yossi Gansburg 905.731.7000

WATERLOO
Rabbi Moshe Goldman........................226.338.7770

WHITBY
Rabbi Tzali Borenstein 905.493.9007

YORK MILLS
Rabbi Levi Gansburg........................647.345.3800

QUEBEC

CÔTE-S.-LUC
Rabbi Levi Raskin 514.485.7221

MONTREAL
Rabbi Ronnie Fine
Pesach Nussbaum........................514.342.3.JLI

TOWN OF MOUNT ROYAL
Rabbi Moshe Krasnanski
Rabbi Shneur Zalman Rader........................514.739.0770

WESTMOUNT
Rabbi Yossi Shanowitz
Mrs. Devorah Leah Shanowitz........................514.937.4772

SASKATCHEWAN

REGINA
Rabbi Avrohom Simmonds........................306.585.1359

SASKATOON
Rabbi Raphael Kats........................306.384.4370

CAYMAN ISLANDS

GRAND CAYMAN
Rabbi Berel Pewzner........................717.798.1040

DENMARK

COPENHAGEN
Rabbi Yitzchok Loewenthal........................45.3316.1850

ESTONIA

TALLINN
Rabbi Shmuel Kot................................372.662.30.50

GEORGIA

TBILISI
Rabbi Meir Kozlovsky...........................995.593.23.91.15

GERMANY

BERLIN
Rabbi Yehuda Tiechtel......................49.30.2128.0830

HAMBURG
Rabbi Shlomo Bistritzky....................49.40.4142.4190

HANNOVER
Rabbi Binyamin Wolff.......................49.511.811.2822

GREECE

ATHENS
Rabbi Mendel Hendel.........................30.210.520.2880

GUATEMALA

GUATEMALA CITY
Rabbi Shalom Pelman..........................502.2485.0770

ISRAEL

ASHKELON
Rabbi Shneor Lieberman........................054.977.0512

BALFURYA
Rabbi Noam Bar-Tov............................054.580.4770

CAESAREA
Rabbi Chaim Meir Lieberman...................054.621.2586

EVEN YEHUDA
Rabbi Menachem Noyman.......................054.777.0707

GANEI TIKVA
Rabbi Gershon Shnur...........................054.524.2358

GIV'ATAYIM
Rabbi Pinchus Bitton..........................052.643.8770

HAIFA
Rabbi Yehuda Dunin............................054.426.3763

KARMIEL
Rabbi Mendy Elishevitz........................054.521.3073

KFAR SABA
Rabbi Yossi Baitch.............................054.445.5020

KIRYAT BIALIK
Rabbi Pinny Marton............................050.661.1768

KIRYAT MOTZKIN
Rabbi Shimon Eizenbach........................050.902.0770

KOCHAV YAIR
Rabbi Dovi Greenberg..........................054.332.6244

MACCABIM-RE'UT
Rabbi Yosef Yitzchak Noiman...................054.977.0549

MODIIN
Rabbi Boruch Slonim...........................054.300.1770

NES ZIYONA
Rabbi Menachem Feldman.......................054.497.7092

NETANYA
Rabbi Schneur Brod............................054.579.7572

RAMAT GAN-KRINITZI
Rabbi Yisroel Gurevitz.........................052.743.2814

RAMAT GAN-MAROM NAVE
Rabbi Binyamin Meir Kali......................050.476.0770

RAMAT YISHAI
Rabbi Shneor Zalman Wolosow..................052.324.5475

RISHON LEZION
Rabbi Uri Keshet..............................050.722.4593

ROSH PINA
Rabbi Sholom Ber Hertzel......................052.458.7600

YEHUD
Rabbi Shmuel Wolf.............................053.536.1479

KAZAKHSTAN

ALMATY
Rabbi Shevach Zlatopolsky.....................7.7272.77.59.77

LATVIA

RIGA
Rabbi Shneur Zalman Kot......................371.6733.1520

NETHERLANDS

DEN HAAG
Rabbi Shmuel Katzman......................................31.70.347.0222

PANAMA

PANAMA CITY
Rabbi Ari Laine
Rabbi Gabriel Benayon............................507.223.3383

RUSSIA

ASTRAKHAN
Rabbi Yisroel Melamed...........................7.851.239.28.24

BRYANSK
Rabbi Menachem Mendel Zaklas.............7.483.264.55.15

CHELYABINSK
Rabbi Meir Kirsh..7.351.263.24.68

MOSCOW: MARINA ROSHA
Rabbi Mordechai Weisberg......................7.495.645.50.00

NIZHNY NOVGOROD
Rabbi Shimon Bergman............................7.920.253.47.70

OMSK
Rabbi Osher Krichevsky...........................7.381.231.33.07

PERM
Rabbi Zalman Deutch...............................7.342.212.47.32

ROSTOV
Rabbi Chaim Danzinger...........................7.8632.99.02.68

S. PETERSBURG
Rabbi Zvi Pinsky.......................................7.812.713.62.09

SAMARA
Rabbi Shlomo Deutch...............................7.846.333.40.64

SARATOV
Rabbi Yaakov Kubitshek..........................7.8452.21.58.00

TOGLIATTI
Rabbi Meier Fischer.................................7.848.273.02.84

UFA
Rabbi Dan Krichevsky..............................7.347.244.55.33

VORONEZH
Rabbi Levi Stiefel.....................................7.473.252.96.99

SINGAPORE

SINGAPORE
Rabbi Mordechai Abergel.........................656.337.2189
Rabbi Netanel Rivni.................................656.336.2127
Classes in Hebrew

SOUTH AFRICA

CAPE TOWN
Rabbi Levi Popack....................................27.21.434.3740

JOHANNESBURG
Rabbi Dovid Masinter
Rabbi Ari Kievman....................................27.11.440.6600
Rabbi Dovid Hazdan
Rabbi Shmuel Simpson............................27.11.728.8152

SWEDEN

STOCKHOLM
Rabbi Chaim Greisman.............................468.679.7067

SWITZERLAND

BASEL
Rabbi Zalmen Wishedsky.........................41.41.361.1770

LUGANO
Rabbi Yaakov Tzvi Kantor.......................41.91.921.3720

LUZERN
Rabbi Chaim Drukman.............................41.41.361.1770

UKRAINE

DNEPROPETROVSK
Rabbi Dan Makagon.................................380.504.51.13.18

NIKOLAYEV
Rabbi Sholom Gotlieb..............................380.512.37.37.71

ODESSA
Rabbi Avraham Wolf
Rabbi Yaakov Neiman.................38.048.728.0770 EXT. 280

ZHITOMIR
Rabbi Shlomo Wilhelm.............................380.504.63.01.32

UNITED KINGDOM

CARDIFF
Rabbi Michoel Rose 44.792.866.9536

CHEADLE
Rabbi Peretz Chein 44.161.428.1818

EDGWARE
Rabbi Leivi Sudak
Rabbi Yaron Jacobs 44.208.905.4141

LEEDS
Rabbi Eli Pink 44.113.266.3311

LONDON
Rabbi Mendel Cohen 44.77.7261.2661
Rabbi Nissan D. Dubov 44.20.8944.1581
Rabbi Mendy Korer 44.794.632.5444
Rabbi Gershon Overlander
Rabbi Dovid Katz 44.208.202.1600
Rabbi Yossi Simon 44.20.8458.0416

MANCHESTER
Rabbi Levi Cohen 44.161.792.6335
Rabbi Shmuli Jaffe 44.161.766.1812

THE JEWISH LEARNING MULTIPLEX
Brought to you by the Rohr Jewish Learning Institute

In fulfillment of the mandate of the Lubavitcher Rebbe, of blessed memory,
whose leadership guides every step of our work,
the mission of the Rohr Jewish Learning Institute is to transform
Jewish life and the greater community through the study of Torah,
connecting each Jew to our shared heritage of Jewish learning.

While our flagship program remains the cornerstone of our organization,
JLI is proud to feature additional divisions catering to specific populations,
in order to meet a wide array of educational needs.

THE ROHR JEWISH LEARNING INSTITUTE,
a subsidiary of *Merkos L'Inyonei Chinuch,*
is the adult education arm of the Chabad-Lubavitch Movement.

Torah Studies provides a rich and nuanced
encounter with the weekly Torah reading.

MyShiur courses are designed to assist students in developing
the skills needed to study Talmud independently.

IN PARTNERSHIP WITH CHABAD ON CAMPUS

This rigorous fellowship program invites select college
students to explore the fundamentals of Judaism.

IN PARTNERSHIP WITH CTEEN: CHABAD TEEN NETWORK

Jewish teens forge their identity as they engage in
Torah study, social interaction, and serious fun.

The Rosh Chodesh Society gathers Jewish women
together once a month for intensive textual study.

TorahCafe.com provides an exclusive selection
of top-rated Jewish educational videos.

This yearly event rejuvenates mind, body, and spirit with
a powerful synthesis of Jewish learning and community.

Participants delve into our nation's rich past while
exploring the Holy Land's relevance and meaning today.

Select affiliates are invited to partner with peers and noted
professionals, as leaders of innovation and excellence.

THE SAMI ROHR
RESEARCH INSTITUTE

Machon Shmuel is an institute providing Torah
research in the service of educators worldwide.